ANIMALS
and Other People

ANIMALS
and Other People

by

LOUIS BROMFIELD

Drawings by Paul Laune

THE WOOSTER BOOK COMPANY
Wooster • Ohio
2008

The Wooster Book Company
where minds and imaginations meet

ANIMALS AND OTHER PEOPLE

ISBN: 978-1-59098-106-1

∞ This book is printed on acid-free paper comprising at least 50% post-consumer recycled fiber.

FOR FLORENCE AND HELEN WORKMAN

Two of the finest people I know

in gratitude for their humane and noble work

with forgotten animals.

Contents

"He prayeth well, who loveth well
Both man and bird and beast.

"He prayeth best, who loveth best
All things both great and small;
For the dear God who loveth us,
He made and loveth all."

THE RIME OF THE ANCIENT MARINER
Samuel Taylor Coleridge

Introductory Note

THIS BOOK came into existence at the suggestion and request of many people, some of them old, experienced, mellow, some of them mere children. It is about wild and domestic animals and about people who are "teched" and have that inner sense of mystical feeling which makes them one with Nature and with animals and birds. Some of the material is new, much of it has been selected from earlier books, revised and edited.

Now and then I discover persons who appear to have no relation in any way to the things written in this book. Some rather withered, bitter and limited characters seem insensitive and actually hostile to the values which are set forth here. Such people are not for me and I find in them very little that is warm, commendable or even human. Every man to his own taste; but I can't help wondering how much such people miss out of the richness and glory of this admirable, intricate, complex and exciting universe of which we ourselves are a part.

One of my grandfathers, a somewhat cantankerous character with a general distaste and even scorn for the human race, once remarked that "a man who did not like dogs, children and music had only half a soul and was not worthy of conversation or even association." It was his belief that as most men grow older they become increasingly corrupted in their sensitivity and perceptions and that the fortunate ones are those who manage somehow to maintain the simplicity of children and animals. He may have exaggerated; I am not sure. The quotation from Samuel Coleridge used elsewhere in this book expresses my own feelings.

It has also been said, with considerable truth, that those who have become disillusioned with their fellow men and their greed, intrigue and false values are likely to turn more and more to Nature and to animals for satisfaction. Certainly one of the falsest and most absurd of all beliefs is that the mere fact of being born human gives man a superiority and imposes upon his fellow men the obligation of treating him differently from animals. In the last analysis we are all animals and the fact of being born a man does not endow us with any special rights or virtues; rather it imposes upon us obligations of a high sort indeed, which animals and birds do not share—obligations of intelligence, ethics, decency, loyalty and moral behavior. The sad thing is how frequently these obligations are ignored and violated by man himself.

In any case, here is the book. Turn away those of you who are not "teched" because there is little in it that you will understand or which will give you pleasure.

ANIMALS
and Other People

Of Boxers, Scotties,
a Cat, and a Mongoose

*(To be skipped by demon housekeepers and
people who don't like animals.)*

THE BOXERS began with Rex, a king among dogs. He arrived one
afternoon at the house in France, big, golden brown, with a muscular body, a black face on a snub bulldog head, a broad chest, an
appearance of great ferocity and an air of immense dignity. He was
the gift of a friend and he had been spending several days with her
twelve Norwegian elkhounds in her house near Chantilly. Now elk-

hounds are not exactly lap dogs and they can fight like demons, and they resented the presence of the newcomer from Germany. There were three days of fighting, and in the end, Rex the boxer won, if not the victory, the right to go his dignified way, unmolested, to be let alone. He arrived at our house with the sense of victory still strong in him.

It was not like having a puppy arrive in the house. That was an experience we had had countless times, mostly with Aberdeens, for we had come to have several dogs instead of merely one, because when anything happened to one the sense of loss was too great. So we were always having new litters of puppies or buying new ones. Later, we discovered that having more than one dog didn't make much difference because each one has its own personality and is an individual and when he dies, the sense of loss is not softened by the fact that he left behind several companions.

Rex was the first grown dog who had ever come into the house, and it would be hard to imagine a dog of more awe-inspiring appearance. I get on well with dogs, but I confess that on first sight I had my doubts about getting on with Rex. He came into the room with an air of complete self-assurance. He did not wag his tail or growl or sniff about. He walked in with dignity and stood there looking at us. It was clear that we were not looking him over. The process was quite the reverse. He was a personality which expected no nonsense and no familiarity. With some misgiving I patted his head and spoke to him. He neither growled nor wagged his tail. It was as if he were permitting a favor.

That night I fed him and took him to sleep in my room. He went along graciously, but with the same dignity and detachment, and in the morning when I wakened he was there on the rug beside me, awake, with his head between his paws, watching me out of his big brown eyes. It was then I think I realized for the first time what lay behind the eyes—the affection, the devotion, the loyalty, the dignity and the independence.

But still he gave no outward sign, either of affection or even acceptance. When I went downstairs he went with me into the garden, and while I had breakfast he sat in the dining room near me, never begging, taking no notice of the fact that I was eating. He had been a show-dog, and like all boxers was a gentleman. I did not know then that he had never really had a master or lived with a family, and that he was desperately hungry for a master and children to whom he could attach himself.

For three days he lived with us, still with the same dignity and detachment, never once growling or wagging his tail, and then, on the fourth morning, when I wakened, he got up off the rug and came and put his big head on the bed beside me and looked at me with his great brown eyes. He did not wag his tail. He simply looked at me. I put out my hand and rubbed his ears, and I knew that we were friends. When we went downstairs he went up and sniffed at each member of the family and did the same trick of resting his head on their knees, and then suddenly he wagged his stump of a tail. He was telling us that he had accepted us after looking us over for three days. From that moment on there was never a more devoted dog. He took over the whole family. He watched the house. He was happy really only when the whole family was at home and together. Even then he kept trying to round us up and keep us all together on the terrace or in the library or the salon. We were his responsibility. When part of the family went to Paris for the day, he would sit all day listening for the sound of the car, an old Peugot, which he could distinguish from every other car passing the house. When he sprang up and barked and ran to the garden gate, you knew the family had returned safely and he would be happy again, because we were all together under his watchful eye.

As the days went by, his character softened and at times he would become almost demonstrative, although he never lost his dignity and he was always a little ashamed of displaying any emotion. I think he must have had an unhappy experience as a puppy, of being shipped about at dog shows and finally sold and put on a train and shipped to a foreign country and sent to a strange house filled with strange dogs where he had to fight to assert his domination. I think he had come to distrust all people and perhaps all dogs. That is why he had looked us over until at last he decided that we were all right and that he had no reason to distrust us. I do not use the word fear, for there never was in Rex in all his life any sign of fear.

In the house at Senlis, he had two rivals, one of whom he dominated, the other he never managed to subdue, although she weighed less than one of his own big paws. The first was the grandfather of the Aberdeens—a grizzled, tough old Scotty called Dash. Dash was both a tramp and a Don Juan. All the town knew him and certainly every lady dog in the town was acquainted with him. He would fight dogs of any size. I have seen him lying on his back snapping and biting at a sheep dog four or five times his size, until the bigger dog would yield the day.

There was a square in the town where all the stray dogs had a habit of gathering, perhaps because in the square there were three butcher shops which, like most French butcher shops, had open fronts and the butchers had a habit of throwing scraps into the street for the dogs to fight over. When any of the family went up the hill to the market, Dash always went along. He liked any excuse for going to town. And when you turned into the square Dash would rush forward at full speed into the midst of the little army of mongrels sunning themselves or scratching peacefully on the cobblestones. At sight of him they would scatter in all directions into alleys and doorways. He never failed to perform this same trick.

He was, in addition to being a tramp and a Don Juan, a good deal of a show-off. He knew all the butchers well and his showing off paid good dividends, for the spectacle of the fleeing dogs always amused them. When the square was cleared, Dash, sometimes accompanied by a lady dog, would quietly visit each shop in turn and receive scraps which he devoured in peace without any vulgar fighting.

Every family in town with a bitch sooner or later would announce that their bitch had had puppies and that Dash was the father. They always had a certain pride in the event since Dash was not a mongrel but a *chien de race*, a pedigreed dog, and that fact, no matter what the breed or ancestry of the female, made the puppies in French eyes, distinguished and valuable.

But of all his conquests the most remarkable was that of a huge German police dog bitch called Marquise. She was the property of Picquet, the gardener, and I doubt that a more ferocious dog ever lived. She had come to Picquet full-grown, and most of her life she had spent chained to a laundry delivery wagon. She appeared to hate all mankind and all other dogs. Picquet kept her attached to a kennel by a heavy chain near his house in the vegetable garden, and each time anyone opened the gate she would lunge forward growling and showing her teeth. She grew steadily more savage until, fearing for children and guests and even for myself, I asked Picquet to get rid of her.

Picquet himself was "teched" and was what might be called a "natural." He was not very bright, but he had a wonderful way with flowers, vegetables and animals. I doubt that anyone else living could have gotten on with Marquise. He came from the Pas de Calais and spoke the ugly half-Flemish Pas de Calais *patois*. He could wait at table, take care of the pony and the children, poach trout out of the clear-running Nonette by luring them with Swiss cheese or stunning them with *eau de Javelle*. Together, he and I grew wonderful vegetables and flowers and I learned from him many a trick about gardening and farming which I hope never to forget. I think in all that world he was the only person who loved Marquise. I promised him another dog if he would send her away.

He agreed as to the danger of having Marquise about, but asked that he might keep her a little longer. She was, he said, *enceinte*, which in English merely meant that she was about to have puppies. I received this news with astonishment, as I knew that not only was Marquise kept chained up but that the garden was surrounded by a high wall topped with broken glass, which no dog, not even a St. Bernard, could cross. The only dog who ever came into the garden was Dash, who worshiped Picquet and left him during the day only on the occasions when he went to market to break up the dog *Kaffeeklatsch* in the Place Gallieni and receive his daily handouts from the butchers. Considering the difference in size between Dash and the immense and ferocious Marquise, a mating seemed highly unlikely. I said to Picquet, "But what dog could be the father? No dog but Dash ever comes into the vegetable garden."

Picquet bowed his head and said, *"Mais monsieur, J'ai aidé un peu"* (I gave a little help).

Marquise remained until she had weaned her puppies, and then went off as the companion of a forester living in a lonely house on the road to Aumont. Everyone was happy, including Marquise, for in the forest she could run at liberty. Picquet kept two of the puppies, who grew up into odd-looking dogs—half-pint police dogs with smooth black coats, Scotty heads and magnificent sweeping black tails arching over their backs.

On one occasion Dash very nearly destroyed a famous dog, the handsome white poodle called Basquette, belonging to Gertrude Stein. Basquette, a big pink and white dog, trimmed and tonsored always by the best dog hairdresser in Paris, arrived with Gertrude for lunch one Sunday, and Dash, after one look at Basquette, decided, I think, that the poodle was not a dog at all, but some monstrous strange, unknown animal that asked for extermination, an intolerable sissy to a tramp Don Juan like Dash. In any case, he leapt to the attack and while the pampered, marcelled Basquette howled, Dash went for him. Two tables were overturned, one guest kicked accidentally in the shins by another, and two others bitten before Basquette was rescued, his beautiful, marcelled white coat streaked with blood.

Only once did Dash ever attack a human, and on that occasion I felt that he was justified. His victim was a pompous bore, the town jeweler, by name, Monsieur Bigué. It has often been said that bores recognize and avoid each other, but this was certainly not the case with Monsieur Bigué, who had chosen to marry a bore even greater, if possible, than himself. By some ill fortune, the pair had one of the common gardens which adjoined our own, and they had a dreadful habit of leaning over the fence to make long, involved, formal and deadly conversations on politics, the weather, the foreign exchange. They were childless and incredibly avaricious as only a French provincial jeweler can be. Madame Bigué lavished all her affection upon a wretched little female, pocket-sized dog called Frou-Frou which fortunately never left the jewelry shop or house save to go into the little walled garden at the back. No virgin heiress was ever protected as fanatically as Frou-Frou. She was, I think, the only female dog in the town which Dash had not seduced. Madame Bigué would, I think, have preferred the grave to bringing Frou-Frou with her when she and her deadly husband came to work their little garden or sit in the summerhouse which dubiously ornamented it. Dash's evil reputation had long since preceded him.

For years Dash took no notice of Monsieur Bigué, although he passed the kitchen steps almost daily, always carrying an umbrella and a basket. (In addition to being bores, they were a mistrustful, suspicious pair, who never for a moment trusted anyone or anything, even the weather.) Then one morning, without visible provocation, Dash sprang from the kitchen steps and tore the seat out of Monsieur Bigué's pants as he passed with his basket and umbrella. Marguerite, the fat cook, rescued Monsieur Bigué, and when I heard of the incident I went to wait upon Madame Bigué at the jewelry shop. She received me with dignity as I explained my regrets and said that I wished to make reparation.

All would be forgotten, said Madame Bigué (while the virgin Frou-Frou yapped in some hidden portion of the house) if Dash were left with the veterinary until it was determined whether he had hydrophobia and if I paid the doctor's bill and for a new suit of clothes for Monsieur Bigué. It just happened, said Madame Bigué, that Monsieur, although he was bound to work in the garden, was wearing his best suit, and as it was obviously impossible to buy a new pair of trousers that would match the rare pattern of Monsieur Bigué's choice, a mere new pair of trousers wouldn't suffice; it had to be a whole new suit. I inquired for Monsieur Bigué, but was told that he was prostrated and that his leg was swollen to elephantine proportions.

The story ended happily enough. I paid the doctor's bill and bought a new suit for Monsieur Bigué. Dash, it turned out as I expected, did not have hydrophobia. I think he merely had great wisdom. I never knew whether Dash attacked the jeweler because he had heard about Frou-Frou and the seclusion in which she was kept or whether he did it because Monsieur Bigué was an intolerable bore, and Dash could not support watching him pass one more time with his basket and umbrella. I only know that if Dash hadn't attacked him, I should have bitten Monsieur Bigué one day myself.

That, then, is the history and character of Dash, not a dog who, after ruling the dogs in his own house and indeed in all the town, would welcome the arrival of a big boxer from Germany.

On the first morning after Rex's arrival, the two dogs encountered one another in the garden. They did not growl. They did not sniff at each other. As for Rex, he walked past Dash with perfect dignity, ignoring him. For once in his life Dash did not attack on sight. His tail went straight into the air and twice he walked the length of the garden on his toes, very stiff-legged, like a ballet dancer, every hair on end. He attempted to ignore the big bulldog, but couldn't quite succeed. He kept watching him out of the corner of his eye, sizing him up. For once, it seemed, he decided he had met his master. Presently, with an air of the utmost casualness and dignity, he re-entered the house and went through it to his post on the kitchen steps, where he could watch what went on in the street and attack any unfortunate dog who happened to pass by. As a tramp, the kitchen steps were just the place for him. As for Rex, the newcomer, Dash simply treated him exactly as if he were not there, either in the house or the garden. On Rex's part, the tactic suited him: like most big men, he was neither pompous nor aggressive because he did not have to be. He merely wanted to be left in peace to look after his family.

Relations between the two dogs never improved, although they continued to live in the same house. When they encountered each other, Rex ignored Dash and Dash walked past Rex with the aggressive, stiff-legged dignity of a very small Scot. Rex was the only dog that Dash failed to attack in the whole nine years of his life. I think it was not the size of Rex which awed him, for he had fought even bigger dogs and sent them howling down the street; it was the awful, regal manner which Dash had never encountered among the mongrels of the town.

But Rex's other rival was of a different character. She was tiny, with gray and black speckled hair which made her coat appear less like hair or fur than like the feathers of a guinea fowl. She weighed a little over a pound and had a tiny, pointed head and a delicate pink nose with brown, shoe-button eyes. When she was angry she would sit up, balancing herself on her tail, and chatter. All her hair stood on end so that she took on a bushy appearance, and the brown, shoe-button eyes turned red. She had tiny brown paws which gave her the effect, when she sat erect, of a very chic lady wearing brown gloves.

George and I had found her in a market at Madras being dragged along on a string by a Pathan six feet six with a foot-high turban and a menacing appearance. Then one of those things happened for which one is forever grateful. Obviously, she did not like being dragged along and had no intention of giving in. She chattered, her eyes turned red and all her hair stood on end. There seemed only one way of rescuing her and that was to buy her. After some double talk haggling with the big Pathan we bought her for thirteen rupees which was a big price for a mongoose but it turned out to be much less than she was worth.

The moment the Pathan stopped dragging her along on a string her temper began to cool. I put her in the pocket of my coat with the string still attached and she went along perfectly happily. She had to have a name and there was but one universal name for a mongoose. She became Rikky after the mongoose in Kipling's famous story.

The odd thing was that she settled in at once on George and me. Mongooses are curiously sociable animals and like to live with people, so long as their freedom is not restricted. All over India mongoose families live in peace and contentment in and under bungalows, driving away the snakes. And so, although we removed the string almost at once when we returned to Government House where we were staying, she did not run away, but stayed about, following me everywhere and putting her pink nose into everything.

If a mongoose has one outstanding characteristic it is curiosity of an unbelievable violence. I have an English friend who lived for years in India and christened his mongoose, quite rightly, "Parker" after "Nosey Parker." Rikky was no exception; she had to open every drawer and box, get inside every piece of luggage to see what was there. If a cigarette or matchbox offered difficulties she would work over it until she found the secret. One afternoon her curiosity brought disaster. I had sat down, all dressed in white flannels for a visit to the palace, to write a letter, and no sooner had I begun than Rikky was up on the writing desk, watching the movement of my pen. She reached out with her little, brown-gloved hands now and then to touch the pen. When she had divined approximately what I was doing, she turned her curiosity elsewhere, this time to the ink pot. I pushed her away once or twice, but instantly she was back again and, eager to get on with my letter, I forgot her until suddenly she jumped from the table into my lap and then I saw what she had been doing. She had been dipping her tiny paws into the inkwell and as she ran from my lap up to my shoulder she left footprints of ink the whole length of my white flannel suit.

Sometimes during the day and always at night, she would disappear. At first, I was alarmed, but always she came back. And then one day I discovered where she went—inside the springs of the mattress. Later on, I discovered the trick and why she did it. Being an immensely active animal with a restless, lightning-like movement all during the waking hours, she slept soundly when she slept, so soundly that on occasions when I found her hiding place I had at first the impression that she was dead. It sometimes took as much as a full minute to rouse her. And gradually I came to understand why she hid herself away when she slept. It was the ancient instinct of protection. She would never sleep in her basket, but always sought a place where she would be completely hidden away, where no enemy could surprise or attack her while she was sleeping. Once while we were traveling in a small launch down the backwaters of the Malabar coast, she hid herself away so thoroughly between the floor and the hull of the launch that we had to tear apart the boat to find, waken and recover her. It cost me money for repairs, but by that time I had become so attached to her that I would, I think, have bought the whole launch rather than lose her.

She came back with us to France, most of the way in my pocket, on a P. and O. boat. I was troubled about the difference in climate and how she would survive. The moment she reached the house and garden she looked things over and decided somehow that this was home. For the first night she slept inside a big, upholstered sofa, but after a day of reconnoitering, she came to the conclusion that she had found a better place. I should have had no concern about her coming halfway around the world to a new country and a new climate, for never was there a small animal more capable of taking care of herself. She had, in fact, chosen the space between the roof of the stable and the flooring of the attic above. There she built herself a nest of old rags and bits of newspapers, salvaged from the dust bin. She slept amid fragments of the *Figaro*, *L'Illustration* and the *Revue des Deux Mondes.*

Before I knew how well she could take care of herself, I drilled a small hole in one of the doors so that she could come in and out at will when the nights were frosty. In my stupidity I believed that she did not know when the weather was too cold for her outside. I had a small slide of wood fixed so that, once inside, I could close the opening and keep her in the house. In order to teach her what the hole was for (a piece of presumption and nonsense on my part) I put her through the hole, and then went inside and pushed the slide across the opening. And instantly, as she had done so many times, she made a fool of me. She sat up on her hind legs, took one look at the slide, pushed it aside and went out. Not to be baffled, I fastened a hook to the slide to thwart her. Again I put her through the small hole and this time fastened the slide with a hook. Immediately she attempted to push back the slide and at once discovered that the trick wouldn't work. After studying the situation for a second with her tiny head a little on one side, she went to work on the hook and in less than a minute discovered how it worked. She lifted the hook and went out again.

After that experience I gave up and left the hole in the door open and then I discovered that she knew perfectly well, far better than myself or any weather forecaster, when it was cold enough to come into the house. Indeed, she became a perfect weather forecaster. If there was to be a sharp drop in temperature, she would come into the house and sleep inside the springs of the sofa. Otherwise, she stayed in her nest in the stable.

She would come to the sofa on other occasions, usually when there were people for lunch or visiting dogs. Then she would thrust her nose out from under the cushions and lure the dogs toward her. When they thrust their noses into the cushions she would give them a sharp nip that sent the dogs away howling. On more than one occasion she startled guests seated on the sofa, and sometimes unaware even of her existence, by dashing in the door and into the sofa between their ankles. Even more startling was her occasional performance during the Sunday lunches which took place in the happy days before World War II at the old Presbytère in Senlis. In those days there was always a big buffet lunch with sometimes as many as fifty people or more and then once the buffet began to be set up a sharp eye had to be kept out for Rikky. She loved hard-boiled eggs and had the passion of a dope fiend for sardines or cold salmon trout and unless an eye was kept on the buffet without relaxation, the sardines and salmon would be raided by Rikky and all have disappeared long before the guests arrived. At such lunches, the guests sat where they liked all through the house, some of them choosing unwisely the very sofa where Rikky had long ago established a nest for herself. And frequently enough Rikky was *inside* the sofa when guests seated themselves and began to eat. There was not always time to explain to guests that the family included a mongoose and more than once a shriek arose when from the inside of the sofa and from under the cushions there appeared a small sharp-nosed head with a pair of shoe-button eyes, looking this way and that with the greatest excitement and interest. The results were even more violent if the guest had never seen a mongoose. She had a trick of showing great interest and curiosity in people who were terrified of her. Malice, indeed, was as much a part of her character as curiosity.

One of her favorite tricks was to climb inside my shirt into the sleeve and come down my arm, thrusting her pink nose and bright eyes out of the cuff to watch what was going on. She would sit on my shoulder and nibble at the lobe of my ear with her sharp teeth, gently, without ever harming me. I think it was her one way of showing affection. If I went into the garden and called her she would either give no sign of hearing me or would put her head out of a crack of masonry in the old walls and chatter impudently without any sign of coming down. But, sooner or later, she would appear, *casually*, on the garden path as if she had just happened along on her own. And she had another trick, done out of malice with every evidence of a sense of humor. While I worked in the garden with my mind far from her, she would sneak up under cover of the vegetation and jump suddenly on my head, clinging there with her tiny feet. She never failed to get the expected result of a yell.

She was death on rats and frogs. The big river rats from the little river which ran through the garden were too big for her to kill, but she had her way of dealing with them, and before long drove them away altogether. I have watched her at work. She would hide and, when a great rat came lumbering out of the water, she would dart out like lightning, give him a thorough clawing and biting and disappear again before he knew what was happening. When you heard wild squeals from the riverbank, you knew she was at work. On more than one occasion she killed a whole litter of young rats in the old chapel or the garage, and always she left them, laid out neatly on the garden path in a row. I do not know why she did this, but it was as if she said, "See what I have done!" She would play eternally the cobra game. I would strike at her with the striking gesture of the cobra and at the fraction of a second my hand struck at her she would leap straight upward three or four feet in the air. Never was I quick enough to touch her.

She did not eat the rats. She liked snakes and frogs and the eggs of the white fantail pigeons and had a great fondness for hens' eggs which were given her once a day. To a stranger it was always a source of amusement to watch her cope with the problem of breaking the shell. She would stand on her hind legs and with her front paws push the egg backward between her legs, in the fashion of a football center passing the ball, until it struck a stone step or wall and the shell was broken.

When she first came to the house in France her playmates were two puppies, a Scotty and a mongrel fox terrier called Albert, after Albert de Mun who found him abandoned on the roadside between Senlis and Paris and brought him to us, and a Siamese cat called Sita. With the puppies the games were all play, but with the others, there were times when the jungle emerged in both Rikky and the cat, moments when on the ground or in a tree they went for each other with teeth and claw. It was always Rikky, with her lightning quickness, who had the advantage.

It was Rex, the big boxer, who aroused her jealousy. The other dogs she did not mind or the Siamese cat, but a few days after Rex arrived, she divined, I think, that he had a special place in my heart, and from then on she gave him no peace.

At first he chased her and I feared that he might do her harm. Each time I called him off, until, with his good boxer character, he controlled himself and adopted a new tactic of ignoring her. This only made her more malicious, and she would follow him about, trying to lure him into chasing her, sometimes even running between his legs while he walked with me in the garden. If he sat or lay on the grass she would come sneaking toward him, her little eyes red with jealousy and anger, every hair standing on end, her tail suddenly inflated to the size of a fox's brush. I have seen her creep close to him and put her pink nose against his big, black muzzle while he trembled all over with restraint. If he made a sudden move she was off like lightning up the nearest tree or wall. She knew that he never had a chance against her quickness. At last, unwilling to see the well-mannered dog tormented by her malice, I said, "All right. Get her!" After that he chased her whenever she began the tactics of annoying him. He never had the remotest chance of catching her, and I think she enjoyed the game of being chased, knowing perfectly well that she was safe.

It was a feud, a jealousy between the tiny mongoose and the big dog, which never died until the day Rex and I left France and were forced to leave her behind.

This happened when Mr. Chamberlain went to Munich with his umbrella and rubbers to meet Hitler. On the day the meeting was announced any sensible, well-informed person knew that there was no longer any hope of averting war and the collapse of Europe. I sent my family home to America. When, after months, I listened to the counsel of Louis Gillet that I could do much more good for France in the U.S. than I could in Europe, and returned home, I could not take Rikky with me because no mongoose was allowed to enter the United States.

I made the discovery nearly a year before when Mrs. Lehman, who loved animals, cabled me suddenly from New York—"AM SENDING MY MONGOOSE TO YOU STOP NOT PERMITTED TO ENTER THE U.S." Ten days later there arrived a box and in it a mongoose. I had received the cable with pleasure, thinking that Rikky would have a mate or, at least, a companion, but when I opened the box I had a disappointment. What came out was not a gay, wicked, malicious, slim creature like Rikky, but a rather heavy animal with black rings around its gray body, looking more like a rat than like Rikky. From the first it appeared to be a stupid and ill-tempered beast which, despite its apparent tameness, would bite at the least provocation. It was a mongoose all right, but an African one.

Rikky would have none of it and clearly did not consider it a mongoose at all but merely some striped form of river rat. After circling about it suspiciously for a time, she attacked it, using the same hit-and-run methods she employed on big rats. The African mongoose had none of Rikky's quickness, and after a few moments bewilderment, fled in the direction of the river. I rescued it from the water and took it into the house, thinking that at a second or third encounter Rikky might become used to it and accept its company. But it was no good. Rikky considered her African cousin a stupid monstrosity and after she had twice again driven it into the river I gave it away to Charlotte Erikson who lived in the same town. She kept it and managed to cure some of its ill-temper, although it always remained a treacherous beast which never learned Rikky's trick of sitting on your shoulder to nibble your ear quietly and affectionately.

When life in Senlis came to an end forever and we left the old house by the Nonette, George took Rex with him on the *Normandie* straight to America, since the quarantine on dogs in the British Isles made it impossible to take him with me to London.

Rikky was left behind with Picquet, the friend of Dash and Marquise, who was next, I think, in her affections to me. The thought of leaving her with Picquet softened the sorrow of parting a little, for I knew that, with his "teched" quality as a "natural" he understood animals and would care for her and feed her even if he sacrificed food from his own table. For more than a year she took over Picquet, not as a master, since she never accepted a master, but as a friend. Dash was dead, having passed away of premature senility, owing, I think, to a disreputable but highly enjoyable life. The one remaining Scotty, not a very bright or affectionate dog, I left with a friend. Sita, too, was gone, after having become paralyzed from having too large a litter of kittens by an alley tomcat. The old life had come to an end.

But at last the mobilization caught up with middle-aged Picquet and he went off to war with the older men to do what they could for the defense of France. For a time the Senegalese troops were quartered in the house and these were followed by Communist riffraff which pilfered what remained and finally the Germans took over but failed to occupy the place because it had been so badly damaged. Finally a bomb tore off the shutters and part of the roof and kind neighbors repaired the damage and boarded up the desolation. When finally the occupation took place, it became more and more difficult to get any news from France and I sometimes wakened in the night, troubled over what had happened to Rikky. And then one day I had a letter through the Underground, passed from hand to hand until somehow it reached Casablanca and was posted there. (Much mail came that way, some of it with no more than my name and U.S.A. written on the envelope.) The letter was from a good friend of mine, a master pilot who brought in and took out the great oceangoing ships that came to Antwerp. He had been a refugee and presently, when he and his wife were repatriated, they went by chance through Senlis and stopped off at the house where once all of us had been so happy. They both saw Rikky, who thrust her tiny head out of the crevice in the wall of the garage and chattered at them and then came down to greet them exactly as she used to do with me again and again. They wrote that she seemed in excellent health and quite able to take care of herself.

Afterward, I had news of her from time to time from neighbors in Senlis, always through the Underground. She stayed by the deserted house, living in her nest in the garage and perhaps going now and again into the silent and deserted house. She was quite able to feed herself on frogs and mice and even young rats, but the neighbors saw to it, even during the privations of rationing, that she got occasionally the eggs she liked so well, and it is a great tribute to her personality that people took time and even grave risks just to tell me that she was alive and flourishing. But the French are like that about pets; they do not believe in any arbitrary line that sets one group of God's creatures aside from another. On the whole the Frenchman, even the poorest and most wretched, looks upon animals as brothers who have never quite grown up or learned to speak. That is one reason I have for them so great a respect and affection and believe them to be by far the wisest of all peoples.

And then the war was over and my daughter Hope went back to visit the house at Senlis where there had once been so much happiness and gaiety before the war. She found it deserted and partly ruined and wept. In the garden she called for Rikky but this time the tiny head with the shoe-button eyes did not appear in the crevice of the stable wall, and when she talked with the neighbors, she learned simply that they had not seen Rikky for a long time and believed that she was dead. She had simply disappeared but I am quite sure that I know where she went. She was very old for a mongoose and had had a very interesting life ranging from the hills of Ootacamund in India to Senlis in France. She had known a great many distinguished and famous and fashionable people and even raised shrieks of terror from some of them. She had survived a great war and lived through shellfire, bombs and occupation.

Sometimes I have wondered what the German troops or the black Senegalese thought when suddenly the strange little animal, the like of which they had never seen before, appeared in the garden. Did she climb up on their shoulders or jump suddenly on their heads? I think not, for she was both a cautious and an intelligent little beast and possessed of a sharp instinct for those who were her friends and those who were not. If she did they were probably so startled that they made no attempt to harm her. In any case, she was always too quick for a pistol shot ever to end her life. I like to think of her tantalizing the Germans as she tantalized Rex.

I think that one evening, with all the instinct and resignation of an animal (which indeed we might well envy) she went up to her little nest made of *L'Illustration, Le Figaro* and *La Revue des Deux Mondes* and fell into one of those deep sleeps from which it was always so difficult to awaken her. Only this time she did not awaken, and if some day the ancient stable is pulled down, someone will find there deep within its walls the bones of a tiny animal, curled up into a little ball, and they will wonder at what kind of beast it was and how it came there.

But somehow little Rikky has led me a long way astray from Rex, the big boxer, on his way back to America to avoid the quarantine regulations in England. London, which I love very much, seemed to me under the Chamberlain government to be an uncomfortable and at times intolerable place, immersed in a sense of doom which could perhaps have been avoided. But now it was too late and I stayed there only a little time on my way home. Friends came to see me off at Waterloo Station, and a moment before the train pulled out there appeared far down the platform a tall, slim handsome Georgian carrying in his arms a half-grown puppy. It was Mito Djordjadze, who with his wife Audrey gave us the big boxer Rex who had become an indispensable part of all our lives and as much a part of the family as one of the children. As Mito came near I saw from the dark, snub-nosed, wrinkled, little face that the puppy was a boxer, not a golden one like Rex but a dark brindle with one white paw and a white star on her chest.

Breathless, Mito said, "I've brought you a wife for Rex!" And I remembered the promise of Mito and his wife Audrey that they would one day give us a mate for Rex.

I took the puppy into my arms and realized that she was thin and ill. "It's the best I could find," said Mito. "You went off in such a hurry. She's just got over distemper. The kennel people say she'll be all right."

She was indeed "all right" as later on I was to discover. It is difficult to suggest how much friendship and pleasure she was to bring into the lives of all of us.

The train started, and I jumped aboard with a puppy I hadn't expected.

There was trouble about keeping her in my compartment, and I went to the luggage van and sat there all the way to Southampton. If ever a dog could not be left alone, it was that puppy. She was ugly and thin and ill, but in her eyes there was something which I think I recognized even then as humor and gaiety and independence.

Aboard the ship she had to stay in the kennel on the top deck with the other dogs, but I spent nearly the whole of every day with her and saw to it that she got warm milk and brandy. Most of the time she lay listlessly in my lap, but she attracted an admirer who evidently liked frail ladies. He was the biggest, ugliest English bulldog I have ever seen. His name was Harry and he had a heart as big as he was ugly. He was being shipped to a kennel in America, and he had no master, but he soon took care of that by adopting me and the pup. All the way across the Atlantic he insisted on lying on the bench beside us with his head on my knee. By the time we reached New York I would have bought him if I had known to whom he belonged. We said goodbye to Harry and he was put back in his box to be shipped somewhere in New England. I have never seen him since but he was one of the most charming, if sloppy, personalities I have ever met.

It seemed obvious that the wife of Rex should be called Regina and so that became the puppy's name. She was still very sick while I stayed in New York, and most of the time she spent on a sofa in my mother's flat, languishing like a mid-Victorian invalid.

Like many a woman who is never strong until she has a baby, Regina was sickly until she had her first litter of six pups at Malabar. From that moment on she was strong as an ox. Since then she has had twenty more pups and is many times a grandmother and great-grandmother, but even today none of her offspring are gayer or stronger. She has always been a good mother, but a stern disciplinarian with no "Momism" or Oedipus nonsense about her. With each litter there comes a time when she feels they should go on their own and out they go. She will have no more of them, but in an odd fashion she continues to discipline them. Even though Prince, her eldest son, is only about eighteen months younger than herself, she took no nonsense from him or from any of her other children or grandchildren. She was affectionate, but independent and hardy, and often enough when all the other boxers are inside in winter, Gina stayed out sunning herself by the greenhouse with the cocker spaniels.

Rex and Regina became the founders of a long line of boxers at Malabar. Three of their sons—Prince and Baby and Smoky—lived there until they died. Their brothers and sisters are scattered all over the country, with owners who feel about boxers as we do, that there is something special about a boxer which makes them different from other dogs. Usually the extra pups are given away but they are never given or sold at any price to people without proper references; which means simply that they have to be a little "teched" like all of us at Malabar and understand that animals can be people and sometimes better people than a good m any I know.

There is a kind of fraternity among people who own boxers. You can speak to them on the street, anywhere in the world even though they are total strangers, and stand there indefinitely talking about the virtues and personality of the breed. I have in my time owned fifty or sixty dogs of many breeds and I have always made friends with dogs, even in the end with poor savage Marquise, but the boxer is different from them all. He is stubborn and gay and comical. He may be devoted to you but never in a worshipful way. He knows your faults and accepts them. He is not a pet. He is a companion and friend and equal. Wherever I go on Malabar, five or six boxers go with me. They are as companionable as any friend. They race off after rabbits, vainly, for they have little nose and none too good sight, but their sense of hearing is fantastically acute, which accounts, I suppose, for the fact that they have always been watch and police dogs. I have sometimes seen three or four of them racing up hill in pursuit of a wild rabbit with the rabbit running unnoticed in their midst.

Their origin as a breed is somewhat obscure. But there is one story that they are one of the oldest breeds in the world, coming originally from Manchuria and North China, where they guarded caravans and compounds, and, indeed, it may be true, for the ancient stone dogs one sees in China guarding the entrance to compounds are very like the modern boxer. There is another story that they were bred as far back as the Middle Ages for the sports of boar hunting and bull baiting, and indeed this may be true for they have an inbred aversion to hogs (which may be only their jealousy of the hogs' intelligence and my personal liking for hogs) and they are poor cattle dogs for they usually go to the head of the beast. However, these faults do not matter, as faults are unimportant in one's companion and best friend.

Yet they are good farm dogs, for they do not go off hunting as hunting dogs will do and rarely run across country chasing cattle or killing sheep like the terriers. Like Rikky, the mongoose, they are happiest when they are with people and rarely go a hundred yards from the house unless someone goes with them. To them the prospect of going for a long walk across the fields is as exciting as going for a walk can be to a dog bred in a city apartment.

There is probably no family of dogs which suffers so profoundly from claustrophobia as the boxers. I think this is so because I have never known any other animal or breed of dogs which comes so near to being human. They cannot abide being shut up and left alone, and frequently take violent measures to escape. Part of their resentment arises undoubtedly from being deprived of the company of their masters, and on the whole no person should have a boxer who shuts him up for long periods without companionship. Nanny, who possesses an incurable British stubbornness, attempted more than

once when I have been absent to shut one or more of the boxers
into my bedroom and office. She never succeeded and only cost
me considerable expense in repairs of the damage they did to doors
and window frames on which they attempted to chew their way out.
Baby, the show-off and clown, resented being shut up and left alone
more than any of the others and all the doors and the window frames
of my room are scarred with the signs of his efforts, always successful in the end, to escape. The resentment and suffering at being shut
up and isolated is closely akin to the feelings of many an imprisoned
human. They are certainly not kennel dogs, as indeed is no dog. On
one occasion during a farm tour, some ostentatious person closed all
the car windows of the station wagon with Baby inside; on my return
I found him outside, his jaws bloodied; he had literally chewed the
glass from one of the windows and found his liberty. Twice when he
was accidentally shut into the greenhouse, he literally chewed his
way out through glass, frame and all.

In the big house at Malabar it is rare indeed that the dogs are left
at home alone. Even though the whole house is left open on such
occasions (for the boxers are all one needs to protect the place),
the dogs resent being left alone and on one or two or three occasions when they have been left because all the household went to
a high school graduation or the annual minstrel show of the Lucas
High School Mothers' Club, they have wreaked havoc, very clearly
with the intention of "getting even." On one occasion we returned
to find the living room floor strewn with bits of cloth and what were
evidently the remnants of artificial flowers. After piecing them together, we discovered that the bits were all that was left of a hat and
a scarf belonging to a close friend who was staying in the house. But
even worse had taken place in her room, for when we investigated
we found that the dogs, who were all perfectly house-trained, had
lifted their legs on the bedposts. I can only assume that they decided
among themselves that the friend and guest, as a new element in the
household, was responsible for their being deserted, and so they had
stolen her hat and scarf and messed up her bedroom. Fortunately
the friend felt as I do about dogs.

A friend of mine in New York returned home to his flat late one night to find the entire flat strewn with feathers from the cushion his boxer had torn apart and scattered throughout the flat, simply I think because he had been imprisoned and left alone for too long. As there are always many dogs at Malabar, most of them boxers, it is obvious that the fact of who is boss must sooner or later be established and a dog government set up. Always it is the oldest dog who takes over and what he says goes with all the others. When the oldest dies or gets so old that he spends most of his day sleeping, the next oldest takes over. The successor at once changes his character, obviously quiets down, and assumes his responsibilities. Sometimes the change, as with Rex II, is a startling one. When Baby at last died, Rex II, who was a gay and frivolous dog who wrestled violently with all the boys and the children, settled down and became middle-aged and full of authority. There was no more nonsense, he had a serious job to do. The change in Baby, the great clown and show-off, was even greater when the faithful, suffering Prince died suddenly. He stopped abruptly showing off. There was no more high-diving to the applause and cheers of visitors and no more clowning with sticks, wheelbarrows and beer cans. Virtually overnight, he settled down.

In all this it is evident to me that dogs not only understand much of what we say but perhaps have an understanding, instinctive and intuitional, of many things which we do not understand. They certainly know when I am going away and they are obviously reassured when I tell them I will be back soon. Although Prince died at the veterinary hospital and simply left Malabar without coming back, I am quite certain that Baby knew that he was dead. There is no other explanation for Baby's abrupt change in behavior and his assumption of responsibility as head of the family. Ostensibly Prince was not simply there any longer, but it did not require days or weeks for Baby to become aware of the fact that he was never coming back; he knew it almost from the hour Prince died.

Those people who brush aside these instinctive and intuitional powers of dogs, and indeed of all animals, as merely unreal and sentimental, seem to me to be very stupid people, like all those who in conceit or egotism or mere stupidity, believe that there is nothing more to be discovered in life. The evidence is, of course, all against them, even in the most scientific circles. Indeed, concerning the universe and its law, we know almost nothing in comparison with what there is to be learned. It is foolish and sometimes cruel to underestimate the intelligence, the intuition and the instinct of animals. It is clearly evident that many humans are deficient in these qualities of intuition and instinct, especially those who are themselves possessed of individual limitations so great that whole realms of experience are forever closed to them. It is among these that we are most likely to find the egotist, the bore, the tactless, the pretentious, the vulgar and, despite any amount of degrees or diplomas, the stupid and the ignorant. The very basis of all this has been admirably put by Alexis Carrel, one of the greatest medical and physiological scientists in our time, when he wrote that simply because we have discovered pretty much everything about the mechanistic physiological workings of the body, there is no reason to suppose that there are not whole worlds of mysticism, intuition, inherited instinct, mental telepathy, and other traits and manifestations, which exist and are quite as real as the tangible, material substance of a body with which we have become thoroughly familiar. We cannot assume that what we do not understand and have never investigated does not exist simply because we fail to understand or to penetrate the mystery.

The children of Rex and Regina each had his own personality. Prince, the eldest son, never left me by more than three feet from the time I rose in the morning until I went to bed at night. There was nothing groveling or worshipful in his devotion. It was simply that I was his best friend. He came to understand that when I went away, it was not for good and that I always came back, but the mere sight of "store" clothes brought out of the cupboard threw him into a depression. From that moment on until I left the house, he sat at a distance from me, watching every move with a sad, reproachful eye. Even when I got into the car to go to the station, he would not come near me. He was a great worrier and always filled with anxiety. His son, the second Rex, has the same traits and habits, save that he has a happier, more philosophic disposition and worries much less than his father.

Prince's brother, Baby, was in a sense an orphan, for he was the only one to survive from a litter born prematurely to Regina after she threw herself gaily into the middle of a dogfight. He was brought up on a bottle by Venetia Wills, who as an *evacuée* from bombed England was staying with us, and he had his own special character. He was both a born farmer and a clown, with a great attachment for the horses. All his days were spent out-of-doors on the farm, mostly with Charley Martin, who ran the vegetable garden in those days and did a bit of everything. He would spend a whole day walking up and down a field beside the horses when they were plowing, perfectly happy. He was never popular with the other dogs, chiefly, I think, because they recognized him as a show-off and a ham actor. Also they may have resented his position as the principal farmer among the dogs.

He drank Coca-Cola from a bottle and water straight from the tap, lapping the water as it fell. To him a wheelbarrow was meant to ride in and if he was with you working in the garden, he would jump into the wheelbarrow the moment it was empty and stay there until he was wheeled up to the house. But his best trick was his high-diving from the high platform into the pond just below the Big House. With a running start he would go off the platform at a height of twelve feet and leap twenty feet into the water for a stick. Despite the fact that boxers are not water dogs and Rex and Prince had to be driven outside on a rainy day to step high and with distaste in the wet grass, Regina, Baby and Smoky all took to the water like retrievers. I think this is so because they grew up with two cocker spaniels and a golden retriever who, even in zero weather, would break the ice of the pond, go for a swim and then come out and roll in the snow. During the hot days of midsummer, Regina would sit in the pond a whole morning with only her head above the water, looking for all the world like a rather ugly hippo.

No one on the farm ever bothered to teach them any tricks, for there was never time. Baby invented all his own bag of tricks, begging as a born show-off to perform the high-diving stunt whenever visitors arrived. He was the only one of the dogs who held long conversations with you, answering each question with different intonations, a trick which infuriated the others, notably his elder brother, Prince, who, after the death of Rex, took over as boss of the farm dogs. He kept them in order, aided by Regina who never gave up disciplining them, even her oldest son, Prince; and as Baby turned older, he turned out to be the only rebel against authority. The rebellion led occasionally to fights, such as took place more and more frequently as Rex grew old and ill and was no longer able to assert his authority. A fight among four or five big boxers is a terrifying spectacle to behold for one not used to them and unable to assert his authority. I have scars on one wrist and one ankle where Prince, in the midst of a fight, got hold of me instead of Rex or Baby. His shame when he made the discovery that it was I he was biting was moving to behold.

In the evenings all four, Regina, Prince, Baby, Smoky and a new-comer called Folly, came into the house and now and then they took over and staged a fight which wreaked havoc. As the source of most such rows was usually the question of who could sit or lie nearest to me, the fights were likely to take place under a card table. As a fight between two became a general brawl, cards, drinks, score pads and all were likely to go flying into the air. Now and then a fight occurred under a table with *bibelots* or a vase of flowers, and the result was the same. On occasion the breakage was extremely expensive. The most celebrated fight of all took place one evening under the dining room table during a children's party with twelve kids present. Before it was stopped two chairs were broken and there were milk, cake and ice cream on floor, walls and ceiling.

Big dogs, indeed, have no place in the life of demon housekeepers. Fortunately, all our household prefers dogs to an immaculate house. Five boxers sleep in my room which serves as office, bedroom and workroom and fortunately is on the ground floor and has many windows and two outside doors leading into the garden. Prince slept on the foot of my bed, Folly in a dog bed at the foot, Gina on the sofa, and Smoky and Baby on chairs. Long after Baby had outgrown the chair he chose as a puppy and hung over both ends, nothing would induce him to give it up. Each place belongs to a different boxer, and if one attempts to take over the property of another, the fight is on. Now and then, other members of the family complained that my room is a little "high" and Nanny attacked it with Lysol, taking over usually while I was away and could not protest. I am afraid that I prefer the smell of dogs to the smell of Lysol.

When there are many dogs in a big house, the problem of letting them in and out in time becomes a burden and long ago we solved the problem by constructing in my office-bedroom on the ground floor a "dog's door." It is simply a door, about three feet high, which like a pantry door swings both ways. It permits them to go and come as they like and, if at night they become aware that there are trespassers outside anywhere near the house, they can rush out and attack at will, regardless of the weather. For the boxers it also provides the great freedom of movement which they crave so frantically. This freedom involves only one fault—a great one perhaps in the eyes of many people but one to which I have become by necessity thoroughly accustomed. There are times when the disturbing intruder which the dogs sense outside the house turns out to be a skunk and more than once in the night I have been awakened when the dogs returned, not by light or by any sound, but by the sense of smell alone. As a rule it requires very little time for the pups to learn that a skunk is something to be left alone, but there is always that somewhat distressing period when they are learning their lesson the hard way. One of the youngest of our boxers, however, a professional beauty called Rocky, has clearly decided that he will become a famous and distinguished skunk hunter and has chosen to concentrate on skunks. I have grown quite used to the smell by now and for me it is less obnoxious than the smell of many chemicals and disinfectants. Indeed, when one becomes as accustomed to it as I am there is a definite musky cleanness about the smell.

The Great House at Malabar is no place for the house-proud woman or the demon housekeeper. It is a very big house but it belongs to the dogs and the children as much as to the grownups. The boxer family are permitted to use the chairs and the sofas and sooner or later each one establishes his liking for a given chair. All this, combined with their own dog's door, allows them all the freedom of the people they live with. It is true that the boxer family are very agreeable companions with whom to share a house, for they are short-haired and, like cats, are forever cleaning themselves; they cannot abide dirt or mud. Only in the winter and early spring, do they provide a problem when outside the house the mud is everywhere; but even then they probably track in less mud than many of the grownups, including first of all myself.

I have never had any great fondness or even tolerance for the kind of woman who is forever emptying ash trays or becomes alarmed if her husband or one of his friends or her son accidentally drops a bit of cigarette ash on the floor. There are many things in life far more important than the woman who keeps a "spotless" house, including the house itself. Often enough she belongs to the category of women who drive their husbands and sons to refuge in the nearest poolroom, bar or bowling alley.

If I were to give a bit of advice for a young man contemplating marriage, it would be, "Beware of the 'dainty' woman—the woman who shudders when she is approached by a dog, the woman who is forever brushing spots off your tie or straightening it, the woman who won't take a drink herself but drinks out of your glass to 'save' you." All of these traits betray a hidden monster who, if one day you marry her, will tread you underfoot or drive you from your own house to find comfort and peace. Beneath the "daintiness" she is both a phony and a steam roller, possessed of an iron will and determination to run you and everything connected with her. She has a sense of values which is both common and perverted. The best bet is to marry a child of one of these women. They have suffered and will abhor all the characteristics which made their mother a "good woman" and a demon housekeeper. That is, if you are able to keep the mother-in-law at arm's length and prevent her from extending her pernicious influence and authority into your own life and that of your family. In the small world at Malabar we come to find spontaneously, and to protect ourselves and warn each other, expressions to describe certain categories of people. Cranks are commonly known as "earthworm people" and house-proud women are always known as "little Lady Dainty."

As a rule such women keep the dog in the cellar or outside the house the year round. They are the kind of women who use the whole common abominable jargon invented by interior decorators and women's magazines. They are the sort who refer to "lovely homes" and "gorgeous drapes," to "scatter rugs" and "occasional chairs" and sometimes even to "chase lounges" (an expression with concealed comic qualities and lewd implications). Of all these expressions which send a shudder up the backbone, I think I heard the very peak when on one occasion a "dainty" woman asked me at a cocktail party if I would like a "cold shape." I replied that during a lifelong experience I had encountered several "cold shapes" but was probably not thinking of the kind she meant. It turned out that what she meant was an abhorrent "molded" salad which I passed by for something more edible.

There is much that I admire in the British and especially in the life that once had its center in the great English country houses and frequently even in the small cottages lived in by civilized people. It was, in its heyday, the finest and most civilized life that perhaps has ever existed, and best of all perhaps was the fact that dogs were considered as members of the household and even of the family. In many a French household, the pets are given greater consideration than the members of the family, which is probably very good for the members. Inez Robb, who comes regularly to stay at Malabar Farm, once remarked that her greatest desire was to die and be reincarnated as a dog at Malabar, since they had the best life she had ever encountered in years of travel and experience throughout the world. It was, I thought, a great compliment which I accepted graciously.

Even as I write, in my combination bedroom and office, Rex II lies curled up on the sofa beside me watching me with his great brown eyes. I would rather have him there than a great many people I know. He is a better companion; he is more amusing and entertaining and he has much greater tact, instinct, intuition and sense of companionship. If he is not a friend, then I have none at all. Even though the Great House is always filled with children and boys and other dogs and he is never shut up in a kennel or even confined when I go away, he waits for me, sitting on the terrace or in winter in one of the upper windows, watching every car that comes up the long drive. When I return, the welcome from him and the other dogs is so great and so violent that whatever I am wearing must go to the cleaner. Sometimes it has to go to the mender as well. One thing is certain—they are not welcoming you in this violent fashion because they want to get something out of you; they have no plans or calculations nor any afterthoughts. So whatever I have is theirs as well as mine.

There was a time, far back when the Great House was still new, when the sofas and some of the chairs wore slip covers of expensive and beautiful Jimmy Reynolds chintzes and there was a pink and yellow Savonnerie rug in the dining room. They have all long since disappeared in a house where living, I think, is valued above antiques and the protection of inanimate fabrics, however beautiful. For a long time now, the chairs and sofas have been covered with strong and heavy materials, plain green or tan which can be washed frequently, and the dining room floor, itself beautiful when waxed, is bare; the Savonnerie rugs, which tempted the dogs with an irresistible temptation to make nests, has ended after constant repairs on the farm dump heap.

Fortunately there is no one in the house who worries about a fleck of cigarette ashes or the sight of a dog on a chair or sofa. We are all the happier for it and I think I can say that if the Great House has a characteristic of which I am proud, it is that neither furniture nor rugs nor chairs nor dust nor stains are regarded as more important than dogs or children or the comfort of the people who live in the house and visit us there. It has, I think, achieved that mellowness and warmth which makes an English country house the warmest, most charming and most civilized house in the world.

As I grow older and more cantankerous and perhaps more eccentric (which is only saying that I have earned the right to be myself) I leave the Great House less and less frequently and more and more rarely enter any house presided over by a house-proud woman. Even the sterile, characterless quality of a hotel bedroom is preferable to the "well-kept" house, filled with "gorgeous drapes" and "scatter rugs" and "occasional chairs" where one is offered "cold shapes" to eat. I am very blessed in having children and even grandchildren who feel exactly as I do.

On one occasion a summer guest observed, "I can't believe this house is new. It looks so old and well-worn. Nothing looks new!"— to which George, who for a generation was my secretary and right-hand man, replied, "Dogs and children take care of that. It looked like an old house six months after it was built."

Prince, the oldest son of Rex and Regina, had his own intelligent tricks. The doors of the house do not have knobs but French door handles, and almost at once Prince learned that he could open any door at will by turning the handle. It became impossible to shut the dogs in any room. The moment a breakfast tray goes into the bedroom of any guest, it is a sign to the dogs that the day has begun and a procession, led by Prince, who opened the door, visited the guest.

They learned long ago that few guests resist the impulse of feeding them bits of toast and bacon.

Prince not only opened all the doors inside the house but learned long ago to open the outside doors, which do not have handles but thumb catches, and to hold back the screen door while he opens the main one. He knew, too, how to open the doors of an automobile and more than once visitors have looked out of the window on cold days to observe five or six boxers sitting in their car with the doors all *closed*. For Prince learned too that closing the door behind him prevented cold air and drafts from entering the car.

But the ancient Ford station wagon was their delight, for they knew that when any of us got into it, it meant that we were off to some remote part of the farm where the other cars could not go because of the mud or the roughness of the roads and fields. In summer in the early morning they would go and sit in it to prevent its getting away without them. Once it arrived in a big field, they were all out at once to run and hunt. Boxers are not clever hunters and the only things they ever catch are ground hogs which abound over the whole of the thousand acres. They know every ground hog lair on the whole of the farm and long ago learned the trick of going straight to the lair as quickly as possible to get *between* the ground hog who may be out feeding and his safe, underground refuge. Each one of the dogs, as a pup, has had a good mauling by a big ground hog and the lesson has never been forgotten. Rex I, the German, nearly lost an eye in his first encounter. A big, old ground hog can weigh as much as forty pounds and will fight and claw like a wildcat, but the boxers learned long ago that the trick is to get their opponent behind the head and break his neck. It is all over in a second.

Although killing anything at all gives me no pleasure, the dogs do serve as a check on the ground hogs, which otherwise might dig us out of house and home, for with lynx and wildcat and wolf gone from our country there is no longer any natural check on the ground hog. No fox dares attack them. The digging of a groundhog can start bad gullies and they can destroy a whole young orchard in a week or two. There are still plenty of them left to dig holes and make shelters, not only for themselves but for rabbits and other game. A female raccoon, hard put to it for a lair in which to have her young, will share a ground hog hole with the owner.

There are always plenty of other dogs on the place. There was a female boxer called Kitchey and one called Susie Parkington, who also knew the Ford station wagon trick and joined every expedition when possible. If Susie saw or heard the station wagon she would come across country any distance to join in the picnic.

There is no more sociable dog than a boxer and there is nothing they like so much as visitors or a party. As they come rushing out they are likely to scare people to death, since they are ferocious in appearance, but they are in their hearts all amiability. All they want is to sit in your lap.

In that respect they are ideal watchdogs on a place like Malabar, where there are hundreds of visitors a year. No one can come near any building without the boxers knowing it and setting up an uproar; but biting is not a part of their natures. The golden retrievers were different, for nothing could persuade them that a part of their duties as watchdogs was *not* to *bite* and on occasion they went beyond bluff and took pieces out of Charley Kimmel, the game warden, whom they knew well, and out of two or three other visitors. In the end we gave them away, although regretfully, for they are the most beautiful of dogs.

But the boxer is by nature the most amiable of dogs and no dog is so qualified as a baby-sitter. They have a natural affinity for children and will endure every sort of poking and tail-pulling and teasing. When they have had enough, they do not growl or bite but simply walk away recovering and carrying with them their own peculiar boxer dignity. Each day at Malabar, all of them save the boss, who is always the oldest dog and rarely leaves me, go from house to house on the farm to visit the children, of whom there is a multitude of all ages. It must be said that often enough there are handouts involved with the attention and petting they get.

Many breeds of dogs have strong characteristics and in many breeds, all the dogs seem to be alike; but every boxer is an individual

with an immensely strong personality. The one most beloved by the
children over a long period of years is a very handsome dog called
Rocky, who is by nature a scamp and a gigolo. He is, as I have men-
tioned, the skunk specialist of the family and I am afraid that he prefers the night to the day. He is not only beautiful but lazy and charming as well and very nearly impossible to tease or torment; he does
not fight back but simply sits and in a lazy good-natured way takes it
all, so that there is no satisfaction in the teasing—a knowledge and
wisdom that many a clever person learns sooner or later in his life.
Rocky is also a swindler. After he has made certain that everyone in
the house is sound asleep he raids the kitchen, even to opening the
catch on cupboard doors. And when the busses and private cars arrive on a general farm tour, he knows that usually inside the busses
or cars there are box lunches, and unless the bus driver is vigilant
and the cars well closed, sooner or later two or three people are
missing their box lunches. But he is generous in his thefts; on more
than one occasion, he has stolen a couple of lunches and delivered
them to the other dogs before making off with one for himself. And
he can charm most of the food right out of the mouths of workmen
who come to Malabar.

The boxers, used to square dances and picnics and meetings,
learned long ago that a group of automobiles meant a party and a
party meant that they were going to have a feast of hot dogs, of steak
bones, of pie and cake and doughnuts. No party ever had more welcoming hosts than the boxers and the two cockers on the occasion of
farm festivities. Usually the next day meant indigestion for them and
the consumption of great quantities of grass and zinnia leaves, which
boxers seem to regard as a cure for indigestion. But apparently the
party is always worth the indigestion.

I cannot write of the dogs at Malabar without mentioning the
two small female cockers, Patsy and Dusky, who came to the farm
as pets of the children. Dusky was all black and very feminine and
very sporting. When the dog party went out in the old station wagon,
Dusky and Patsy would go off hunting, *really* hunting and not just
rushing about rather aimlessly like the boxers, deep in the woods,

to come back all wet or covered with burrs hours later. They were inseparable companions who lived out-of-doors and slept in the potting shed, silky, affectionate and charming.

Of the two, Patsy had the eccentric character. She was a very small cocker, black, with tan-colored spots and big brown eyes with a slight squint, which gave her a hopelessly comic expression. Despite her small size and good nature, she took no pushing around from the big boxers. Although in play they sometimes sent her rolling end on end, she always came back making hideous snarls and growls. In a way, her life was a tragedy of frustration, for her one overwhelming desire was puppies. With her first litter she caught pneumonia and all of them died. Shortly after that she ran under a car and suffered a broken pelvis. It mended badly, and after that there was danger in her having puppies and we did not breed her, but twice each year she had an hysterical pregnancy, even to producing milk. Whenever Gina, the mother of all the boxer clan, had puppies, which was about once a year, Patsy acted as nursemaid and babysitter. Apparently she and Gina had some agreement, for, although Gina would allow no other dog, male or female, to come near her puppies, she made no objection to Patsy sitting beside the straw-filled box in which they lay or even to sharing the box with her and her puppies. Patsy would never leave the vicinity of the box save to eat, and when Gina went out she would get into the box with the puppies and even attempt to feed them. I think she got satisfaction out of all this, and she helped Gina to bring up four litters of pups which, before they were three months old, were twice as tall as Patsy herself.

During the last summer of her life she showed all the signs of hysterical pregnancy again, and none of us, accustomed to the phenomenon and certain she had been safely shut up, took any notice. But this time the pregnancy was real. Somehow she had been bred, probably to one of the big boxers. The puppies were born dead and Patsy died too later, happy, I think, in the illusion that again, after years, she had produced a family. Anne wrote a poem about her—

It matters little to the world
That one small dog
No longer trots these dusty lanes.
The canny eyes, untidy hair
Brown dots for eyebrows
Have faded in the dark unknown of death
Much like a pebble in a dark smooth pool.
Still she is here, trotting busily
The steep fern-covered hills
So long as we who were her friends, remain on earth.

On Being "Teched"

THERE ONCE LIVED in our country a remarkable woman whose name was Phoebe Wise. Vaguely she was a relative, her grandfather and one of my paternal great-grandfathers having been brothers. I have written of her many times, although while she still lived I called her by other names than her own. It was useless to attempt to disguise her character and personality by using an invented name. No one who knew her was deceived by the strategy and I am told that she, herself, was the least deceived of any, and that the stories I wrote about her caused her pleasure and even mirth, since the invented portions were, she considered, entirely outside her character, especially on the romantic side. For Phoebe, it must be said, had contempt for nearly all men, to the point of actually having murdered one, half-intentionally. Indeed, I have written so frequently of her that at times I have very nearly worn out the subject, like an etching plate which has grown old and blurred from use. Yet I cannot stop myself even now, for I think I never met any individual who left upon me so profound an impression. In all the years I was away from the Valley I never forgot her. The first time I saw her I was about seven years old and the last time I saw her I was seventeen. She died at the age of ninety-three while I was on the other side of the world.

My memory of her is of a tall woman with a remarkably fine figure and carriage even at the age of seventy when I saw her last. At that time her hair was still black as a crow's wing. I think it stayed black because of her remote Indian blood. Her grandfather, my great-grandfather's brother, who was a circuit-riding preacher in the days of the first settlements, married the daughter of a Delaware Indian chieftain who was one of his converts, and all her life Phoebe bore the stamp of that remote Indian blood, in her carriage, in the blackness of her hair and in the fierce intense blackness of her eyes.

The last time I saw her I was home for a few days before leaving for France and the war of 1914 and she stopped to talk with my father and me, to wish me goodbye and good luck. In a torn, bewildered world in which a whole somewhat unsavory epoch of human experience and history was dying, I was going into a distant and foreign part of the earth which she had never seen but which she knew and perhaps understood better than most people of her time. This to Phoebe Wise was a prospect of great interest, especially since I, a callow but eager youth, was the potential instrument in this potentially exciting and enriching experience. She was dressed, as she always was, in an extraordinary fashion. She wore a yellow taffeta dress with a bustle and many flounces, very long with a slight train which she did not lift, but permitted to drag grandly behind her. Weather, mud and dust had discolored the yellow taffeta to about the height of her knees. On her hands she wore black lace mitts and her fingers glittered with cheap rings, purchased from time to time at Woolworth's, in which were set imitation diamonds, emeralds and rubies.

On her head she wore a large rusty black picture hat, and on it, for ornament, she had pinned a garland of real wild asters plucked from the roadside. For as far back as I or anyone else can remember she had worn the same hat, changing the fresh flowers each time she came into town, according to the flowers in season. During the winter she pinned sprays of wheat or oats to the hat. Over one arm she carried a basket in which were collected the purchases she had made on her trip into town from her house which stood a mile or two from the factories in the shadow of the state prison.

I remember on this occasion that Phoebe, who had probably never been outside the county, observed, "You are a very lucky boy. Don't miss a thing. Keep your eyes and ears open and remember always remember that it is impossible ever to learn or know too much. Just go on seeing and learning and then try to make sense out of what you know and you'll be all right." She turned briskly to my father, "What about it, Charley?"

My father agreed, although I am not certain that he knew what she meant, for he was a simple kindly man who greatly loved his fellow men, his own lovely countryside, his horses and had never been troubled, as his young son was troubled all his life, by wild temptations toward adventure, color and human experience in all and any of its forms. I myself by no means understood at that time the full sense of what she was saying; it is only now, nearly half a century later, that I have come to understand fully what it was she was trying to tell me and how right she was. Everything out of the past, everything out of experience, becomes automatically a reference, a standard of values and a perspective which enriches everything which follows and gives every experience a depth and value which it could not have otherwise.

She made one more observation, "Never say 'no' to life," which, after so many years, seems a strange observation to have come from Phoebe who all her life, so far as anyone knew, had said "no" to the greatest of all human experiences—that of love; for Phoebe never married and she never had any children. But perhaps she was, with a sigh born out of her own experience, making an observation which was based upon this very negative fact of her existence, something which she had perhaps realized when she was old and it was too late.

I remember the flash of her cheap rings in the sunlight and remember having wondered why women like Mrs. Hanson, the Banker's wife, found pleasure in spending hundreds and even thousands of dollars on expensive jewelry when Phoebe's own rings made quite as pretty an effect as any diamonds or emeralds I had ever seen up until then, or indeed have ever seen since then. I still wonder what is the peculiar pleasure of an honest woman in wearing a fortune in real precious stones when artificial ones or semiprecious stones like tourmalines and zircons and topazes are frequently more intrinsically beautiful than many a dull precious stone. I think it is that in the minds of many it is the cost and not the real beauty which impresses, as it does with the middle-class matron who must have an expensive new car every year to impress her suburban neighbors. I can understand the trollop who collects precious stones as an investment or the refugee who turns his money into precious stones which can be easily hidden as he flees from one country to another. But it must be a shallow soul indeed which chooses to pour great wealth into stones weighing only a few carats which frequently enough do not enhance a woman's appearance but merely render it vulgar and betray an inward greed or an unsatisfied vanity.

Phoebe, of course, could never have been able to purchase real gems but I doubt that she would have done so even if she had possessed millions, for it was the general effect of her appearance (however bizarre) which concerned her rather than the desire to impress a friend or a stranger by her wealth (which she did not have).

In the evening when Phoebe had made her purchases in the town and had spent the better part of the afternoon chatting with old friends and acquaintances from one end of Main Street to the other, she took off on foot again, ignoring the trolley line, and stamping along through mud or dust in her yellow taffeta, to walk to her house three miles away on the Olivesburg Pike.

It was a tiny house with a small turret and a great many tiny gables and much fretwork, overgrown, rotting and forced apart at the eaves and cornices by the thrusting shoots of wisteria and trumpet vine. The little garden which surrounded it was a jungle of old-fashioned flowers—lilacs, mock orange, day lilies, petunias and a hundred other shrubs and plants. Here she lived alone, surrounded by all sorts of animals, both wild and tamed. Between them and her there existed an extraordinary relationship. She allowed no hunters on or near her place and she had been known to drive them away on more than one occasion with an old-fashioned musket. Although it was doubtful whether the rusty musket could have done anyone the least harm, she carried great prestige and inspired considerable awe for once having shot and killed a man. Trespassers did not pause to argue with her. Her only guardian was not a dog but an old white horse which she had raised from a colt without once having harnessed or bridled it. The old horse would run at trespassers, showing his teeth and kicking out viciously with his forefeet. You could not enter the place unless she called off the horse which obeyed her exactly as if it had been a watchdog.

From the description I have given you may gather that Phoebe's appearance was that of a dowdy scarecrow. Actually, the effect was exactly the opposite. In the first place the old-fashioned clothes had about them an air of great style, even the real flowers were pinned on the old hat with a sense of style that would have brought credit to a great Paris milliner. Unquestionably Phoebe had that mysterious quality possessed by some women which the French, who understand it best, have chosen to call "chic"—a quality which cannot be invented, imitated, bought or even adequately described or taught. Some women—a few—are born with it and so are able to invest even a Mother Hubbard and a sunbonnet with great style. Other women never achieve it even with vast expenditures on dressmakers and milliners. It has, I think, something to do with carriage and the tilt of the head, with long legs and the instinctive way clothes are put on.

But why attempt to define this curious quality? Hundreds have tried and failed. It turns up in the most unexpected places, as with old Phoebe in a half-frontier town in Ohio. I have seen it in coal-black, half-naked African women and even in one or two Indian women in the jungles of Mato Grosso. It is a quality which causes a man to take a second look, regardless of whether the woman is beautiful or plain. It has nothing whatever to do with the mere prettiness which afflicts many *unchic* women nor with the curves and busts which seem to possess a kind of exaggerated, naïve and infantile preoccupation for so many American men.

There is in the Luxembourg Palace in Paris a picture which is surely one of the most stylish and worldly that exists. It is a portrait of Sarah Bernhardt by Carolus Duran, and the first time I ever saw it, I thought at once of Phoebe Wise in a yellow dress of stiff and rustling taffeta with bustle and flounces such as Sarah wears in the portrait—the very dress indeed which Phoebe was wearing the last time I saw her outside the Bank Saloon near the corner of Fourth and Main Streets in Mansfield, Ohio.

Beyond this quality of chic, the old woman had an air of immense dignity, almost of majesty which, together with her strange but clear brain, not only demanded but commanded the respect of all who knew her. No one ever laughed at her and she never suffered the mockery of children, who are born small savages. In the county Phoebe was known as a "smart woman" and what they meant, I think, was that she was remarkably well informed, that her brain was like a proverbial steel trap and that she was quite able to care for herself. One did not tangle with Phoebe by choice, unless one were a fool. No one ever attempted to make a "smart deal" with Phoebe. On the last day I ever saw her she talked of Europe and the war there with astonishing clarity, perception and knowledge.

At one time, as the state grew rapidly and with it the population of the prisons, the state sought to buy Phoebe's birdcage house and later even attempted legal proceedings to take possession of it in order to enlarge the area of the prison farm. But Phoebe fought back; embattled with her old musket and guarded by the old white horse, she permitted no one to enter on her property and brought interminable proceedings in court to prevent the seizure of the little turreted cottage in which she had been born and had lived all her life. At litigation she was very good and quite learned, for at the time she accidentally murdered a man she made a thorough study of the law concerning the circumstances of such a case and defended herself in court and was acquitted. But in this case I think she was concerned not so much with maintaining possession of property as defending the principle that the rights of sturdy individuals must not be submerged and defeated however great are the impersonal and inhuman pressures from the masses—a principle with which I have always heartily agreed.

The story of the man she killed was a simple enough one. He was an unwelcome suitor, one of the many who sought to marry her when she was left an orphan with a small inheritance at the age of eighteen. At that time she lived alone in the same little house without even an old white horse as a guardian. The ill-fated lover, an eccentric man not notable for his attractions, was unwilling to accept her rejection of him and on more than one occasion had come to the house late at night and attempted to force his way in. At last one night, her patience gone, she called through the door that if he knocked again, she would fire through the door. He made one more attempt to enter and she fired. She heard no more sounds from him that night, but in the morning, when she opened the door, she found him outside on the doorstep, dead.

At the trial Phoebe insisted upon defending herself and was, of course, acquitted, but the knowledge that she had killed a man set her somewhat aside from the other members of her community and undoubtedly strengthened her determination never to marry. From then on, although she walked to town once or twice a week, her life became more and more solitary and her natural intimacy with birds and animals increased.

The odd thing was that she really liked society and intelligent conversation, but she satisfied the liking not in her own little house to which few people ever were admitted but on street corners where she would stand, in her fantastic clothes, talking for hours with the men and women whom she liked or respected. She had a sympathy for the simple ones and the eccentric characters like herself. My father she deigned to talk with because he was a simple and friendly man and vaguely a relation. She always called him "Cousin Charley." Usually you found her talking with Gus Douglass, a brilliant but eccentric lawyer whose own sense of mockery and humor destroyed his respect for legal processes and blighted what might have been a great but a far less human and satisfactory career. Or it might be Susie Sturges, another eccentric as strange in dress and appearance as Phoebe herself, or anyone who she felt was free or simple and direct or intelligent. She was immensely selective—Phoebe—and, in her own way, a snob. She could not tolerate conformity and regarded timid conformists as dull or fools. She had no time for the conservative or the conventional whom she held in contempt as limpets clinging to the rock of security.

I have written at length about Phoebe because the memory of her has always been so much a part of my own life and because her legend, like that of Johnny Appleseed, has persisted and grown as a part of the life of our own beautiful country. But there is another reason, perhaps more profound, which has a bearing upon this story. The memory of it is still vivid, although the observation was made by Phoebe when I was about seven years old.

I had gone electioneering with my father and we stopped at Phoebe's little house out of sheer friendliness because Phoebe, being a kind of Rousseau anarchist, held all politics in contempt and did not vote. While my father talked with her, I played in the jungly garden which surrounded the house, making friends with the animals, both wild and tame, which lived there. Among them, I remember, was the white horse which at that time was only a colt perhaps not more than a year old. There were also a tame raccoon and a fox. I don't know what kept my father talking with Phoebe for so long a time, but presently I was aware that they were both coming down the path toward the springhouse, Phoebe dressed in the practical man's clothing which she always wore around her own place.

I was sailing boats made of twigs on the surface of the spring pond. The white colt was standing beside me, playfully dipping his muzzle into the cold water and then raising his head and tossing it so that the water fell in a shower over me. It was a comic, clownish trick, one of those which at times convinces me that animals know far more than we suspect, that some among them possess even a sense of humor. I was absorbed in my play and did not look up but I heard Phoebe saying, "Cousin Charley, that boy is *teched* too."

As I turned, I saw her watching me with her burning black eyes and suddenly there passed between us a strange current of sympathy and knowledge, which bound us together forever afterward. Because of that look I remembered her in strange, far-off places. Sometimes I dreamed of her. Because of that look I was glad that on the day I left for the war, the unearthly, witchlike Phoebe was almost the last person I saw on a street corner before the Bank Saloon. When she wished me good luck, I had a feeling that nothing would happen to me. Curiously, the feeling persisted throughout the war even under circumstances in which it appeared unlikely that any man in our company would ever come out alive.

Afterwards on that day my father and I visited her, as we were driving away from Phoebe's in the buggy, I asked my father what "teched" meant. He laughed and replied, "She means a little crazy, like herself." And then after a little time he added with a sigh, "A lot of people think Phoebe is crazy, but I don't. I think she's awful smart. They're just fools. They're lucky because they'll never know what fools they are or how much they've missed."

It took me a good many years to understand to the full what Phoebe meant by being "teched." It needed a lot of experience and a lot of observation, but I think I know now what it was that lay behind the remark. I know today that any good farmer has to be a little "teched," and when I go over the list of good farmers, I know there is not one of whom it could not be said, "He is a little teched," for it means that he loves his land, his animals and his trees and understands them all. He farms not in order to make money but because of the pleasure and the satisfaction there is in it, because it is a destiny he would not change for any other in the world. Success and profit follow, but they are merely incidental.

And that, I think, is a rule that holds through all of life; the ones who set out in life with the sole object of "getting rich" rarely succeed in their ambitions, and as a rule they lead narrow, pinched, hard lives unilluminated by the warmth of idea or ideal, wholly empty of that intense internal satisfaction belonging to those who create things all the way from a simple table or a garden to a cathedral or a symphony. They remain shallow egotists, isolated both from man and Nature. The man who has set money as his only goal and failed is perhaps the bitterest and most perverted of all specimens of humanity—and as my father suggested, the greatest of all fools.

I think all that was a part of Phoebe's strange wisdom, and now, when I am a middle-aged man and Phoebe is in her grave, and I have acquired a humble stock of experience and wisdom and humility, I know that the casual observation made beside the spring is the finest praise I have ever had. And I know that all the real satisfaction I have ever known in life as well as all the improvidence, the extravagance and carelessness with regard to money, has come from the fact that I was, as Phoebe had already observed by the time I was seven, a little "teched."

I have made a great deal of money, but I have saved none to speak of. In the years before and even during the Great Depression,

I spent the money I made, more rapidly sometimes than it came in. I traveled where I wanted to go. I gave money away. I spent it on what sometimes turned out to be rash experiments. During the same period, I had friends who denied themselves the extravagances in which I indulged myself and my family, who stayed at home and saved their money and invested it, and when the Great Depression came, it was swept away and they had left neither money nor the liberty and good things which money could have brought them, in experience, in warmth, in richness, in memories. They were left with very nearly nothing. What I had acquired (which, after all, is the greatest and perhaps the only value of wealth) was not cash or stocks or bonds, all of which can be destroyed overnight by a depression or an inflation. Neither these friends nor myself had any money when the war and taxes and the Great Depression almost destroyed the fabric of our existence, but I did have left a great store of experience and memories and friendships in half the countries of the world out of which I could write and make a good living for the rest of my life, even though I lived to be over a hundred. What I had was indestructible capital. I know now, in this tottering and impermanent world, how little folly my seeming folly really was. I take no credit for being motivated by wisdom, although the long experience of war and shortages and inflation outside my own country taught me many things which I was able to turn to the advantage of myself, my family and sometimes my friends. I acted as I did only because I was, as Phoebe said, "a little teched." I really could not help myself. By many I was regarded, and perhaps still am, as a fool.

And so the whole big adventure of Malabar Farm came too under the head of being "a little teched," and out of a philosophy not far removed from that of Phoebe Wise. A "smart" fellow would never have put so much money into so many acres of half-ruined hill land. A "smart" fellow would never have gone out and worked hard to earn that money. A "smart" fellow would never have attempted anything so extravagant as "The Plan" which has taken years and mountains of hard work to bring to fruition. And more than once the "smart" fellows have laughed at what we were trying to do. Fortunately, I come of a hard-shelled family. Scottish and New England by blood, which was never very much concerned about the opinions of others. For generations, most of the members have set a course and to hell with the rest.

Some have failed, in a worldly sense, some have succeeded, but I cannot think of one among them, either among the grandparents or the aunts and uncles or my own parents, who set out simply to "make money." I know too that whether my experiments succeed or fail in the long run, whether I die in the big house I built or whether I die in a cottage with only an acre of ground around it, there will, at least, be no bitterness and no envy, so long as I have a couple of dogs and a garden, with birds and springs and forests near at hand, and that huge stock of adventures and memories, which Phoebe counseled me to collect and cherish. Among them all the adventure in Pleasant Valley will be the brightest and most exciting of all. I also know that I will have left my mark on the surface of the earth in at least two places, one in the heart of France and one in Pleasant Valley in Ohio. There will be two spots at least which will be better and more productive and more beautiful because I stayed there for a time. I think all that comes of being a little "teched"—a condition which is undoubtedly a fact and which I do not regret.

That is why for me, the memories of those two "teched" characters, Johnny Appleseed and Phoebe Wise, will always be respected. Both of them have become legends in our country because they represented something which all men and women at some time envy and seek to attain—that poverty, that simplicity, that *richness* which is the essence of true Christian teaching and experience and far above all worldly riches. In a way the two of them acquired, like St. Francis, that intimacy with God and with Nature and birds and animals, that lack of all envy or ambition or greed, which is the ultimate "oneness with God." That is why they have become not only legends but in a way saints of our green and rich Ohio countryside. They represented something which men, even the hardest and most perverted, yearn for, sometimes secretly and with shame.

One of these saints was a Swedenborgian, the other had no formalized faith at all beyond her love of all that had to do with Nature, yet they will be remembered in our county long after the millionaires, politicians, the great manufacturers are forgotten. When factories are silent or in ruins and the industrial population is without food and perhaps shelter, the forest, the hills, the valleys, will still be there and the wild things which live in them will still be coming out of the forests and swamps at nightfall to harvest the wild, spicy apples, descended from the trees which Johnny Appleseed planted centuries before. About Johnny's legend and the hills and valleys there is an eternal quality, an ultimate refuge, which the mechanical civilization of man, with his automobiles and bathrooms, can never wholly provide or even approach.

My father was always a little "teched." He was improvident and dreamy and never really succeeded at anything in terms of money and acquisitions, but until after middle age, when he left the small town and country life for the city, he had a happy, rich and satisfactory life. In *The Farm*, I have painted of him a loving, full-length portrait. His only significance here is the fact that he was an understanding friend of Phoebe Wise and that he fashioned and encouraged in me a love for all that had to do with animals and the out-of-doors. When he died he left me in money only debts, but in reality he left me the greatest fortune a man can leave his children—a good and rich and satisfactory way of living, in which all animals and all Nature provided the very foundation.

My father undertook many things in life in order to feed his wife, his offspring and the visiting relations and to put a roof over their heads. He was at various times an oil operator, a bank cashier, an agent for the Great Northern Railroad in its campaign to open up the great fruit and grain country of the Northwest, the employee of a wholesale grocer's firm, an agent for the sale of farm properties. There was also a brief career in politics, and for years he was secretary of the County Fair Association. None of these things made him rich; for his heart was really in none of them save the secretaryship of the Fair Association and that paid nothing whatever.

During all his life he was passionately interested in two things—
the restoration of ruined farms, and the reformation of run-down
or unruly horses. Of the latter we had an endless procession in my
childhood and boyhood, ranging from the pintos which he brought
into the county from the West, to a team of wild and unruly Belgian
mares which on one occasion ran away, destroyed a farm wagon,
fifteen rods of a neighbor's fence and nearly killed my father and
myself. Always there was something about the horses which needed
reforming; they bucked or balked or had hard mouths or were vicious and unmanageable. They were the only horses I ever knew
until I was nearly grown, and my experience with them banished all
fear of horses forever. Some of them we succeeded in reforming for
both of us had the "teched" quality and understood animals, but a
good many of them were hopeless. I suffered a broken arm and still
possess a shoulder which can be dislocated at will as a result of attempts at reforming horses. Of course, nobody made any money out
of these reformation projects, but all of us had a lot of excitement
and fun.

The restoration of run-down farms was no more profitable than
the horse project and it usually tied up whatever liquid capital my
father was able to raise. In my boyhood in our rich county there
were farms which were already out of circulation through erosion or
greedy farming. We always had two or three of these farms at a time
and my father's efforts to restore them were primitive in comparison with what can be done in these times. At that time there were
no county agents and few agricultural bulletins and the efforts and
information of the Soil Conservation Service were primitive or non-
existent.

My father's ideas were sound as far as they went. He cleared
away the underbrush that were already moving in upon deserted
fields, and reseeded with clover the fields which had been left bare
by the last farmer to leave the place. And he fought gullies by filling
them with cut underbrush and with rolls of rusted fence wire, and he
spread the manure left in the deserted barns over the starved fields.
Sometimes it had accumulated without having been hauled out for a

period of two or three years and the beams above were worn smooth from the backs of the cattle rubbing against them.

Most of the restoration work was done by ourselves with the aid of small boys and sometimes girls who were friends of my sister, my brother and myself. There was never anything tiresome about the work; indeed, it was never really work at all, for my father by his spirit, and my mother with the good meals she prepared and carried along, invested the whole project with the air of a lark and a picnic. Every Saturday, Sunday and holiday and sometimes on days stolen during the week from the office where my father should have been working, a procession set out for one or the other of these ruined farms. It consisted of one and sometimes two buggies filled with axes, shovels, picks, food, women and children. Always there was a dog or two and a troop of boys on bicycles which careened up and down the road like a convoy guarding the buggies.

On arriving at the farm the horses were unhitched and turned loose to graze and we went to work, cutting undergrowth, building check dams, demolishing ruined fences and reassembling snake rail fences by picking out the good rails and burning the others. There was always the smell of wood smoke and of coffee and steak cooking under my mother's direction. The dogs ran rabbits and once or twice during the day the boys went swimming, and in May, in the old abandoned woods and thickets, we found quantities of spongy morels which I discovered later in life were regarded by the French as the greatest of all delicacies. There was no need for any of us to be told that the "mushruins" were delicious, for in this world or the next there is no better food than morels cooked in butter and served with steak broiled over an open fire in the woods.

Evening came at last and, tired and sunburned and smoky, the whole procession started back to town, sometimes in the moonlight, those in the buggies singing old songs in chorus to the light of the moon, while the tired smaller children slept soundly. Sometimes in the course of the day there came up one of the majestic and beautiful thunderstorms typical of that Ohio country, and then everyone took refuge in the decaying barn to watch the spectacle of warm rain and lightning and black clouds swooping down quickly over the Valley and the wooded hills.

So the whole of my childhood was involved with ruined, worn-out farms, and even then, despite all the fun we had in the process of bringing them back to life, I was always aware of something tragic and awful about the manure-filled, half-ruined barns and the houses left by the last tenant who had not even taken the trouble to close the door when he left. Inside on the rotting floors beneath the half-ruined ceiling there was always an assortment of half-wrecked furniture, and on the hooks along the wall, a row of worn-out Mother Hubbards and overalls. Mournful ghosts they seemed to me—the ghosts of ignorance and shiftlessness.

I did not understand then what all those farms and hundreds of others like them meant to the economy of the nation, nor did I speculate as to what became of that last tenant, moving to another dying farm or into the slums of an industrial city or, worst of all, taking to the road with his family as an indigent tramp. I only knew that the desolation I saw was somehow evil and wicked.

The ghosts that haunted those tired and lonely farms were too the ghosts of people who had been not only cruel to their land but to their beasts and often enough to their own children. They were of the accursed—the misfits, the deformed of Nature which put to mockery the mere idea that there is something sacred about being born human. For so long as the land is rich, the sunlight shines and the moon comes out, there is no need for man to be either poverty-stricken or miserable. The roots of his failure come not from the past nor even from the present but from within himself, out of his egotism, his envy, his laziness, his selfishness, his self-pity, his isolation from all that can make of a life a colorful and satisfactory existence. He has all the universe in which to live, all of Nature to delight and comfort him and good honest work to give him strength and his reason for existence. What more could one ask of paradise?

All that was, I think, a part of the wisdom of old Phoebe Wise in her gown of soiled and dusty yellow taffeta and her jewels from Woolworth's.

Of Green Hills and Valleys

ONE DAY Mr. Jarvis, the bee man, came to look over the hives and put on new supers. He is the county bee inspector, and we run thirty hives of bees on shares, the farm furnishing the equipment and bees, the inspector caring for them.

The thirty hives stand on the side of the hill above the Big House, sheltered from the north winds in winter and thunderstorms in summer by a ledge of pink and red sandstone rock. Time, frosts and wind have worn and pitted the sandstone and its face is covered with ferns, and wild red and yellow columbine. Each winter, pieces of the rock break loose and fall down the steep slope below to lodge among the wild raspberries and gooseberries that grow in the thin, flickering shade of a grove of black walnut trees.

Until we placed the beehives in the grove and took to frequenting the place, a pair of red foxes had their den in a crevice that ran far back into the rock. It was a cleverly arranged home, with three or four different entrances. The main hole could only be reached from above, by coming down a narrow ledge among the ferns and columbine. Twice I caught the vixen slipping delicately down the face of the rock toward the entrance, so delicately that she scarcely disturbed the foliage on the face of the rock. As she passed, brushing the ferns and columbine aside, she put down her little paws so deftly that the leaves swung back into place as she passed, leaving no evidence that there was any path there at all. Indeed, unless one stood looking down very closely there was never any evidence that an animal went up and down the face of the rock many times daily. Once I caught her returning with one of our Leghorn pullets in her mouth, her tiny, shrewd head held high to keep the dangling bird from trailing across the ferns. Perhaps if I had had a gun I would have shot her, for we are, after all, in the poultry business, and each summer foxes take forty or fifty pullets off the range; but I had no gun, and afterward I was glad I had none.

I have seen foxes many times, but I have never seen one when I had a gun. There was a big, bold dog fox who would come across the open field in broad daylight, select a fat pullet and carry it off, ignoring your shouts and even an ill-aimed stone or two. One summer, three young foxes used to sit in a row on the high ledge, silhouetted against the evening sky, their tails curled around them, not more than two hundred yards above the Big House, watching us in the garden below. I saw them there many times, but never when there was a gun handy. I do not know how they knew it, but they did know. If I went back to the house for a gun the three young foxes sitting against the sky had always vanished when I returned.

But one summer one of the dogs caught them out. Baby, one of the boxers, came down the hill carrying what appeared to be a big Maltese cat. He was inclined to be wicked with the barn cats and I thought that at last he had got old Tom, who had tantalized and scratched his nose and ears since Baby was big enough to put up a fight. But when Baby came up to me proudly, I discovered that it wasn't old Tom at all, but a half-grown, gray fox cub. After that, the foxes, both gray and red, left the ledge above the house. They have not been back since, save at night, when in the mating season they bark and call all along the ridge above the Big House. At night, they come close in so that the sound of their barking is mixed with the sounds of the sheep and cattle in the barns.

One of the most pleasant things about living in rich, half-wild country, like ours, is the feeling that when evening comes and at last darkness falls, live things stir and come to life all about us. My room, where I work and write and sleep, is a big room with a bay window and two outside doors leading directly into the garden. A little way off, the half-wild garden merges imperceptibly into underbrush and forest, and the animals at night come close in to the house. In winter on a moonlit night I have seen as many as twenty rabbits feeding on the terrace just outside my window, where we throw down grain for the turkeys, the fighting chickens and the guinea fowl. You can sit inside in the darkness and watch them nibbling at the grain, suddenly raising their long ears in alarm, hopping off hysterically at the slightest sound, to return presently, in little, tentative, sudden advances, until their alarm is dissipated, and they begin their nibbling all over again.

In spite of the grain, they have during a hard winter gnawed their way around the flowering crabs and slaughtered rosebushes and young blueberries; yet I have never been able to bring myself to shoot one of them. After you have watched them like that, night after night, silently in the moonlight, something happens to you. I do not know exactly what it is, save that they come somehow to be your friends, that you would feel a bully even to open the door and frighten them away. Watching them, living very close to them, gives you a vague and curious sense of participating in the mystery of Nature itself, of yourself being not a specimen of dauntless, clever, all-powerful mankind, but of being only an integral and humble part of something very great and very beautiful. You feel a sudden intense and unattainable desire to step out on the terrace to speak to the timorous rabbit, to make friends with him, to talk with him there in the moonlit, glittering snow.

For me religion and faith have never come through churches and rarely through men. These things have welled up in me many times in contact with animals and trees and landscape, at moments when I was certain not only of the existence of God but of my own immortality as a part of some gigantic scheme of creation, of an immortality that had nothing to do with plaster saints and tawdry heavens, but with something greater and more profound and richer in dignity, the beautiful dignity of the small animals of the field, of a fern growing from a damp crevice in the rock, or a tulip tree rising straight and clean a hundred feet toward the sky. It is the dignity and beauty which man managed to translate into the stone of Chartres and St. Cernin, but somehow missed in the ecclesiastical manifestations of his spirit.

In the daytime, mourning doves come to the same terrace to feed with the guinea fowl and turkeys—small, silver-gray doves with rings of darker pink beige for collars. Sometimes they stay with us all through the winter, living on the dry, sheltered ledges of the sandstone rock above the house. With them feed the chickadees, the song sparrows, three or four varieties of woodpeckers, the cardinals and the noisy, vulgar sparrows. They all feed together in peace save when that beautiful and arrogant fellow, the blue jay, drops down and bullies them all away.

In the mornings the borders of the pond are marked with footprints of the raccoon who has come down in the night to wash his face and his food before eating. A little while ago, I found among the wild iris growing at the edge of the big pond, the body of the grandfather of all raccoons. He was very nearly as big as a dog and very gray, even to the spectacles which outlined his eyes. He was lying on his side, quietly, dead. I think he had come down for the last time to his beloved pond to die in peace of old age.

One autumn I was awakened in the early morning for the first time in my life not by a sound but by a smell. As I opened my eyes, I knew what it was—pure essence of skunk. Beside my bed were three of the boxers, wriggling and shaking themselves, their eyes smarting. They had gone out of my room as usual in the early morning and on the doorstep they had encountered a skunk. The encounter had been brief, and, following Prince, who was clever enough to open doors (for this was before the happy era of the special dog's door), they had returned to tell me of the encounter and ask me to do something about it. I went to the door and there on the opposite side of the ravine I saw Mr. Skunk. He was making his way back to the shelter of the forest and he was in no hurry at all. Had he not just put to rout three big boxers? He even stopped now and then to tear at a stump or turn over a stone, delicately, in search of a fat grub or two. The skunk is an animal of great dignity, because he can afford to be.

And opossums too come close to the house. I have seen them on the driveway late on autumn nights in the lights of the car apparently enjoying the warmth that has remained in the gravel. The possum is a slow-moving, lazy fellow whose glands will not permit him really to run, but if he is caught on the ground he will put up a ferocious battle with teeth and claws. Not long ago, Pete ran one down on foot by the lights of the jeep. He brought it into the house by the tail to show the children. The possum seemed to take the whole adventure lethargically. He was a young fellow, and even when you put him on the floor he made no attempt to run away, but only nosed about the floor without any sign of alarm. Possums are comical beasts which look and act a little like clowns, and this one was no exception. Now and then he would stop moving and look up, blinking in the light, with a wicked twinkle in his yellow eyes. When you held him by the tail he would turn and lazily try to climb up his own tail and bite you. A mother possum on a branch with a whole family clinging to her back is one of the most comical sights in the world. I have seen it only once. The possum family are the only marsupials outside the continent of Australia, and they have an air of belonging to another world, survivors, as they really are, of a prehistoric time.

Twice I have seen one of them actually "play possum." Once in the Jungle, the dogs, running ahead of me, collected about some object on the ground. I discovered that it was a possum, on his back, with his feet in the air completely dead. The dogs sniffed the funny yellow body. When it did not move or run, they lost interest and went away. I touched the possum with my toes. He was still soft and flexible and I thought, "He can't have been dead for long" and went on my way. Ten minutes later, returning by the same path, the possum was not there at all.

And another time the dogs caught a possum in the open in broad daylight. Gina was shaking him when I came up and called them off. He was a big fellow and must have weighed about fifteen pounds or more. I picked him up by the tail to carry him back to show the boys, who were shelling corn by the lower barn. I was nearly a mile from the barn, but during the whole of the long walk, while he grew heavier and heavier, he showed no sign of life. His size created interest among the boys, and I tossed him into the back of the wagon to be dumped into the field for the buzzards. He lay there in full sight of the boys, who went on shelling corn; but all the time the possum must have kept one eye open, watching them, for when they had finished and looked in the wagon, there was no possum there. Looking about for him, they discovered him making his way lethargically across the bluegrass two hundred yards away. They let him go to return to his family and no doubt describe in possum language his remarkable adventure.

On a moonlight night you can sometimes look out of the window and see a muskrat or two swimming across the pond—a tiny dot which is his nose with a great V wake spreading out about him in the still water. If you go outside for a closer view the dot will disappear at once beneath the surface. They are shrewd and bold little beasts, very nearly as shrewd and bold as the fox. In winter, they will move up from the big lake and the marshes in the Clear Fork Valley and dig themselves homes in the banks of the little brook that flows only fifty feet from my window. You know that all through the night they are there, quite near you, feeding on the roots of your best iris, even coming up to the terrace outside the door to eat the grain scattered for the guinea fowl. But you never see them, or at least you see no more than a fleeting shadow, so swift you cannot identify it. Only once has one of the dogs ever killed one of them. The honor went to

Lady, Max's pointer, who had a nose fine as a needle. All through the marshes in our county there are millions of them. Their fur in winter is of high quality, and more than once, dyed and plucked, it has been mistaken in a theater or a restaurant in New York for sable. They are one of the reasons why Ohio ranks third among the fur states of the Union.

Cheeriest of all the night chorus is the music of the frogs. They make a kind of part singing, ranging from the shrill call of the spring peeper to the "jug-o-rum" of the bullfrog. The tree frog, especially on hot nights, sings a kind of obbligato, and the leopard frog sings baritone. Some years ago a friend in the Game Control gave me five hundred giant tadpoles of the big Louisiana frog prized for its legs. I distributed them among the ponds, dubious of their survival in the cold northern winter, but some of them at least managed to live, for in the first summer there was a new voice in the part singing—a deep basso like that of Wotan. Since then they have survived and propagated until there are Louisiana bullfrogs in every pond and marsh on the farm. Now and then a fishing friend takes one on a fly by accident and at first he does not know what kind of monster he has on his line. They have legs ten inches long and the size of a fine capon leg.

Night in our country is far from silent, as many city-dwelling friends have discovered when they come to stay. There is always the chorus of the frogs, and at certain seasons there is the barking of the mating foxes back and forth from the wooded ridges on both sides of the Valley, and in autumn the baying of the fox and coon hounds running the woods, a distant beautiful sound which sometimes comes near enough to rouse all the dogs on the place to a frenzied barking. And there is the discordant, squeaking-gate noise of the guinea fowl disturbed in the night, or the gobble of the field turkeys, or the hysterical cackling of the fighting chickens. They all choose to live in a tree just outside the window of the large guest room. Or from the lower farm may come the calling of the geese, disturbed by a fox or a weasel. A lonely farm never need be unguarded while there are geese and guinea fowl. I doubt that any intruder could come within five hundred yards of the house or barn without rousing an unwelcome din that would echo up and down the Valley.

But we have come a long way from Mr. Jarvis, the county bee inspector. He is a frail little man who took up bees because his health was too bad to work any longer in the shop where he made his living. That was a long time ago, and the years have made him expert. He has bees of his own, placed in orchards all over the county. Indeed, bees are his whole life. To be a good beekeeper that is necessary, for bees are a complicated business, or rather a profession in which there is a need for art. There are some people who naturally rouse the bad temper of bees, and they are very temperamental creatures. They suffer from the heat, and become, like humans, uneasy and short-tempered in the hot, muggy stillness which precedes a thunderstorm.

We had been having that kind of weather for days on end, the kind of weather which makes the corn grow so fast that if you stand quite still in a big cornfield on a warm night you can hear the faint crackling sound as it pushes upward and the stalk increases its circumference cell by cell. Corn has to grow fast in our country, since it is planted in late May and has to ripen by September. It has to grow eight to ten feet tall, blossom, bear ears and ripen them in a little more than three months. There is a rich, dark green, tropical beauty about corn that none of our other temperate zone crops possesses and on a hot night there is a tropical smell about a lush field of corn; the air is filled with the scent of pollen and fertility.

But the weather which corn likes is not the weather for bees. They like clear, sunny weather with cool breezes and blossoms that open to the sun.

Three times Mr. Jarvis had come to our shaded hillside beneath the fox lair that week, and each time sudden thunderstorms had made the bees angry and hard to work with. And now on the fourth visit the air was hot and still and there were thunderclouds like great heaps of lemon sherbet in the west. It was still not a good time to work with the bees, but Mr. Jarvis was worried about some of the hives swarming while he was away. He knew that in each hive there were queen cells. If the ruling queen neglected to open one of the cells, tear out the grub and murder it, as was her habit, a new queen might hatch and take part or all of the swarm with her. It had happened before. We had lost swarms that went off to establish themselves in hollow trees in the deep woods. They had a liking for hollow boxwood trees, perhaps because just outside their door in the spring of the year hung the most delectable of nectar-filled blossoms. I know where there are two of them, one above the big cave, the other near the raccoon tree in the old orchard.

So Mr. Jarvis put on his bee bonnet, rolled up his sleeves, picked up his smoke-bellows and went to work. Usually he scorns both bonnet and bellows, but on this day the bees were, as he put it, "very sassy."

On the doorstep of each hive the worker bees were standing with their backs to the opening of the hive, their feet anchored, their wings fanning briskly to force fresh air inside. Bees are tidy creatures and hate stuffiness as much as do sensible human beings. And inside the hive a great deal of work was going on. Cells were being built, some to harbor eggs to keep the population going on; honey and pollen were being stored for the winter; the eternal house cleaning was in progress. Heat or no heat, they were getting on with their work. It was no time to disturb them.

But Mr. Jarvis went to work with his bee bonnet tied about his throat and his sleeves rolled up. A whiff of smoke from his bellows, meant to stupefy and calm the bees, had very little effect. The hive was what beekeepers call "a strong one," with a big and healthy population. He lifted off the top "super" where the first honey of the season, drawn from the spring wild flowers, the apple and pear blossoms and the blossoms of the black locust trees, was stored. Already, in June, it was so heavy that it taxed Mr. Jarvis' frail strength. Inside, there were hundreds, perhaps thousands of bees busy at their marvelously organized work, moving about capping cells, feeding the young grubs that were to become drones and workers. Somewhere among them was the queen, surrounded by the cabinet of workers who constantly attend her.

Prince and I sat at a little distance watching. Prince, who would not leave me, even when I went among the thirty hives, was uneasy, with eyes and ears cocked against the assault of an angry bee. He knew them well for as a pup he had, like all frolicsome young boxers, tried to catch them and been stung on the nose.

Despite the heat and the distant thunder, it was pleasant there on the hillside among the ferns and columbines and wild raspberries. And there was pleasure in the sight of the hives heavy already with honey—the kind of a pleasure which in a countryman raises up pictures of long winter nights with a cellar or storeroom well stocked, of wood fires and fat cattle standing in clean straw to their knees in the great barns.

Mr. Jarvis got stung once and then again and again. They couldn't get at his face because of the bee bonnet, but they attacked fiercely his bare hands and arms. "Darn!" said Mr. Jarvis, "They're really ornery today."

Beekeepers say that after you have been stung many times you don't feel the pain in the same way greenhorns feel it. It must be true, for Mr. Jarvis, as he worked, taking out comb after comb to look for queen cells to destroy, was taking a terrible beating without any special evidence of discomfort.

Then, as we watched, a dive-bomber bee came out of nowhere, and landed on one side of my head. There was a sharp pain followed by a burning, itchy sensation. I had been stung before when I helped Mr. Jarvis. It wasn't exactly a pleasant sensation, but I wanted to learn about bees and anyone who has ever had to do with bees knows that one doesn't learn overnight. Nor can you learn out of books. Any book on bees requires as much study and concentration as a whole college course and, even when you have finished, you are nowhere. A great many people believe that to have unlimited quantities of honey all one has to do is set up a hive and place a swarm of bees in it. It is not like that. I have the same respect for Mr. Jarvis that I have for a great scientist. He *knows* about bees and that is something—something which can't be learned out of books. You have to *live* with bees.

Then, as I watched, another dive-bomber struck Prince. He yelped and rolled on the ground, snapping and biting at his nearly invisible attacker; but he did not go away. Then one struck me on the nose and another on the throat. One entangled himself in my hair.

Mr. Jarvis said, "You'd better put on a bonnet. I'll get you one from the car. I'm going to give them another good whiff of tobacco smoke. Fun is fun but I've had enough."

He must have been stung twenty or thirty times. With each clap of thunder the bees seemed to grow angrier.

I thought that with a bee bonnet I could watch more closely, but as soon as I put on the bonnet a strange thing happened. My eyes began suddenly to stream and my face to itch intolerably. I could feel my features losing their shape. I was ashamed in front of Mr. Jarvis, who went calmly on getting stung, so I said nothing at all. But the sensation became more and more unbearable, and I could feel it spreading downward from my face and head into my shoulders and arms. It was as if I could feel the poison moving through my whole body following every small vein, nerve and artery. I wanted suddenly to throw myself on the ground like Prince and roll among the ferns. At last, it could be borne no longer, and I said to Mr. Jarvis as casually as possible, "Well, I must get back to work." I took off the bee bonnet and turned toward the house.

The hives are not more than five hundred yards from the house itself but by the time I reached my room, the itchy, burning sensation covered the whole of my body. I could still feel it spreading downward from my head as the blood carried the poison through me. It was an extraordinary sensation, like some subtle torture, as if you could feel every artery and vein and nerve throughout the body.

When I looked in the mirror my eyes were bloodshot and watery and nearly swollen shut, my nose swollen to twice its size. When I undressed, my body was covered with red welts. Quickly I had a bath with the green soap which was kept in the house for poison ivy. It did no good, and then suddenly the shock of the poison brought on a violent chill. When that had passed, there came into my mind from somewhere a forgotten piece of knowledge—that bee venom was highly acid and that probably it was too much for a system which naturally suffered from acidity, and so I took a giant's dose of bicarbonate of soda dissolved in water.

Just as I had drunk this, Bill Windsor, the fish and game manager of the Conservancy appeared. Clad only in a silk dressing gown with my eyes swollen nearly shut, I met him. He took one look at me and said, "Bee stings, eh?" I told him about the red welts that covered my body. "Hives!" he said. "Some people can't even eat honey without getting hives." I told him about the bicarbonate. "That was right," he said. "Go and take some more. It neutralizes the acid."

In an hour the itchy and burning torture was gone completely. My face, however, remained swollen, and the next day one eye had a beautiful shiner.

These thirty hives of bees play a large part in the economy of Malabar. They cost us nothing beyond the original investment, for Mr. Jarvis tends them and we share the honey. During the war when at times sugar became unobtainable, it did not matter to the families of Malabar, for honey and maple sugar took its place in baking cakes, in tea or coffee, on breakfast food, in all the countless uses for sugar. When supplies of sugar are normal, it is more profitable for the farm to sell its honey and maple syrup and buy sugar.

But the economic benefits do not end there. The thousands of bees work for us in pollinating fruit—the apple and peach and pear and plum trees, the strawberries and the raspberry blossoms for which they appear to have a passion. From plant to tree, from blossom to blossom, they go dusting flower after flower with the pollen carried on their tiny, furry legs. They work the wild white clover, the Dutch clover, the Ladino, the alfalfa, the alsike, pollinating flowers which otherwise might go sterile, and slowly, as the years passed, the evidence of their work showed up not only in yields of clover seed and the thickening of pastures and meadow growth, but along the roadside and in long-dead gullies where the seed of white, Dutch and Ladino clover drifted mysteriously in and started legumes growing where before there had been only weeds or bare ground. The bees played a big role in the balance of Nature, which we were endeavoring to set up again on poor, wrecked land.

Their big cousins, the bumblebees, went to work for us too in ever-increasing numbers on the mammoth and the red clover and upon certain small fruits. Ecologists have long since established the fact that bumblebees, like pheasants, shun poor, worn-out land, and their population increases as land is returned to fertility. Taking a census of bumblebees is not a simple and easy operation, and we have never attempted it, but in the plot consisting of the flower garden and the adjoining raspberry plantations their numbers have unquestionably increased as much as tenfold. And when the fields of red and mammoth clover are in blossom, the bumblebees work there in platoons and whole armies. On a still day you can hear the drone of their buzzing chorus a hundred yards away. They, together with proper land use and steadily growing fertility, have increased the yields of clover seed as much as two hundred percent.

But there is nothing remarkable or startling about all this. It is a part of the whole balance of Nature, from the bacteria and earthworms working deep in the topsoil to the crests of the ash trees high above, which no longer die out at Malabar because now there is plenty of moisture and underground water. The bumblebee prefers to build his nests underground in fence rows where the leaves and decaying vegetation lie in thick layers, or in loose rich soil full of humus and decaying organic material. On a barbaric farm where fence rows are burned over and the soil is like cement, the bumblebees will die out quickly. Since only the bumblebee can pollenize properly giant and red clovers, many a dying farm which made a good income out of the seed of leguminous plants has been forced to abandon the project as the bumblebee disappeared.

Slowly, week by week and month by month, year by year, the whole of the landscape about us has changed, imperceptibly at first, until now, it seems almost a new world. The same outlines are there, the same soft contours, yet there is a difference. The thin, half-starved look is gone, save for a few bare hilltops on the Bailey Place. The bees have played a big role, from the nitrogen which the legumes, beloved by the bees, fix in the soil to the natural reforestation which comes from blossoms which the bees have helped to pollinate.

What was once the hog lot and swamp just below the Big House is a garden now, with a clear spring stream running through it all the year round—the spring stream which once flooded and tore out roads and bridges after a heavy rain and dried up during the hot months of August and September. Where once there was a gullied hillside, there grow now a multitude of flowering shrubs and in spring the whole hillside is bespangled with the white and yellow of narcissus and daffodil.

Even during a cloudburst the water no longer rushes down across that slope from the old orchard and steep pasture and cultivated fields on the little plateau above.

The story of what happened there is on a small scale the story of any well-managed farm. It begins really at the very top of the hill on the little plateau above the Big House by the orchard. Once, after a rainfall, the water poured down the rows between the corn across the steep little pasture, cutting its way through the old orchard below, and finally across the steep slope that rose above the swamp and hog lot. These floods never occur any more because on the little plateau the row crops are contoured and the water stays and sinks into the ground. Later there will be no row crops at all on the little plateau above the Big House, but only grass, alfalfa, clovers and wheat grown in rotation—hay year after year until it thins out, and then wheat in order to seed it back again into hay.

On the steep slope of the little pasture the scars of the old gullies have seeded themselves over with bluegrass and white clover. In the old orchard, where once crops were grown and the soil left bare all winter to wash away with the winter rains and frosts and thaws, there is a thick sod of orchard grass, and between the rows of hundred-year-old apple trees grow peaches, pears and plums and grapes—Concord and Niagara, Delaware and Moore and golden muscat. And in the half-shade grow also red raspberries, healthy and extravagant, and blueberries and blackberries, all mulched but never cultivated. No water cuts across it now, no topsoil slips away imperceptibly yet by the ton if one took the trouble to measure it.

On the steep slope above the garden the ugly, deep gullies are healed across with growing shrubs and flowers, day lilies and peonies and poppies and iris. The steep hillside took care of itself once the run-off water was stopped and held on the land above. That slope has never been cultivated. Nothing was ever done to the flowers and shrubs and trees which grow there, save to mulch them heavily with barnyard manure once a year in November. Each year, the mulch was left on the ground, and gradually, beneath it, in the earth which once in summer dried out into a hard bank of yellow clay, there grew up whole colonies of earthworms, hundreds of thousands of them, which fed on the decaying mulch and the grain in the manure. Year by year, it was possible to see the clay bank change into topsoil, imperceptibly, yet with extraordinary rapidity. On the surface there grew up, first of all, a layer of dark loam soil and, beneath it, the clay itself, permeated by the slow infiltration of manure water and churned over and over by the action of the worms, began to disintegrate and grow soft and loose and a little darker in color. It was rich enough, that glacial clay; it needed only mulch and humus, bacteria and earthworms to turn it into the richest of soils. At any time of the year, you can dig beneath the mulch and sod and find the soil loose and moist. And all the moisture does not come from the rain which falls directly upon it. It comes, much of it, from the water caught and held on the little plateau a quarter of a mile away and nearly two hundred feet higher up, and from the rain held by the sod and mulch among the grapes and apple trees and raspberries and small fruit trees of the old orchard just above. On what was once a bare clay bank grow today the finest flowers in the garden, healthier and finer than the flowers in the cultivated, carefully prepared borders in the flat part of the garden below. On two spots of the once dry bank there are seepage springs, from which water oozes all summer long.

And the bluegrass and white clover of the steep little pasture below the outcrop of pink sandstone grows lush all through the dry months from the water which, instead of rushing across its surface, seeps through the ground from the little plateau above.

And in the flat garden, the little stream no longer goes wild and tears out small trees and great clods of earth. It flows as it must have flowed when the first settler came into the Valley, limpid and clear and steadfast, because the springs above which feed it are in turn fed by the trapped rainfall which no longer uselessly flows off the bare land to flood the Valley below.

And the new pond, below the old still pond which silted up with the good soil from the hill fields above until it became first a swamp and then a garden, is almost free from silt. It will be there a hundred, two hundred years from now, still free of any silt save that which creeps in from the near-by roads during a heavy rain. The spring over which the first settler, John Ferguson, built his little cabin more than a century and a half ago now flows clear and cold all year, out of the roots of the big, black walnut tree.

Ours is naturally a county of springs, rolling country, with glacial moraine piled on top of the thick layers of pink sandstone, and what happened to John Ferguson's spring happened to all the other twenty-odd springs on the place. As the forest was turned back to Nature, the hills contoured and stripped, the earth kept covered in winter by an even green blanket of wheat or rye, the water no longer ran off the four farms, carrying with it the precious topsoil. Instead, it sank into the ground to come out again in clear flowing springs. As year passed into year the flow of the old springs increased and new ones appeared.

One morning in the third year Pete came into my room and said, "Come with me, up to the Ferguson place, I want to show you something."

He wouldn't tell me what it was he wanted to show me, but by the grin on his face I knew that it was something good. We couldn't go farther than the gate in a car, because it was early April, and even the old Ford had been known to become mired in the lower spots of the big hilltop pasture. We walked up over the crest of the hill, where you have a view of three counties, and halfway down the far pasture in a grove of walnut trees we came to what had excited him.

There, at our feet, bubbling from the very roots of the trees, was the most beautiful of sights—a new spring, with a three-inch stream of clear, cold water bubbling up in the midst of the pool which had formed in the depression among the trees. From somewhere deep underground a vein of water had suddenly forced itself up through the soil of the pasture. Once, long ago, there must have been a spring on the same spot, for nearby grew the red daylilies and the pale green star-of-Bethlehem which always mark the site of a settler's cabin in our country, but as the land above had been farmed more and more badly, the spring had diminished and finally died. Then we had come to the place and anchored the soil above and covered the bare earth in winter with cover crops and turned much of the land back to sod, so that the falling rain no longer ran off the high hill above, but sank into the earth to accumulate deep in the strata of the underlying sandstone. And so, as the underground reservoir grew, the accumulated water at last reached a level where on this April in 1942 the old spring was reborn, gushing out from under the walnut trees as it had done when the first settler came upon it.

That spring has never failed since, even during the bad drought of 1944 when farmers all about us in Ohio were hauling water for their livestock. During that drought, the worst our part of Ohio had known for fifty years, only two or three small springs out of the twenty-odd at Malabar showed signs of failing. Never for one day were our cattle without water in any pasture of the thousand acres.

And then a few years later, when we were building a pond near the newly revived spring, we made a remarkable discovery. In excavating, we uncovered the original site of the spring beneath nearly six feet of topsoil which had eroded from the fields above and buried it completely, forcing the newborn spring to find a new outlet. There it was—the small basin walled in the sandstone, built more than a century before by some settler or trapper who had built a cabin there because there was a spring. No one in all the valley remembers who once lived there and no one is alive who remembers even the time when there was a cabin; day lilies and the star-of-Bethlehem and the walled-up basin which we uncovered are the only evidence. But the reborn spring now has two outlets, one where Pete found it on that April morning and one from the little walled-in pool build long ago. What we had done was a simple thing, simply to restore the balance of Nature, to keep the water where it belonged, on our land rather than turning it loose down the long course of the rivers, finally to reach the Gulf of Mexico. And now, in drought time, we had the water we had stored up underground during the seasons of good rainfall.

There is something beautiful and exciting about a deep, clear flowing spring, even in the rich, well-watered Ohio country. It is a sight, I think, which strikes deep into the ancestral memory of man, going back thousands of years into Mesopotamia and Egypt and India, to the very roots of man's beginning and civilization.

There is on the Bailey Place a famous spring, one of the largest in all Ohio, where a whole brook gushes out of the sandstone outcrop behind the old house. It flows through an ancient springhouse with great troughs hewn from single blocks of the native stone. In the troughs filled with icy water stand cans of milk, crocks of cream and butter. In late summer, cantaloupe and watermelon float there, chilled by the living water. The stone walls are damp, and moisture hangs in drops from the ceiling and outside, where the icy brook flows swiftly down toward the barn to water the cattle, the steep course is choked with crisp, spicy watercress. In summer, the small boys go there to fill the big jugs they carry to men working in the fields at harvest time.

What happened in the little garden and the springs and the steep slopes above has happened over nearly all of the four old farms at Malabar. Now, when one stands on the little porch in front of the Big House, the whole of the landscape has a look of lushness that had not been there for fifty years or more, perhaps not since those first years after the settlers cut away the great oaks and beeches and maples and began to farm the thick, black, virgin soil.

In the bottom pasture the bluegrass and white clover grow like an extravagant lawn, the kind of lawn an English gardener dreams of. The lime and the phosphate have made it dark green and thick and juicy, and the moisture from the blocked drainage tiles and the mulch which has been built up by pasture mowing keeps the bluegrass cool and growing throughout all but a bitter drought.

Along the road at the edge of the pasture and around the barnyard of the big barn is a row of big locust trees planted there to feed the bees. They serve not only the bees but they add immeasurably to the beauty of the landscape, and in the still evenings when they are in blossom their heavy perfume drifts all the way past the bass pond up to the Big House. Beneath them the bluegrass grows sweet and lush because the locust is itself a legume and pours nitrogen into the soil. They represent neither much expense nor much trouble—a few hours' work with a spade and a few cuttings thrust into the ground.

And below, around the little bass pond on the Fleming Place, where the geese and ducks have their world and are joined spring and autumn by their cousins, the wild ducks, the once bare banks are covered now by the feathery green of the Babylonica willow and the red-stemmed water dogwood and a few young sycamore trees. A little above the pond there grows on land that otherwise would have been wasted a young orchard of pears and apples. The geese and ducks nest among the forsythia that covers the banks, its golden yellow reflected in the pond.

All of this transformation involved little expense or trouble. The willows and the water dogwood came from bundles of cuttings carried under my arm during Sunday afternoon walks and thrust into the damp soil along the shallow edges of the pond where the big bass and the bluegills and the red-winged blackbirds make their nests. The forsythia came from young layered plants sprung up beside their parents and carried along on Sunday walks and put in with a child's spade. The sycamores seeded themselves and were not cut down ruthlessly by a man with a scythe and more energy than intelligence.

That little corner with its bass pond had been bare as the head of a bald man when we came up there. The same tenants who left piles of old tin cans and rubbish outside of their door took the trouble to scythe it clean of all growing things once each summer, for what reason neither God nor man can, I think, divine, unless it was the atavistic instinct inherited from pioneers with a fear of the encroaching forest or the precautions of those insatiable farmers who admire bare wire fences and monotonous fields.

Today the pond and the little corner in which it is set have become a place which produces fish and fruit and are pretty to look at, not only for ourselves but for the passers-by on the Hastings Road. Frogs and turtles and muskrats live in it. Killdeer and red-wing blackbirds and song sparrows nest along its edges, and big, gray Toulouse geese and Peking and Muscovy ducks live there and breed and raise their young, feeding themselves most of the year, with only a little grain thrown them in the bare winter months. It has become a little world of its own, full of life where exciting things happen—tragedies like the advent of a great and ancient snapping turtle, which killed the baby ducks, until one day the dogs caught him offside in the pasture and I put an end to him, and the endless comedy of the big, bold, gray geese who fear not to grip an old sow by the ear to drive her away from the corn, or to chase the big boxers if they come too near a nest. And the antics of the big male bass guarding a nest who will attack your finger if you thrust it into the water near him. And the breeding frenzy of the toads in the early spring in the shallow water, a spectacle which surpasses in lechery and urgency the most terrible Babylonian orgy. And there is the compensating and satisfactory beauty of the wild iris and the bulrushes, and the tragedy of the big water snakes that prey on the frogs and small fish and have to be killed by Baby, the biggest of the boxers, who inherited his propensity for snake-killing from his noble father, Rex I. And there is always the scent of crushed mint underfoot as one walks along the edge of the pond on a hot day.

It was not much trouble—that pond and the little world surrounding it. I think I love it best of all the spots on the whole farm, better even than the lofty, remote and beautiful world of the Ferguson Place. Up there against the sky looking across thirty miles of Valley and stream and lakes and woods and hills, one comes close to God with that sense of remoteness and grace and insignificance which the Hindu knows, but down below in the Valley by the pond, one comes very close to all that lives, to the geese and fish and birds and frogs and turtles. Beside the little pond one is no longer insignificant, a mere atom in a vast universe, beyond comprehension, which produces in the spirit a remoteness and peace not untouched by terror; in that smaller world one understands everything, with all its tragedies and comedies. One sees that even among geese and ducks there are braggarts and bullies, heroes and knaves, clowns and heroes. It gives one a pleasant reassuring feeling of belonging to a whole scheme of things, of being a part of the whole plan of Nature. One begins to understand exactly where man fits in.

And beyond the pond and the white and green barn of the Fleming Place, lie those fields which were abandoned and grown up in weeds when I first saw them again after thirty years. Now they lie in long strips of green following the soft contours of the low hills left long ago by the icy, glacial rivers, green with alfalfa, with the lighter green of corn and the sea green and, later, the gold of wheat and oats. And, in the near end, where once there was only desolation, grow the rows of potatoes, the sweet corn, the peas, the lima and string beans, which provide six families with all they need and more for all the summer and the long winter that follows.

What one sees there is a kind of miracle made by the hand of man with work and intelligence and an investment of money which has been repaid many times over. The old square fields are gone and in their place are the strips of green following the contours of the earth itself. Where the slopes are steep, grows only green hay or alfalfa or wheat which binds the soil and fills it with roots and keeps it from wasting uselessly away. And each year that soil, anchored by trillions of tiny small roots and sheltered by the grass above, grows a little deeper, a little richer with nitrogen and bacteria and worms and the manure that is spread over it by the wandering cattle in the autumn and by the man-made machine when the ground is frozen and covered with snow. And the fence rows along the roads and between the fields are not merely bare wire fences; they have been allowed to grow into hedgerows which check the moisture and provide shelter for the quail, the pheasants, the rabbits and wild game of every kind. And as I write, the hedges of multi-flora rose which have gradually replaced the fences are in full bloom, filled with the nests of the great thrush family. Their perfume drifts through the open windows of the Big House into the room where I am working.

Beyond the fields the distant, high, bare hill of the Bailey Place, the last of the farms to be acquired and the poorest, have already begun to turn a deeper green as the lime and phosphorus seep into the starved hillside and disintegrate and feed the new growth of bluegrass and white clover. And, each year, the cuttings from the pasture mowings will build a little thicker the blanket of mulch and humus which keeps the earth beneath cool and moist and the blue-grass growing through the long, hot days where once the vicious heat on the bare, overgrazed earth burnt the roots and all but killed it.

But perhaps the woods have changed more than any part of the landscape. Only a few years ago the ground was bare beneath the high trees. There were no seedlings and no fine roots and the leaves as they fell blew away to pile up against the fences in drifts. The little grass that grew there was shaded and sickly. It contained little nourishment for the cattle and sheep, who were expected to pick up a meager living on the pasture they found off the fends, the wildflowers and the young seedling trees. Gullies scarred the bare hillsides where the natural processes of forests were checked or destroyed.

Once the cattle and sheep were kept out of those woods, a transformation began to take place on the floor of the forest. The first year a whole crop of seedlings came in—tiny oaks and beech and ash, hickory and maple. And, as year passed into year, the seedlings grew and new ones appeared, until presently the woods began to take on again the appearance of a real Ohio forest. The seedlings grew and produced leaves, which dropped to the ground, and their trunks prevented the leaves which fell from their tiny branches and from the big trees which spread overhead from blowing away. They stayed where they fell, on the floor of the forest, and began again to build up layers of decaying vegetation. And when the rain fell, it no longer fell on bare earth, but seeped into the ground to feed the big trees and the new seedlings. And the water trapped on the fields above the hillsides by the sod and the contours began to form seepage springs again all through the floor of the forest. The ash trees, which like cold, wet feet, stopped dying at the tops when they reached the height of fifty or sixty feet, and each year the yield of sap from the sugar maples increased. And nowadays, when one enters the woods, one enters a green jungle with a tangle of seedlings twice as high as a man's head, in which it is possible to lose oneself completely during the hot, summer days when the trees are in full leaf.

Over the years it has been fascinating to watch the vegetation of this woodland grow through several cycles, very rapidly under the existing conditions. The changes have in essence followed in pattern those which occurred on the face of the ancient world, as the eroded rocks gradually built up the soils so that the benevolent vegetation could grow and so support in the end far higher and more complicated forms of life. In the first stage there was little ground cover at all, for the grasses would not grow properly in the heavy shade from the few enormous maples which had been left to supply sap for the making of syrup and sugar. What tree seedlings or wild flowers had persisted somehow were quickly eaten off by the half-starving sheep and presently, without any protective covering for the land, the gullies had begun to appear and the whole natural process of building up soils was disrupted, and rapidly the whole area had begun to go backward to the prehistoric times when all the world was bare eroding rock. As the moisture receded and the temperatures rose, even the lichens on the outcrops of sandstone began to disappear and with them the ferns, the pre-glacial vegetation, the wild columbine.

The shutting out of the cattle worked a miracle and provided a demonstration of what Nature herself will do if given only half a chance. During the first year seedlings not only of trees but of the wild plants and flowers suitable to a thick forest began to appear, here and there singly or in sparse, sickly clusters. Next came the brambles—the blackberries, the wild black raspberries and in the more open spaces the elderberries and the dewberries. For three or four years, until the forest seedlings began to grow rapidly and take over, the brambles established complete possession until the whole forest became a veritable and impenetrable thicket. Under this cover the wild flowers and ferns tended to recede a little, but presently as the thick tree seedlings became sturdier and thicker, the cycle of brambles began to disappear beneath the increasingly thick shade. Then within the next three or four years as the saplings grew stronger and more vigorous, the brambles gave way, rapidly and at last completely and the cycle of ground plants and wildflowers and ferns, typical of the thick hardwood forest everywhere in the world, began to return, almost as if they had invaded the forest overnight. In the thick cool shade, the dripping moisture and the still, damp air, they had found their proper climate once more. While the forest had only a few gigantic trees and the vegetation was eaten bare by the sheep and cattle, fallen twigs and branches had lain for months and even years, bare and dead but undecayed like the bones of prehistoric animals; but now in the changed climate, there appeared everywhere countless kinds of mosses, fungi (including the delicious morel), molds and lichens, and within a little time the fallen twigs and leaves and branches began to disintegrate and disappear in the eternal cycle by which life on this earth is maintained—the cycle of birth, growth, death, decay and rebirth. On the sandstone outcrops the lichens appeared again to break down the rock into good and fertile soil in which plants and shrubs and trees might grow again. The wild columbine, the wild ginger and an immense variety of ferns, springing from spores which had remained dormant or blown in from some distant place, appeared everywhere on the rocks and in the woodsy decaying leaf cover.

And finally as the saplings turned into trees thirty or forty feet tall, the beautiful hardwood forest, typical of Ohio, began to return again in its full, luxuriant almost tropical splendor. The new young seedlings began to languish and fade away and the last of the brambles disappeared, and along the edges of the forest appeared great writhing vines of wild grapes like the lianas in the tropical forests of Brazil. The forest floor became carpeted with yellow and white, purple and pale mauve violets, with trillium and in the wet spots with the opulent skunk cabbage, with Dutchman's breeches and squirrel corn and jack-in-the-pulpit, with wild ginger and trailing partridge berry with its shining evergreen leaves and brilliant red berries. By now many of the saplings, and especially the fast-growing white ash and the black walnut, have risen to a height of fifty to sixty feet. But most glorious of all are the brilliant white clouds of the dogwood, which likes to grow and flower in the deep cover of the woods. The birds too have come back and the bee trees and all manner of squirrels and raccoon. Most beautiful of all perhaps is the darting brilliant flight of the shy scarlet tanager, which likes the deep woods.

In 1950 in Virginia I had an experience which has quite possibly never known been known to any other watcher of birds, save the Paul Mellons and my wife who were with me. We had been discussing the vivid beauties of the North American birds and how they were only rivaled in variety and splendor by the birds of Brazil and India. We had been talking of the beauty of the scarlet tanager, which is very different from the beauty of the friendly cardinal, when just ahead of us, where a small crystal spring stream crossed the back country road on the edge of the forest, we saw an indigo bunting and a male goldfinch bathing and drinking from the little stream. Stopping the car to watch the lovely sight, we sat there for a long time and then the miracle occurred; they were joined in their bath by a scarlet tanager. The sight of the brilliant iridescent bunting, the yellow and black goldfinch and the brilliant scarlet tanager bathing and drinking together was one of the most lovely spectacles I have ever seen.

And now in summer the very air beneath the growing trees is green so that as one walks through the forest it is like moving across the bottom of a clear and crystalline sea; and always, even on the hottest days of August, the air is moist and cool. To come directly from the hot rich fields into the forest itself is to enter another climate and another world.

One day the seedlings will be great oaks and beeches and maples and ash, tall and straight and round, as forest trees should be. The time is not too far away when, harvested like crops in the field, they will bring a good return in money. Meanwhile, they are serving to build new soil; they are piling up layers of decaying leaves to absorb rain as a sponge absorbs water, to check the floods which periodically sweep away good land and houses and people all the way from Pleasant Valley to the mouth of the Mississippi. And the water they absorb into the earth comes out again in the pasture and fields of the valley below to feed the bluegrass and the crops when the hot, dry season comes. All these forest seedlings are a good investment, one of the best investments we have made, not only for ourselves and for the immediate future but for our neighbors and for the people downstream on Switzer's Creek, and the Clear Fork, the Muskingum, the Ohio and the Mississippi. They are an investment not only for ourselves but for the nation.

One of the great changes in the landscape in our part of the Valley is in the quality of its greenness. Each year it has grown a little deeper, a little darker, a little richer. It is a new and healthy greenness born of many things, of work, of humus, of elements restored to the soil, of intelligence, of love, of water, of working with Nature instead of fighting her. The job is by no means finished. There are still places where the topsoil is too thin, where there is still not enough humus to hold the moisture, where the pasture is meager or the crops too pale a green. Many things have plagued us; many things have stood in our way—the clamor for greedy production of food, the war and the loss of manpower, the difficulty of obtaining fertilizer and fencing and proper machinery, and sometimes the weather. Our progress has been slowed, but not stopped. We who are interested in the adventure could not stop if we chose to, for it is in the blood of all of us to make that countryside each year a little more lush, a little deeper green in color, a little more productive.

We have set about to turn the wheel of fertility moving forward again. It had been moving backward almost since the day the trees of the virgin forest were cleared away. What we have been doing has been a relatively simple thing. We have sought merely to build as Nature builds, to plant and sow and reap as Nature meant us to do; we have sought to rebuild the earth as Nature built it in the beginning. With man's ingenuity we have been able to do it more rapidly than Nature herself, but only because we worked *with* the law and within the idiom of Nature. Man is never able to impose his own law upon Nature nor to alter her laws, but he can, by working with her, accomplish much, whether it is in dynamos or the airplanes or the earth or the body of man himself. The man who loves Nature comes nearest, I think, to an understanding of God. Even man's religion grew out of Nature itself, and the good earth and true faith have never been removed from one another. They are as near today as they were ten thousand years ago.

The adventure at Malabar is by no means finished, but I doubt that the history of any piece of land is ever finished or that any adventure in Nature ever comes to an end. The land came to us out of eternity, and when the youngest of us associated with it dies, it will still be there. The best we can hope to do is to leave the mark of our fleeting existence upon it, to die knowing that we have changed a small corner of this earth for the better by wisdom, knowledge and hard work, that we shall leave behind upon it the mark left by Johnny Appleseed and my grandfather and Walter Oakes and the other good farmers or lovers of Nature of whom I have written in this book.

Not even one small part of the big program is complete, for there will always be fields and fence rows and woods which can be still greener and richer and more productive of life and food and beauty. And even those fields which have been rescued from barrenness and death require eternal vigilance and the awareness that, to keep them fertile and green, we must pay back our debt to them in kind. Each mistake, even the smallest one, each attempt to cheat or short-cut Nature, must be paid for in the end by ourselves.

The whole adventure has not been without disappointment and heartbreak. There have been droughts that broke the heart as the corn withered and the pastures turned brown, and there have been with us from time to time a man like Lester who broke faith and stole from the others and men like Elmer who sought to disrupt work and to set us against each other, and even a neighbor or two, cantankerous and backward, who sought to obstruct the things we were trying to do. And there were the tragedies of death in the barns and the stables—the death of a calf or a colt, not only valuable, but beloved by all of us. And most discouraging of all were the checks and obstacles growing out of the war when materials and labor and farm machinery were unavailable and the progress both of experiments and The Plan were set back from five to ten years. It was a discouragement shared by farmers over the whole of the nation. But we learned many things out of the trials and disappointments, as every farmer must learn.

The whole field of agriculture represents perhaps the most fascinating of all callings, because no program is ever finished, and each goal attained can be held only by vigilance and intelligence and because it embraces all of science and philosophy, religion and life. In no life, certainly, is there so little monotony, in no life so much of richness for those with understanding. Each farm is a tiny world in itself, with each day its small play of tragedy, of comedy, of farce. Each day is in itself a cycle of the history of the earth.

This much we have done with the land that has come into our hands at Malabar. Each day the forest grows greener and thicker. Each year the soil grows darker and deeper and the crops a little heavier. Each year water in the brooks and streams grows more steadfast and clear. The fish and wild game increase in number as the fertility increases. No longer does the water after heavy rains rush across bare land below us. No longer does the soil vanish by the ton after each rain to darken the streams and leave our own field bare and sterile. On the thousand acres of Malabar no living gully, however small, exists like an open wound today. Each year more water gushes from the springs to water the cattle and the sheep, and feed the little brooks where the watercress, which tolerates only clear, pure, cold water, grows on the gravelly bed.

Where there was once little, we have abundance. The trees we planted bear pears and peaches, grapes and plums and apples. The grapes trained along the fences that border the gardens hang green and yellow and purple in September. The gardens grow beans and cantaloupe, watermelon and broccoli, peas and carrots and sweet corn and asparagus and a score of other vegetables, not only for the season but for frozen storage all through the long winter. There are fat cattle and lambs and pigs in the fields, and eggs and chickens and milk and cream and butter. The bees work for us, and the trees provide maple syrup. Geese, turkeys, guinea fowl, ducks and fighting chickens wander at large over the fields, woods and ponds. Everywhere there is wild game, quail and pheasant, raccoon and possum, rabbit and squirrel and deer, and they too find abundance in the enriched fields, in the orchards and the walnut and hickory and beechnut of the woods and the wild berries and hazelnuts of the fence rows.

The law of Nature is not that of scarcity, but of abundance, and we have followed that law as nearly as we understand it. In all the war period of shortages and rationing we at Malabar took little or nothing from the needed stores of the nation, and we contributed much. In our small world, since the very beginning, we have had both self-sufficiency and abundance. It was there to be had; to achieve it only required application of energy and intelligence. We have lived well at Malabar, and the record is there in the fat, heavy cattle, in the brightness and health of every child on the place. We have been beholden to no one in what we have accomplished. In good times we have done well and in bad times we have always had security and shelter and food and, above all else, the dignity and self-respect without which life becomes, for the reasonable man, unendurable.

I think we have reason to be proud of our record, for we rebuilt the very soil while we worked it, gaining a little way toward our ends, even while we produced our crops and our animals. On the whole, we have lived together in harmony and decency with mutual self-respect and co-operation and as much privacy as we desired, and all that is not easy for as many as thirty-five men, women and children existing on a small co-operative democracy of a thousand acres. I think the record must imply a considerable degree of abundance and health and contentment. We have lived in peace with our neighbors and helped them and received help from them, I think, largely because we were engaged upon a project of considerable size which required a concentration of energies that led us to mind our own business.

We have been rewarded not only in terms of material plenty but in countless other ways in terms of health and the spirit, and we have learned much out of the very soil itself. For the children the rewards have been greater possibly than for the adults. There has been health and good food and fields and woods to roam over, animals to care for, streams to fish and swim in, and all those contacts with air and earth and water which make for wisdom and understanding and judgment and for those resources later in life which are indestructible and far beyond either fame or riches in the long and trying span of life. We all know, I think, the great importance and solace of work, not the aimless, monotonous work of riveting and fitting together nuts and bolts, but of work which creates something, work which leaves its own record, within the natural scheme of man's existence—the kind of work which contributes to progress and welfare of mankind and the plenty of the earth upon which he lives. Wherever the children go in after life they will possess the knowledge of the fields and the brilliant beauty of a cock pheasant soaring above the green of a meadow in October. They will know how things grow and why. They will understand what goes on above the earth and in it. If they are ever bored and defeated it will be in the narrow streets of the city or in some dark office or the thunderous shed of a factory. They will, I think, understand what is decent and tolerant in life and comprehend both the evils of selfish exploitation and the evils of a regimented world in which human dignity and the soaring quality of the human spirit are cramped and stifled.

I believe one day there will be abundance for all as God and Nature intended, an abundance properly distributed when man has the wisdom to understand and solve such things. I believe there will be no more floods to destroy the things man has worked to create and even man himself, and that the abomination of great industrial cities will become a thing of the past, that men and women, and, above all else, the children, will live in smaller communities in which there can be health and decency and human dignity, and that, when that time comes, the people then living will look back upon us and the stupidity of our times, as we look back with unbelief at the squalor and oppression and misery of the Middle Ages.

I am not a partisan of those who believe that in this country we have passed the zenith of our wealth and well-being. The possibilities of the future are boundless. Until now we have destroyed as much as we have constructed, and we are beginning at last to pay for that destruction in terms of reduced living standards and health and intelligence, in subsidies and all manner of politico-social-economic short cuts, tricks and panaceas. There is a tremendous job ahead of reconstruction and restoration, a job quite as big and infinitely more complicated than the job of subduing the wilderness by the first settlers. What we need is a new courage and a new race of pioneers, as sturdy as the original pioneers, but wiser than they—a race of pioneers concerned with the physical, economic and social paradise which this great country could be, if there were fewer exploiters, fewer selfish minorities, fewer self-seeking, vainglorious politicians, fewer social and economic panaceas and fanatics. These new pioneers will have to be men who sit not in libraries working out theories, but men who understand the people of this country and the illimitable wealth of its natural resources and beauties, and, above all, the fact that there is wealth for all and a good life, and that it is founded, as is the wealth and well-being of every sound nation, upon its soil, its water and its forest. When there is no more soil, there will be no more nation, and the American civilization, even in its cruder materialistic and mechanical manifestations, will wither and pass away.

For myself, I am deeply grateful to my parents and my grandparents for the life they gave me as a child in this rich Ohio country, for with it came the resources in life which are indestructible. They are bulwarks against fate, against wealth, against ambition, against poverty, against defeat. An acre is as good an anchor as fifty thousand, for in that acre, as Fabre well knew, there is the whole of a universe and the answer to most of man's problems.

And I am deeply grateful to the French for what I learned from them of the earth, of human values and dignity and decency and reality. And I am grateful to Louis Gillet, dead now of a heart broken by the humiliation of France, for the long talk that evening in the moonlit forest of Ermenonville while we listened to the calling of the amorous stags, for he sent me back to the county where I was born, to Pleasant Valley, and the richest life I have ever known.

Johnny Appleseed
and Aunt Mattie

M<small>Y EARLIEST MEMORIES</small> of Johnny Appleseed are of listening to
my Great-Aunt Mattie talk of him beneath the big catalpa tree on
my grandfather's farm. Aunt Mattie was blind from the age of thirty,
and when I first remember her she was over eighty, a sprightly, very
bright old lady, with a crinkly mouth that was always curling up in a
good-humored, faintly mocking smile. She was a witty, and at times
a malicious old lady, and, like so many blind people since the time
of Homer, a great storyteller. I think that the stories were a kind of
compensation for the darkness in which she spent more than half a

century of her life. Now, nearly forty years after her death, I realize
that you could not always take all her stories as gospel truth, but I
also know that she was in her way a minor artist. If there were facts
missing from one of her stories of frontier life, she supplied them
out of her own imagination; if some fact did not suit one of her tales
she modified and altered it to fit the artistic frame. Those qualities
and methods are, of course, what distinguish the creative artist in
any field of artistic endeavor. Brahms plagiarized simple folk and
provincial dances but when he had finished with them, they were art
rather than nature.

Aunt Mattie said she had known Johnny Appleseed. I do not
know whether this was true or not. She was born in 1826 and by
a curious combination of circumstances her presence and her stories brought me as a small boy very near to the eighteenth century,
for she was the child of my great-grandfather who had visited Vol-
taire at Ferney. She was born when he was seventy-two years old.
But there were other elements which brought her very close to the
strange little man who has become a legend and a kind of saint in
our Middle Western county. She loved the woods and the streams
and the wild birds and animals as Johnny Appleseed had done. Once
or twice as a small boy I came upon her on the edge of the marshes
or the deep forest standing quite still, listening with the intensity of
the blind to the singing birds or even perhaps the rustling in nearby
bushes or marsh grasses which betrayed the presence of small moving animals. On both occasions she was smiling with a kind of secret
knowledge and her lips moved. I was never able to overhear what
she was saying to the birds, the animals and the trees about her, and
so to God as well.

My grandmother told me that when Aunt Mattie was a small
child she had caused much anxiety through her trick of running off
to spend whole days wandering through the swamps and forests of
the still half-conquered Ohio frontier country. In those days there
were occasional bears or wandering Indians about, but no amount of
bloodcurdling tales ever succeeded in instilling fears in Aunt Mattie as to what might happen to her. My grandmother said that, like

Johnny himself, Aunt Mattie never seemed to have any fear of Indians or wild animals.

Even as a blind old woman she kept that love of the streams and forest and wild things. She had a remarkable talent for finding her way about the farm. Of course, she had been born there and until she lost her sight she knew it well, and so even in all the fifty or more years of her blindness she must have known always exactly how it looked. But sometimes on long excursions she did not go off by herself, feeling with her small feet the roads and paths or guiding herself by the sound of the rustling leaves of the familiar landmark trees. Sometimes when she felt adventurous and wanted to make a long excursion down through the bottom pastures where the creek ran on into the thicket and the marshes she would ask one of the children to act as her guide. She would select a spot which she remembered beneath a tree on the edge of the creek and then tell us to come back for her two or three hours later. She did not like us playing about. She wanted to be left alone and at times, even as a child, you had the feeling that she had come there like an ardent young girl for a rendezvous and did not wish to be disturbed or spied upon. She would spend a whole afternoon listening to the sounds of fish jumping or birds singing or cattle lowing.

Since she knew that whole small world through touch and sound alone she undoubtedly understood it in a way none of the rest of us could ever do. She heard and interpreted sounds, small sounds—the symphony made by frogs and crickets and birds and cattle which we never heard at all. Sometimes you would come upon her sitting quietly beneath a tree beside the clear little stream, her head tilted a little in an attitude of listening. Like as not, the cattle would be lying all around close up to her, munching bluegrass and fighting flies. When one sees, there invades one's consciousness a million distractions which serve to block out sound. In a country like ours, one tends to take the sound of the birds for granted, and so not hear at all the whole rustic symphony of their existence—their quarreling and lovemaking, the hungry cries of the young and the glorious arias which greet the freshened earth after a thundershower. It is only when one concentrates on sound alone that this whole glorious world is revealed. And so blind Aunt Mattie heard things and knew a whole world which to most of us remains forever closed. The spirit of Johnny Appleseed haunted that same Valley which Aunt Mattie knew so well. Once, long ago, he had roamed all the region, sleeping in the big sandstone caves or in Indian huts or settlers' cabins. He was welcome wherever he stopped—among the Indians, the white settlers or the wild animals themselves.

With each year the figure of Johnny Appleseed grows a little more legendary; each year new stories and legends attach themselves to what has become in our country an almost mythical figure. A few facts are stated but few are known. It is said that Johnny's real name was John Chapman. Some say that he was born in New England, others that he was born at Fort Duquesne, later to be called Pittsburgh. It is pretty well accepted that he was a Swedenborgian by faith. It is also related that he died at last like the Abbé Constant alone on the roadside during a thunderstorm somewhere near the borders of Ohio and Indiana.

The truth is, of course, that Johnny Appleseed has attained that legendary status where facts are no longer of importance. Long before we returned to Pleasant Valley he had become a kind of frontier saint about whom had collected volumes of folklore and legend. In the natural process of things, as in the lives of all saints, it is the stories and legends and not the facts which have become important. I think Aunt Mattie understood this change of values which throughout all history has imperceptibly translated heroes into gods and hermits into saints. It was a part of her genius as a storyteller, even a poetess or female bard of the frontier country. For Johnny Appleseed has long since become the patron saint of all those who find in brooks and streams, in the beauty of a meadow, or the deep forest or an understanding of animals, great and direct manifestations of God.

She told us children that she remembered him well as an old man when he came to spend nights at her father's big farm. He was a small man, Aunt Mattie said, with a shriveled, weather-beaten face, framed by long, ragged, gray hair. His eyes were a very bright blue, surrounded by fine little lines which came of living always in the open. He went barefoot winter and summer and for clothing wore strange garments fashioned in summer out of a kind of sackcloth or in winter of leather or skins given him by the Indians. His only baggage was a metal cooking pot with a handle, which did not encumber his movements, since when traveling he wore it as a hat with the handle at the back. He always carried a "poke" swung over his shoulder in which he carried seeds and plants.

He would arrive in the evening and have supper with the family, although later on as he grew older and more solitary he would not eat in the house but only on the doorstep or in the woodshed. Sometimes in the evening he would preach a kind of sermon upon love of mankind and all Nature. As he grew older the Swedenborgian doctrines changed imperceptibly into a kind of animistic pagan faith which ascribed spirits to trees and sticks and stones and regarded the animals and the birds as his friends. But the sermons never had the curse of the conventional doctrinal harangue; they were interspersed with wonderful enchanting stories about the wild things, so that for the children, the opossum, the raccoon, the bear, the blue jay all came to have distinct personalities and a sense of intimate reality which many people never understand. Aunt Mattie said that, like St. Francis, he had a habit of talking aloud to the birds and animals as he tramped barefooted through the woods. None of the children ever resented or avoided his "sermons." It is probable that Johnny's visits took the place in that frontier country of theater and talking pictures and comic strips all rolled into one.

He never accepted the hospitality of a bed but chose instead to sleep in the great haymows above the fat cattle and horses. Usually when the settler went to the barn in the morning Johnny had already vanished with his kettle on his head and his "poke" of apple and fennel seed thrown over his shoulder. I think every Indian, every settler, every trader in all that Ohio country must have known him well, much as my great-grandfather knew him.

A good many of the white men and their families humored him and were fond of him, but looked upon him as half-mad. Some of

them owed their lives and the lives of their families to Johnny Appleseed. The Indians regarded him with awe and veneration, for in the
way of primitive peoples, they looked upon his particular kind of "insanity" as God-given, an "insanity" which linked him to the trees, the
rocks, the wild animals which were so much a part of the redskins'
daily and hourly existence. Because of this veneration the Indians
never harmed him and left him free to go and come as he liked, nor
did they conceal their plans from him. More than once during the
early days of the frontier Johnny slipped away with his kettle and
"poke" out of an Indian encampment to journey miles through forest and marsh to warn some lonely family to leave their cabin for
the safety of the nearest village or blockhouse until the tragic raids
were over. If the Indians knew he had used his friendship to betray
their plans, they appeared to have borne him no ill will for he lived at
peace among them, preaching brotherhood and good will until there
were no longer any Indians left in all the region and Johnny died one
night, an old man, in a hedgerow in Indiana.

My Great-Aunt Mattie used to tell about Johnny's friendship with
the King of France and, although I do not remember that she ever
claimed to have seen the King, she certainly intimated that she had a
speaking acquaintance with him. She meant, of course, the Lost Dauphin, that curious and mysterious character who, as a young man, spent
much time in our Ohio country. To the Whites he was known as Eleazar
Williams and to the French traders and the redskins he was known
simply as Lazare. For many years he lived among the Indians and the
French half-breed *coureurs de bois*, wandering down into our valleys
where, undoubtedly, he met and knew Johnny. My great-aunt also said
that when the King, Louis Philippe, then the Duc de Chartres, came
into the Ohio country to investigate the claims and legend of the Lost
Dauphin, he saw Johnny Appleseed and questioned him concerning
his friend Eleazar Williams or Lazare. That too is not only possible but
probable, for the Duc de Chartres, later King Louis Philippe, *did* come
to Ohio accompanied by a commission to determine whether or not
Eleazar Williams was really the son of Louis XVI and Marie Antoinette
who had been spirited out of the Temple and off to America.

More than a hundred years later, when I wrote of Johnny Appleseed and his friendship with the Lost Dauphin in *The Farm* and
the book was translated into French, the ancient controversy was
reopened in France and learned articles on the subject appeared in
the *Revue des Deux Mondes*, *L'Illustration*, and other French pe-
riodicals, and the name and legend of Johnny Appleseed became
known to countless Frenchmen of another time and world.

The whole tale of the Lost Dauphin is one of the fascinating stories of history and I think no one, even today, could say with any cer-
tainty that the Eleazar Williams who frequented our frontier country
was or was *not* the son of Louis XVI and Marie Antoinette. His past,
like that of Johnny Appleseed, has joined the legends and folklore
of the Middle Western country. It is known that there arrived in
Maine mysteriously, at the end of the eighteenth century, a boy of
ten or eleven years of age. He was unaccompanied save by a box of
shabby clothing. The ship's captain knew nothing of him save that
he had been hastily embarked at Bordeaux as the ship was sailing by
unknown persons who paid his passage and left instructions for him
to be put ashore at the first port touched upon in America. This happened to be Bath, Maine. The boy spoke only French and appeared
to be dim-witted or to have been frightened out of his wits by some
terrifying experience. His only memories were those of mirrors and
mobs and torches. A New England preacher named Williams took
him in, it is not clear whether by adoption or as a kind of bound-boy.
As he grew older the boy's wits never seemed quite normal, and
presently he slipped away to live on the frontier among Indians and
French trappers. My Great-Aunt Mattie said he never spoke English very well and that he was blond and big and heavy, with a big
nose and a small chin. I doubt that Aunt Mattie knew what were the
physical traits of the Bourbons, but she described them perfectly in
her account of Lazare, the Lost Dauphin. It is likely that she never
saw him or was too young to remember him and that the description was passed on to her by her father who had visited at Ferney
the old man who did more than any other to bring about the French
Revolution. The Duc de Chartres, sent by the Dauphin's sister, (the

dull, tragic Duchess d'Angoulême) to the wilderness of Ohio to investigate the stories, repudiated the Lost Dauphin, Lazare, but that was inevitable because the Dauphin stood between the Duke and the throne of France.

I like to think of crazy Johnny Appleseed and the Lost Dauphin with his dull wits, wandering our country, protected and respected by Indians because they were both "naturals" and thus close to the beasts and trees.

After I had written of Johnny and the Dauphin in *The Farm*, I had two letters, both from very old ladies, one in Illinois and one in Minnesota. The old lady from Illinois wrote that at one time there was in the state capital of Illinois an unmistakable portrait of Louis XVI which had been brought from France by a deputation of men who believed that Lazare was the son of Louis and Marie Antoinette and sought to persuade him to return to France as a pretender. My correspondent claimed that as a young girl she had seen the portrait but did not know what had become of it. She remembered having heard that the deputation bringing the portrait had come by way of Canada and the Great Lakes and that their ship had been lost in Lake Michigan. Several men were lost but the portrait was saved.

From Minnesota the other old lady wrote that she had known the false Dauphin as an old man married to an Indian squaw. Her description of him was, like that of Great-Aunt Mattie, unmistakably the description not only of a Bourbon but of a son of Louis XVI—that of a fat, soft, blond old man with a scant beard, almost more feminine than masculine. I doubt that anyone will ever know whether Lazare was the true or the false Dauphin. I only know that in legend he has gone down as a friend of our Johnny Appleseed, and that to Aunt Mattie he was always the true King of France.

There is some disagreement concerning the way in which Johnny went about planting apple trees in the wild frontier country. Some say that he scattered the seeds as he went along the edges of marshes or natural clearings in the thick, almost tropical forests, others that he distributed the seeds among the settlers themselves to plant, and still others claim that in the damp land surrounding the marshes he established nurseries where he kept the seedlings until they were big enough to transplant. My Great-Aunt Mattie said that her father, who lived in rather a grand way for a frontier settler, had boxes of apples brought by wagon each year from Maryland through the Cumberland Gap, until his own trees began to bear and then he always saved the seeds, drying them on the shelf above the kitchen fireplace, to be put later into a box and kept for Johnny Appleseed when he came on one of his overnight visits.

Johnny scattered fennel and yarrow seed all through our Ohio country, for when the trees were first cleared and the land plowed up, the mosquitoes increased and malaria spread from family to family. Johnny regarded a tea brewed of fennel and yarrow leaves as a specific against what the settlers called "fever and ague" and he seeded the plant along trails and fence rows over all Ohio. Some people said that he carried flower seeds with him to distribute among the lonely women who lived in cabins in clearings in the vast forest and that today the great red day lilies which grow along the roadsides or on the sites of old cabins long disappeared, were spread by Johnny. They say also that Johnny sometimes carried in his "poke" as gifts tiny seedlings of Norway spruce which he gave to frontier wives to plant before their cabins. Both stories may be true, for in our part of Ohio there is nearly always a pair of Norway spruce well over a hundred years old in the dooryard of every old house, and the red day lilies have gone wild in fields, on roadsides and along hedgerows.

In the next county there is an ancient apple tree which, it is claimed, was one of those planted by Johnny. I do not know whether this is true or not, but I do know that in our pastures, on the edge of the woods and in the fence rows there are apple trees which are the descendants of those planted by Johnny. They bear a wide variety of apples from those which are small and bitter to those, on one or two trees, which are small but of a delicious wild flavor which no apples borne on respectable commercial apple trees ever attain. Their blossoms have a special perfume, very sweet and spicy, which you can smell from a great distance, long before you come upon the trees themselves. They have been scattered here and there long ago by squirrels and rabbits and birds, muskrat and raccoon who fed on the fruit of the trees planted more than a century and a half ago on the edge of clearings out of Johnny Appleseed's "poke." And in our Valley, Johnny Appleseed is certainly not dead. He is there in the caves and the woodland, along the edge of the marshes and in hedgerows. When in early spring there drifts toward you the perfume of a wild apple tree, the spirit of Johnny rides the breeze. When in winter the snow beneath a wild apple tree is crisscrossed with the delicate prints of raccoon or muskrat or rabbit, you know that they have been there gathering apples from the trees that would never have existed but for crazy Johnny and his saucepan and "poke" of seeds. He is alive wherever the feathery fennel or the flowering day lilies cover a bank. He is there in the trees and the caves, the springs and the streams of our Ohio country, alive still in a legend which grows and grows.

Sometimes when I am alone in the old bottom pasture, or the woods, the memory of blind Great-Aunt Mattie returns to me. I can see her again, sitting by the edge of the clear flowing stream where the children left her, surrounded by cattle and the wild birds, her head a little tilted, listening. She has been dead for close to forty years, and only lately have I begun to understand what it was she heard. It was the song of the earth and streams and forests of which Johnny Appleseed has become the patron saint in our country. It may be that while she sat there Johnny Appleseed was with her.

She had a verse, out of one of the most beautiful and certainly the most musical poems ever written, which she used often to repeat to us children:

> *He prayeth well who loveth well*
> *Both man and bird and beast*

> *He prayeth best who loveth best*
> *All things both great and small*
> *For the dear God who loveth us,*
> *He made and loveth all.*

One hot summer afternoon when I was twelve years old, we returned late to guide Aunt Mattie back to the farmhouse. As we approached the chosen spot the cattle were as usual lying in a circle about the place where we had left her. She was leaning against an ancient sycamore tree, her head thrown back a little, her eyes closed. My cousin and I thought she was asleep, but when we spoke to her she did not answer. It was my first sight of death and I felt no more terror of it than the cattle lying in the bluegrass in a protecting circle about her. It was all strangely a part of the Valley, of the whole cycle of existence and the most natural thing in the world. Long afterward, more than forty years later, when for three days I lay on the edge of death, but still conscious, I felt no fear, or even any great reluctance to die. I think it was because I knew what Aunt Mattie knew.

I remember that when I got back to the farmhouse I had an impulse to say, "Aunt Mattie has gone to join her friend Johnny Appleseed." But I was only a small boy and then it seemed silly. I only said, "Something has happened to Aunt Mattie." She was eighty-five years old when she died.

Some More Animals

Sʏʟᴠᴇsᴛᴇʀ is a Guernsey bull. He is the biggest Guernsey bull I have ever known and one of the handsomest. He is also the biggest baby I have ever known.

He came to us from George von Penen who has a farm near Kalamazoo, accompanied by a harem of thirty-four lady friends, of all ages from six months to an old girl of thirteen. At Malabar he found another twenty-seven ladies awaiting him. From then on he occupied, as Lord and Master, the big stall and bull pen in the dairy barn at the Big House save for occasional periods when he was allowed a holiday in lush pasture with the dairy cows and young heifers.

On his arrival he was a young fellow, not quite two years old and he continued to grow and put on weight and muscle for almost another year, but from the first he revealed the fact that there was a broad streak of ham actor in him. He was always a poseur and, as if aware of his own good looks, he spent a great deal of time in the bull pen, striking attitudes and showing his profile to anyone who would care to stop and look at him. Occasionally, the plastic poses would be interrupted by pawing and snorting and butting about the big iron oil drum which was given him as a plaything.

I think he made up stories about the oil drum, converting it most often into a rival to whom he would give an unearthly drubbing. At times he would butt the drum uphill on the slope of the bull pen. When it struck the wall of the barn it would rebound and start rolling downward back toward him. At just the right point he would give it another almighty butt so that it repeated the action. This game would go on for sometimes as long an hour. It began, I think, as his own idea of fun and exercise but gradually, as with all his other actions, it took a show-off form. The spectacle was exactly like that of a middle-aged businessman playing handball and showing anyone concerned or interested that he was just as young as he ever was. The larger the audience the more enjoyment Sylvester appeared to gain from his performance.

In the meanwhile he developed as well some of the characteristics of a spoiled Persian cat. Unlike most bulls he appeared to enjoy petting. Inside his stall, he would come and thrust his head over the edge of the barrier to be petted and talked to. I think it was the sound of my voice or Al's or Jim's he liked more than the petting. You'd say to him, "Well, how's the old stinker today?" and there would be a kind of answering deep rumble from his throat. And then "Want some attention, do you?" and again a rumble. The eyes which a moment before had been showing the whites in his performance in the role of the big, bad bull, would half-close with pleasure. Usually the petting and conversation was accompanied by a treat of some kind—a handful of grain or a fresh ear of sweetcorn or an apple. He knew perfectly well what "Do you want an apple?" meant. Also he clearly knew what we meant when we asked, "Want some attention, do you?"

Only one thing tempted him away from the pleasure of being petted and talked to and that was the presence of ladies who frequently took a timorous attitude toward him. The moment they would start back and, in a feminine way, cry out, "But aren't you afraid of that big brute?" all the ham in him would come to the surface and he would begin at once to arch his neck, to snort, show the whites of his eyes and to flex all the great muscles of his handsome neck. No ham actor, strutting through the lobby of the Hotel Astor, ever did such a job. Indeed, the performance was so impressive that I once had a letter from a lady visitor on her return home begging me "not to trust that ferocious bull" for a moment.

Of course I didn't trust him, nor did Al or Jim, because no sensible farmer ever trusts a bull. Many a farmer has been killed by a playful and friendly bull who wasn't ferocious at all but "simply didn't know his strength." Any farmer knows the playfulness of a bull calf and how he will put his head against you and push. A lot of calf remains in a lot of bulls after they are grown, only by that time the pushing is no fun any longer, at least for the farmer. Sylvester has a lot of play in him but I wouldn't want to play with him if I were sandwiched between the wall of his stall and his big head.

He carries his clowning, his hamming and his posing with him into the lush green ladino and bluegrass pasture. I think he realized that here, in grass up to his knees with the blue sky and the woods for a background, he was his best, and certainly he is a handsome beast. As if he knew it, he plays the Lord to all the cows and heifers. When you first turn him out he does not, like many an eager, unwise male, run wildly to join the cows and heifers. Instead, he steps inside the gate and, striking a pose like the Bull Durham advertisement, lets out two or three ungodly bellows and waits. There is both lordliness and assurance in his manner and he has never had reason to change his tactics for within two or three minutes the silly cows and heifers all appear out of a clump of bushes or over a hill, high-tailing it toward him. Then for a while he paws and bellows and poses, permitting them to admire him.

He has an infallible instinct for those who are afraid of him and bullies them unmercifully. One autumn he discovered he could bully Jesse. Now Jesse, who is himself quite as much a character as Sylvester, was then sixty-five and a man of all jobs with all the raciness and profanity of the Tennessee hills, and a word-by-mouth account of his encounter and feud with Sylvester cannot be set down here with any degree of literalness. Jesse and Sylvester occupied the same pasture while Jesse was engaged with the Ford tractor in ripping it up for re-seeding and Sylvester took to leaving his harem and following Jesse about. So long as the tractor was moving it was all right but once it stopped Sylvester closed in on Jesse. I doubt that he meant any real harm but he knew he could rouse from Jesse a fine stream of Tennessee four-letter words and he also knew that he could keep Jesse on the move. So for Jesse there was no peace. He had to keep on the move from the time he entered the field until he left. Two or three times, standing on the top of the hill, I have watched the comedy.

But worst of all, Sylvester wouldn't let Jesse get a drink at the spring. It was unseasonably hot October weather and Jesse got thirsty, but during the whole week he worked in the field he never once had a drink from the spring. Each time that Jesse turned the tractor in that direction Sylvester, as if divining his purpose, got there first. He even went further than that; when he tired of following Jesse about, he simply went back to the spring and lay down beside it. He knew perfectly well all the time that Jesse was scared of him.

But his behavior with Al and Jim and myself was quite different. If we encountered him in the field from the safety of the jeep or on the opposite side of the fence, he would begin his best Bull Durham performance. After you had watched with amusement for a time, all you needed to say was "Aw, nutz! Come over here and get your head scratched!" And at once the snorting, the pawing and the eye-rolling stopped and he would walk over to the fence or the jeep and have his head rubbed like a pet calf.

Sylvester has never quite understood the jeep. He dislikes all machinery and puts on a terrific show whenever a truck or a tractor comes into the barnyard. I think trucks and tractors and jeeps puzzle him because he cannot figure out why Al and Jim and I can be his good friends on foot and then suddenly become part of a noisy, chugging Behemoth. In the pasture he will come up to the jeep and after his usual show-off performance, smell it, regard it from all sides, clearly and profoundly puzzled. He could of course demolish it if he

chose and once or twice he has put his big head against the radiator
with every intention of doing so, but a single blast of the horn sets
him back on his feet and back again into his chronic state of bewilderment.

His pasture behavior eventually resulted in a climax, however,
when he went berserk and apparently decided that the only subli-
mation of his dislike for machinery was to break it up. There came
the day when Sylvester actually attacked two tractors and chased
Jesse and Kenneth from the field. Both were small-sized Ferguson
tractors and Sylvester, instead of merely following them about bellowing and pawing, actually went for them. With his tail high in the
air, the whites of his eyes showing and with tremulous bellows he
put his head under the back end of the field cultivator and lifted it
off the ground. Jesse, seeing himself and the tractor rolling down

the hill, jumped free and took to the woods. Flushed with his victory, Sylvester set out after Kenneth and repeated the performance with the same results. Then while Jesse and Kenneth watched from the safety of the woods on the opposite side of the fence, he put on a show of regal triumph, posing, arching his neck, pawing the earth and bellowing and at last, when he felt he had shown off sufficiently, he turned and rushed up the hill and out of sight to rejoin his harem leaving Kenneth and Jesse to return sheepishly and rescue their tractors.

It is a pity that Sylvester could not hear Jesse's subsequent account of "The Battle of the Tractors." With each retelling it grew in detail and horror until Sylvester had attained the size of an African elephant and the ferocity of a sabre-toothed tiger. Fire came from his nostrils and sparks from his eyes. The tractor, in Jesse's later versions, was lifted in the air so high that he had to jump several feet to the ground, just in time to save himself. Indeed, Jesse's account of the Battle has reached such proportions that beside Sylvester, Paul Bunyan's Blue Ox seems no more than a sucking calf.

Sylvester developed a lot of idiosyncrasies in his stall and bull pen. The one thing he cannot bear is lack of attention or being ignored. If you pass him without rubbing his nose or at least speaking to him, he will put down his head and pout and grumble like a small child. And at some period and for some reason no one has been able to divine, he took a dislike to the top bar of the gate to his bull pen. At first this was a plank which he proceeded to break in two. When it was replaced he broke the second one and when a steel pipe was substituted he proceeded to bend it and force it out of position. Finally, Al left the top bar off altogether and there remained only the lower bar less than three feet from the ground. Despite the fact that he could step over the remaining bar he has never attempted to do so nor made any effort to leave the pen, even though the cows pass him on his way from the milk parlor. It is useless to replace the top bar for he proceeds at once to smash or bend it. Apparently the top bar seems to present what psychiatrists refer to as "a psychological obstacle," which appears to be all that is necessary. Visitors, seeing him with nothing between him and the outside world, take alarm and say, "Aren't you afraid he'll get out?" He never does. Perhaps some day he will and we shall have to take other measures. The day finally came however when Sylvester got his come-uppance and made a complete fool of himself. It was all his own doing and he was, I think, properly humiliated. For days afterward he was self-conscious and ashamed.

My first knowledge of his predicament came when I began to hear the most prodigious bellows coming from the dairy barn as I was working in my office. He has a good voice, Sylvester, and is never hesitant about using it, but on this occasion the bellows were more like those of a bull elephant ringing from hill to hill in the jungle. Realizing something terrific must be happening, I went toward the barn and as I reached the corner in sight of the bull pen, I discovered a spectacle which set me laughing so much that I could not act.

The head of the oil drum which Sylvester used in his version of handball had apparently rusted out and in some way he had got his head inside the drum where it became firmly stuck. Blind and helpless, he grew madder and madder, and the madder he got, the more he bawled, with variations basso profundo, tenor and even coloratura. No bull—not even the Bull of Bashan—ever bellowed louder.

It was no use trying to get the oil drum off without aid. It was really stuck over his horns. It finally took two of us half an hour to free Sylvester.

Once freed, he appeared momentarily dazed. Then he gave us both one of the most baleful looks I have ever received from an animal, grumbled once or twice, turned his back and went into his stall where he sulked the remainder of the day.

His behavior carried me far back into my small boy memories and the behavior of a tart old lady who once slipped on the ice of the main street in my home town and fell in a most undignified position. Being young and filled with the feeling of "doing a good deed every day," I ran to her rescue, helped her up and aided her in brushing the slush and ice from her alpaca dress. When I said courteously, I hope that you didn't hurt yourself, ma'am," she turned on me savagely and replied, "I guess I can fall down if I want to!" This was exactly the way Sylvester behaved after we had struggled a good half-hour to free him.

Since then, although I have not relaxed my caution, I feel that I have Sylvester under control. I need only say, "Remember the oil drum!" to cover him with confusion.

One of the most remarkable things about animals is the variety of their personalities and the fantastic tricks which, untaught, they will develop. To the average town dweller and even to some farmers all cows or hogs or horses appear to be alike and indistinguishable in characteristics and behavior, but nothing could be less true. A good stockman must have, it seems to me, three characteristics: (1) He must know and love his animals and divine the fact that they are sick or off their feed and what is the matter with them. (2) He must have a "feeling" for them so strong that he can virtually divine what they are thinking and what they are up to. (3) And in a broad sense he must treat them as companions. I have never willingly hired a man to handle livestock who could not imagine himself to be a cow, a chicken or a pig and thus be able to imagine what they would like and what would make them happy. Sometimes I have been forced to hire another type of man but the results have always been unhappy and even disastrous.

The 4-H Club boy, showing his prize steer or lamb or hog in Kansas City or Chicago or Omaha or Toronto, will know what I mean. Many a time I have seen a boy sound asleep in the clean straw of the cattle pen beside the prize steer which he will not leave, and twice at least I have seen tears in the eyes of a farm boy when the moment came to put the steer up for auction. Any good dairyman knows every cow in his herd and knows that each of them is different in personality from all the others and that the understanding of this fact and treatment based upon it means money in the milk pail.

The forty-cow dairy at Malabar is located only a hundred feet from the Big House and I spend a good deal of time there so that I have come to know all the cows pretty well, although nowhere nearly so well as Al and Jim who milk and care for them. In some remarkable way, beyond my own powers, Al and Jim know by sight all the forty milking cows and the twenty-odd which in rotation are dry and awaiting calves. They know them by name and personality and when Al opens the door of the loafing shed many of the cows will come forward at the calling of their names.

Because there are so many cows in the dairy, as well as sixty or seventy-five new heifers each year which eventually pass through the milking parlor for a season before being shipped to the eastern milk sheds, the naming of them long ago became a problem which we solved by calling them for the women and children on the farm and for visiting friends. There are Mary and Dessi and Virginia and Martha and Gwenn, Hope and Allen and Anne and Fanny, Lauren and Inez, and so on. At times the custom leads to mirth and broad jokes: Al or Jim announces "Jenny freshened last night!" or "Wow! Did Fanny kick me in the behind tonight!" or "Myrtle has come in with six teats!"

There is Irene who will take on the milking machine peacefully until she is three-quarters milked and then begin to let fly with rabbit punches which could break your leg. And Essie, a big Holstein, who outdoes even the other Holsteins in her greed and will rattle her stanchion violently until she gets an extra handful of grain. And Mary and Martha and Jean who will follow you about to be petted. Each one is capable of her own set of tricks. Some will not have their heads touched and others will rumble and purr like cats when you scratch their ears. Jean, who clearly has a sense of rhythm, will chew her cud in time to the music from the milk parlor radio, alternating waltz time with rhumbas and fox trots. I think she takes pride in entertaining visitors with her performance, for she gives occasional backward glances (without losing a beat) at a sudden outburst of mirth at her performance.

But oddest of all performances was the feud which developed between Eileen and Mummy, the big female tiger cat who staked out the feed room as her territory and did a first-rate job on the mice and rats who come to the milk parlor to feed off the spilled grain. Mummy was so named because of her extraordinary fecundity. In astrological realm she was probably what is known as the Universal Mother. Naturally she lived in close companionship with the dairy cows and, I believe, really knew them apart. Long ago she learned that by walking along the concrete ledge beyond the feed trough she would get some extra petting when the cows occasionally reached out and licked her coat as she passed. When this happened, she stood quite still, arching her back and purring. It was a performance she carried out regularly at milking time, as much a rite as the milk which she received twice a day.

All went well with the system until Eileen, a very big and greedy Holstein, took an unaccountable dislike to Mummy. I suspect Eileen felt that Mummy had designs on her allotment of grain but I do not know. In any case there came an evening when Mummy, walking along the ledge receiving the usual attentions from the cows, was seized by Eileen and given a good shaking. Al heard the catlike yowls of distress and discovered the astonishing sight of Mummy being shaken by Eileen. With her tail spread to balloonlike proportions and all four feet dangling in the air, Mummy was emitting outraged and furious squalls. For a moment Al was so paralyzed by laughter he could not rescue the indignant cat. A cat is the most dignified of all animals and no animal so resents a violation of its dignity. It was this violation, I think, which outraged Mummy far more than any harm she received by Eileen's astonishing uncowlike behavior. Twice more the incident was repeated, once in my sight, and by that time Mummy had had enough. She did not abandon her habit of parading the ledge behind the feed troughs. She simply gave it up while Eileen was in her stanchion being milked. As soon as Eileen was unlocked and released from her stanchion, Mummy resumed her promenade receiving with purring satisfaction the attentions of her bovine friends.

The life of cats about a farm is in itself worthy of a whole study. They come and go from one set of farm buildings to another, according, so far as I am able to make out, to the rise and fall of food supplies. No animal but a hog knows better how to take care of himself. We have a score of farm cats, fat and sleek and well fed on mice, rats and unwary sparrows, as well as on the milk from the dairy barn and the table scraps from the houses. In summer some of the big toms will take to the fields and thickets leading a sporting life and living off the countryside. More than once when mowing, I have started up out of the thick hay a big tom engaged in stalking field mice. I don't like it when they take young birds and chipmunks but there doesn't seem to be any way of controlling them and in the barns they are not only valuable but indispensable, prowling the rooms, the feed mows and the cattle stalls to keep down vermin. The number which "goes wild" in summer is small for they are well fed in the barns and find an easy living there and at the kitchen doors of the various houses.

As a rule the barn cats are just cats and it is sometimes difficult to distinguish one from another, but occasionally there develops what might be described in Rotarian language as an "outstanding" cat. You begin to notice something different about such a cat, and discern certain quirks of personality or behavior which attract your notice and you begin to have a special feeling for him and watch him and give a closer observation to his behavior. Mummy was one of these cats with her immense fertility and her boldness and arrogance. Sita and Lester were certainly cats possessing violently distinctive personalities.

Sita was originally an alley cat which my daughters got at the Bide-A-Wee home in New York City to share their flat with them. They felt, like all our family, that no home was a home which was not shared by animals, and in New York, where they were away from home much of the time working or at classes, a cat seemed more appropriate than a dog. And so Sita came in as a small kitten and a very beautiful kitten.

She was a tiger cat but instead of her stripes being brown and gold they were black and silver. She had a fine small feminine head and moved with the grace of the angels. But alas, her disposition did not go with her looks. I always suspected that somewhere in her ancestry there was a Royal Siamese. She was arrogant, possessive and above all tough, a quality which may well have come out of her gangster, back alley background as if a Siamese princess had been brought up on the Bowery. Twice she fell off the balcony three stories up and escaped unhurt save for the strain of a fit of bad temper. She insisted on arising with the sun; that would have been harmless but she insisted that everyone else arise with her. She stole things off shelves and sharpened her claws on the furniture. In short, Sita was a real hell-raiser who with her slimness and beauty might better have been christened "Carmen." In the end she made life in the flat very nearly intolerable and my daughters shipped her to Malabar, which has always been a catchall for animals and pets.

On arrival she was promptly given her freedom but instead of taking to the house she chose immediately the barn and the other cats. This was apparently what she had wanted and had been waiting for and from then onward she became a half-wild gypsy cat who would, only occasionally and when she felt like it, turn amiable for a little while and come to you to be stroked. This she did with an air of conferring a royal favor.

Although she was a small cat she at once moved in on the barn cats and completely dominated them. Perhaps it would be more accurate to say that she bullied them. Slaps, scratches and yowls followed her but apparently did not interfere with certain lewd moments of violent courtship, for she produced almost as many kittens as the veteran Mummy. There was no doubt whatever about her success with men although I do not believe she brought happiness to any of them. She was just a natural hellion.

One of her special pleasures was the baiting of the boxer dogs. When she had no kittens she would entice them to chase her, take a sudden stand and after a couple of swift vicious swipes on the nose, make her escape. Chasing cats is the boxers' favorite pastime and it is a profitless one for in a great barn with high and enormous stacks of hay bales, any but the stupidest cats can find a hole or a sweet-smelling cavern in which to take refuge and be safe even though only a few inches from the boxers' noses. Sita certainly knew every hole and cranny and, being quick as lightning, the dogs hadn't a chance with her. All the time Sita lived at Malabar there was scarcely a day when she did not have an encounter with the boxers. Nearly always these encounters were provoked by Sita herself, with the most obvious malice and pleasure. In short, Sita, for all her beauty, was never what you might call a nice cat.

When she had a nest full of kittens somewhere inside a cavern among the hay bales, she did not provoke attack upon herself. She attacked. If the dogs came onto the barn floor there would be a flash of black and silver, a ball of fur and claws shooting out from the hay bales like a meteor. I have seen her chase as many as three big dogs out of the barn at one time. When they were gone she would, slowly and with dignity, her tail inflated to the size of a balloon, walk across the barn floor without even turning to look over her shoulder to see if the dogs returned. They never did and usually for a day or two they nursed long scratches across their black muzzles or on their backs, for Sita had early learned that a cat riding on the back of a big dog can inflict all kinds of damage without much danger to herself.

And then, in the way of our barn cats, there came a day when Sita simply wasn't there any more. She may simply have grown tired of her surroundings and, like Carmen, migrated elsewhere in the way of gypsy cats, or she may have chosen, like some of the big old toms, to take off and lead a completely wild life, or she may have died somewhere off alone in the way of animals, from the cat influenza which visits us every few years in epidemic form and leaves only the strongest still living. In any case she had had a rich and full life "living it up" from the day she was born perhaps in some trash can in a back alley in New York until the day she disappeared at last. She had known life in a back alley, a New York apartment on Madison Avenue, and on a big farm where she had reigned for a time as absolute Queen of the Cats, and perhaps she died at last in solitude somewhere in the marshes and woodlands of Malabar. If we had erected a gravestone to her memory I think we should have inscribed it with a single phrase: "She was a Holy Terror!"

Sita, like all truly passionate women, had no sense of humor but not long after she disappeared there arrived another cat who undoubtedly possessed one and, oddly enough for a cat, could almost have been described as "merry." For years, people who wanted to be rid of a dog or cat or a litter of puppies or kittens, frequently left them on the roadside at Malabar. It is a barbarous custom and an unpleasant one practiced by the lazy and sloppy who are unwilling to accept the responsibility of caring for an animal or for finding it a good home. Such people come within the category known among us at Malabar as "white trash." They leave the animals at Malabar because they know that someone there will accept their own responsibilities and because Malabar has always been associated with two very good women, spinster sisters, who operate the Angell Refuge where, with very little money, they care for stray or abandoned animals, find homes for them or put them painlessly out of the way. The sisters are regarded as eccentric by certain citizens in the town. Some even regard them almost with hostility, perhaps because of their own inborn meanness and cruelty or, as is often the case, because such people really dislike themselves and experience no respect even for their own characters and personalities. The two sisters are among our finest citizens, far better educated and cultivated than most of us, and certainly far superior to most of us in their simplicity, kindness and dignity. The people who leave animals on the roadside know that at Malabar we work very closely with the sisters and that no animal, either a puppy or a kitten or an old dog who has become a burden, will be turned away.

And so Lester came to us. My daughter Ellen found him on the roadside as a small yellow-white and unpromising kitten, dropped or perhaps thrown out of someone's car. He was never at any time even faintly a beauty, but be always knew how to care for himself and very early displayed a great sense of independence. Even as a very small cat he managed the dogs. And as he grew up into a middle-sized tom, he worked his way into the affection of everybody and had his own way in the dairy which he regarded as his home. He was, despite a rich diet of whole milk, a terrific mouser and at times one had the feeling that he regarded mousing as his duty and the milk merely as his wages. At times when the mouse and rat population rose, Lester would go on real binges and gorge himself, and at such times his coat became shabby and, oddly enough, he grew leaner and leaner and more and more disreputable in appearance. He was also a great Don Juan and, judging from the number of white and yellow kittens which appeared everywhere after his arrival, he was especially successful despite his moderate size and lack of beauty. More often than not it is the small ill-favored man who works hardest at his conquests and boasts the most loudly concerning them, perhaps because he must assert his ego and somehow find compensation for his handicaps.

In any case, Lester was certainly successful. There were other evidences also of his battles and conquests. Periodically Lester would appear in the early morning in the dairy, scratched and badly chewed up. And certainly no cat could yowl louder while engaged in fights and conquests. How he came by the name of Lester no one really knows. It is what Ring Lardner once described as a "barbershop" name and it suited Lester. In the old days when I was a boy and barbershops in small towns were in reality clubs for men, there were always two or three rather undersized, battered, lady killers named Lester or Elmer or Homer. They rarely made any bones concerning their conquests or had any scruples in revealing the names of their victims. Lester always reminded me of these characters and his name bestowed on him by someone while he was still a kitten was singularly appropriate and prophetic. I am not at all sure that if the real story were known, Don Juan might well have been really called Lester or Elmer or Homer and have been a barbershop boaster.

Where Sita was a ball of fury with the dogs, Lester was merely a tormentor who led them on into all kinds of small traps and disasters. Lester never really attacked the dogs or put up a fight; he merely liked being chased by them, and if they did not chase him spontaneously, he taunted them into it. In this he was like the mongoose whom we had loved so much. Again and again in the evening when I sat on the lawn with the dogs, Lester—possibly out of boredom—would come out of the narrow passage between the potting shed and a catchall building known as "Collier's Mansion." He would survey the peaceful scene and judge the distance between him and the dogs and between him and the nearest refuge. Then he would wait for a time for one of the dogs to catch sight of him, give the signal to the others and set off a wild chase which ended with Lester in a tree or on a roof laughing up his sleeve. If the dogs were dozing or did not notice him, there came the moment when he would meow faintly to give them the signal that he was ready to be chased. Then the fun began.

He knew in some mysterious way how to get them into trouble. One of his favorite tricks was to lead them across the cold frames. This ended in the breaking of much glass and cuts, sometimes serious ones, on the legs and shoulders of the dogs. Twice I have wakened in the morning to find the heads of two different dogs beaten and bloody, as if someone had hit them with a club. The injuries remained a mystery until I discovered that it resulted from one of Lester's tricks. The barn stalls have Dutch half-doors and Lester would lead them to chase him as a pack at full speed. He always calculated his distances very nicely so that each time the dogs would believe that they had at last cornered their tormentor. Then in the last fraction of a second he would leap through the half-door and leave the dogs piled up against the door. He had certain holes, large enough for him to take refuge but too small for the dogs. He played the same tricks with the holes. When I saw him do the trick the first time, I understood what had happened and that Lester, if a cat can chuckle, was somewhere about chuckling over his success.

Very early he discovered that the cows did not mind him, perhaps because they understood that, along with themselves, he was part of the establishment given over to producing milk. He could wander about among them without ever being harmed. At the same time one of the earliest lessons a puppy learns at Malabar is to keep away from the cows. More than one of them has lost his front puppy teeth from a real rabbit punch kick from a cow. Lester apparently put two and two together and in the milking parlor or the loafing shed he knew that he had only to lie down between the feet of a cow, his tail curled about him, while he pretended to doze or actually did doze. At a little distance the dogs would stand trembling with excitement but unwilling to risk a good rabbit punch kick from the cow. The expression on Lester's face could only be described as a smirk.

Once I witnessed what was very nearly the end of Lester, for it is certain that if the tormented dogs could ever have laid paws on him they would have finished him off, and I am not certain that I could blame them. On this particular day, they caught Lester offside well out in the middle of the pasture where he probably had gone in search of some tender morsel of field mouse. The dogs got between him and the nearest tree and for a few seconds I was certain that I was about to be an unwilling witness to Lester's end.

But Lester was a tactician; sizing up the situation, he apparently saw that he could not run *away* from them and make his escape. In the fraction of a second he adopted the boldest possible tactic. This was to run straight into the midst of a pack of pursuing boxers and take a single flying leap high into the air. The tactic worked, for by the time the boxers had put on the brakes and turned in pursuit, Lester was well up a tree. When I passed the tree an hour later Lester was curled up, sleeping soundly in a crotch twenty feet above the ground. Beneath the tree, still barking occasionally, sat the youngest of the boxers watching the sleeping tomcat. He had yet to learn, as the others had learned long before, that cats cannot only be malicious but infinitely patient. Lester was not wasting his time. He was making up for lost sleep and storing up energy for new prowls and conquests after darkness fell. Very clearly he was not in the least disturbed.

And then one day Lester, like Sita, was simply not there any more. It is a curious thing that out of all the scores of cats in the big barns at Malabar we have rarely seen a dead cat. Perhaps they go off alone to die or perhaps they have, like the elephants, a legendary graveyard where they go to die. Or perhaps they are merely transported, when the time comes, to some cat's paradise. In any case we have always missed Lester with his barbershop ways and character. If we were to give Lester an epitaph it would certainly be: "He led a merry life."

Our parrot was in himself a remarkable bird. Although he was with us until the children went off to school for good and his tyranny became unbearable, we never learned his sex. He never laid an egg but he was a confirmed man-hater and showed a great preference for the ladies. During all the years he was with us he never was locked in his cage, but late at night he would enter it at what he thought was the proper time, go to bed, take his place on his perch and close his eyes.

Occasionally he would make excursions from one of the children's rooms to another but he never made any attempt to escape and fly away. There were moments when all of us wished he would take it into his head to fly straight back to the Jungle. In the end, like the goats, he came to persecute the whole household.

All the children were girls and Nanny shared their part of the house so that there were no men to speak of who could bother him until the girls began to grow up and have boy friends. Then, to put it in an unrefined way, all hell broke loose, and his persecutions could only be controlled by putting him inside the cage and throwing a cover over it. This failed to put him to sleep before the time he considered proper and from the darkness he continued to swear, mutter and grumble until he fell asleep at last.

He was an exceedingly clever bird. No one ever attempted to teach him anything but he picked up plenty. He learned to imitate Gilbert, the gobbler, and the guinea fowl; and he learned to whistle for the dogs and would spend hours at the window alternating shrill whistles, remarkable for their human quality, with sardonic and mocking chuckles. For three or four days after he began practicing the trick he had the dogs crazy but with their sharp hearing they soon learned that Thomas was a fraud and ignored him, I almost suspect, to his fury.

Then one day he began practicing on a new noise and for some time we were all baffled in our attempts to discover what the strange sounds he made were intended to imitate. There was no doubt that he was attempting something complex and difficult, as if a violin player were suddenly attempting to be a whole quartet, or a quartet a whole symphony. There would be a whole string of noises which sounded like "gabble-gabble-gabble" with occasional shrill stretches which appeared to be music, interspersed without rhyme or reason by almost maniacal screeches. He would spend whole mornings practicing in his window directly over the main summer porch. Later, if not too hoarse, he would continue into the evening while we sat below. For a time, we thought that the noise was possibly a manifestation of parrot schizophrenia.

And then one night, after weeks of practice, the imitation took enough form to be recognizable. I might not have understood what it was meant to be save for the fact that, returning from the barn one night in the darkness, I found myself at a spot on the lawn at equal distance from the group of family and friends on the porch and from Thomas at his post in the window overhead. The people below were talking and laughing to the accompaniment of music from the radio inside the house, and upstairs in his window Thomas was practicing. From where I stood, the sounds came to me in about equal volume. And I understood—Thomas had been practicing for weeks to imitate the mixed sounds of human conversation, laughter and radio music which rose night after night during the summer to his window.

When I reached the porch I said, "Would you all like to know what

you sound like?" There was a silence and from abovestairs Thomas'
imitation came out "gabble-gabble-gabble" with interludes of shrill
music interspersed with insane giggles and maniacal chuckles. He
had very nearly perfected it and it was good. What would have happened to him if he had been exposed to an average cocktail party I
do not know. Very likely he would have burst apart in an explosion of
flesh, bone, and feathers.

Where he came from I do not know. We bought him from one
bird dealer who had bought him from another and his origins were
lost in antiquity. We had only three clues to his past life—his hatred
of men, his passion for toast soaked in coffee, and his habit of shriek-
ing on occasion in an unmistakably feminine voice, "Shut up! Damn
you, shut up!"

There came a time when Thomas' disagreeable and cantankerous
personality became a strain, perhaps because he developed a habit
of deliberately scattering the hulls of his sunflower seeds as far as he
could over the whole of the room. I suspect that he enjoyed watching someone clean them up so that he could scatter a fresh lot.

In any case Thomas finally went too far when he began actually
attacking any man who entered the room where he was. My novel-
ist friend David deJong, on a visit at Malabar, told us that he had a
way with parrots and he was sure that he would get on with Thomas.
Despite protests and warnings he went upstairs to court the wicked
bird. We had not to wait, for within three minutes David came down
the stairs at full speed with Thomas clinging to his shoulders beating
him frantically with his wings.

Shaken off, the evil bird remained strutting and chortling about
the front hall until Nanny, clad only in her nightgown, appeared
from abovestairs bearing his cage. Knowing his ways, she placed the
cage on the floor and he immediately hopped on it and was carried
back upstairs, chortling and leering back at us over his shoulder.

At times he was amusing but he was always a malicious bird without warmth or any humor save the most savage and bitter derision,
and as he grew older and dirtier he became an untidy and shrewish
burden like some malicious old man. We returned him to the bird

store and the proprietor sold him to an elderly and very plain widow living alone. I think it unlikely that his antipathy to men is aroused very frequently and I am sure the widow has plenty of time to clean up after him. I suspect that both are now happier—if indeed happiness or unhappiness ever played any part in Thomas' life.

Gilbert, the Tom turkey, died finally of old age. We found him dead one winter morning beside the pond. He was a venerable bird, who must have been ten or eleven years old at the time of his death. Although he was a nuisance at times with his gobbling, strutting and preening which kept interrupting conversations, we missed him.

His bronze wives all preceded him in death from one reason or another but he left behind a relic in the form of a white Holland turkey hen who was spontaneously known by the name of a much photographed dowager famous for her liking for Metropolitan Opera openings, her jewels, and for her wattled throat. She then took on "a companion" much younger than herself from whom she was inseparable. He arrived on the scene as a three-day-old chick, dyed a brilliant green, as an Easter gift. He quickly shed his dyed fluff and emerged as a handsome Leghorn rooster who got somehow the name of Tony. The fighting chickens would have no part of him and he attached himself to Gilbert's white Holland widow. They make a devoted but somehow ridiculous couple and Tony defied all the rules of poultry husbandry by leading a natural out-of-door life and becoming the handsomest show rooster I have ever seen in or outside a poultry show.

There are plenty of other animals at Malabar like Jo, the Border Collie, who is scared to death of cows and Folly and Susie, who are boxers, and so come of a race of watchdogs and fighters but who are excellent stock dogs, and Tex, the handsome five-gaited Kentucky mare who was bred for the show ring but has a passion and an unswerving instinct for rounding up cattle. And there are two Angus bulls called Junior and Pee-Wee.

And there are other boxers, full of personality and intelligence and character, like Little Midge who died young but has lived in our hearts for years. She was the runt of one of Regina's litters but did not deserve such a designation. For unlike most runts, she was not ugly or misshapen and she had none of the grotesqueness which sometimes afflicts a runt. She was always, even as puppy, lovely and delicate but full of life; she was merely smaller than her brothers and sisters. In disposition she was always gay and in her movements she was like a very great ballerina, bouncing high into the air and always landing again with precision and delicacy, never lumbering as her brothers and sisters sometimes did. Even as a small puppy she was never clumsy. And she had a special charm which appeared to attract not only dogs but people. I think it was because she was kindly and gay, for malice or envy or jealousy or greed have no part in charm. One gets what one gives, and during her short life there returned to Midge many times over the gaiety and good nature and affection which she gave out so lavishly.

Outwardly she seemed as healthy and vigorous as the other dogs but inwardly there must have been some flaw hidden in her small, delicate physique, for one evening we found her lying on the lawn under the great walnut tree as if asleep. But she was dead and when Doc Wadsworth examined her he came to conclusion that her heart had been weak and that she had danced one ballet too many. I am sure that if there is such a thing as reincarnation, Midge has come to life again many stages higher up the ladder, for she gave pleasure and warmth and love to everyone about her.

And there was Sophie, whom I loved very much, who was by nature a tramp. If she had been a woman she would have been the kind that every evening visits all the bars along Third Avenue—gay, good natured, cracking dog's jokes and drinking beers. Never a day passed without her visiting every house on the farm to see the children and perhaps get a free sandwich and a beer. She came to an end so tragic and heartbreaking that I cannot even now write about her without a deep sense of wretchedness; yet in the last moments of that tragic end there was a kind of satisfaction, for as she lay dying with her head in my lap, we were nearer to each other in understanding than we had ever been, and in affection. Her death hurt me more than anything that ever happened to me in all my life.

When they heard of Sophie's death, my old schoolmates Todd and Sadie Chesrown, who farm near us, at once sent over to console me a three-year-old boxer female with the odd name of Dagmar. She had been christened Dagmar and registered under that name as a puppy and in the end, as if Nature were imitating art, she never regained her figure after her first litter and maintained a conspicuously prominent bosom.

Dagmar is by nature a real gun-moll. She is a more ferocious watchdog than any of the other boxers and hears distant and unusual sounds before any of them and leads them to the attack. She is also a dog of enormous health and vigor and will take none of the teasing which some of the boys give the other dogs. When Dagmar has had enough, she takes a good bite at them accompanied by ferocious growling, which all is I suppose the equivalent in a dog gun-moll of a slap or a poke in the eye. She is also a dog with an almost incredible intelligence.

When first she was let off the leash by the Chesrowns, she came over at once to investigate me and appeared to like the experience. I put back the leash when the Chesrowns drove home, as I feared that, like many dogs, she would attempt to follow them. She watched them leave, with an air of puzzlement, and after a little time I took her off the lead and she began to make friends with the other boxers who were highly excited at the unexpected arrival of a handsome full-grown female in their midst. By the end of the evening she seemed content and came along with the other boxers to my bedroom. I still doubted that she would remain, but she was still there in the morning and gave me a hearty greeting when I wakened.

Then began a most curious and human performance which could only be described as "casing the joint." She investigated absolutely everything, not only in the house but in the barns, the fields, the woods. Wherever she went with me she smelled and examined everything. Within twenty-four hours, she decided that Malabar was home and that she liked it. Never once did she show any sign of leaving; on the contrary she attached herself to me and became as intimate and as possessive as the noble Prince had once been. Otherwise her character remained tough; she will stand no pushing around and no freshness from dogs, from boys or people. She is quite different in character from any of the other dogs I have known so well. I suppose you might call her a "diamond in the rough" with "a heart of gold." She has been a great addition and I hope she will have a long life with her affection, her toughness, her dignity and her independence.

As Ellen, the youngest daughter, once put it, "The trouble with the animals on this farm is that they all think they're people."

"My Ninety Acres"

I HAD A FRIEND, a big handsome old man, who lived over the hill in Possum Run Valley in a small white house on a farm which is known as "My Ninety Acres." It has never been given that name as farms are named "Long View" or "Shady Grove." The name is not painted on the red barn nor on a fancy sign hanging at the end of the lane leading up to the house; nevertheless, even now long after Walter Oakes died, people throughout the Valley still refer to Walter Oakes's farm as "My Ninety Acres." At first, more than half a century ago, when Walter was still a young and vigorous man, they used to speak of "My Ninety Acres" with a half-mocking, half-affectionate smile, especially the big farmers who owned a lot of land, because

Walter always talked about that ninety acres as if it were a ranch of many thousand acres like the vast King Ranch in Texas, or a whole empire, as if he were Augustus Caesar or Napoleon referring to "My Empire." Some of the old farmers, I think, believed Walter a bumptious and pretentious young man.

But at last, as time passed, and Walter turned into a solid, middle-aged farmer, and later into an old man, the smiles and mild sense of mockery went out and "My Ninety Acres" became simply the name of the place, the way a farm was known as the Ferguson Place or the Anson Place. People said, "I'm going over to 'My Ninety Acres'" or "If you want to see a nice farm, go and have a look at 'My Ninety Acres.'" Nobody in the Valley any longer finds anything confusing or absurd about the name. I think this is so, partly because in places like the Valley people come to accept the name that is natural to a place and partly because as the years passed, old Walter earned the right to say "My Ninety Acres" as Augustus Caesar might say "My Empire."

He had a right to speak of it with pride. It wasn't the conventional Currier and Ives farm one expects from the long tradition of American farming—a bright, new place, with new wire fences, and cattle standing like wooden animals in a pasture that was more like a lawn than a pasture. There was, indeed, a certain shagginess about it, a certain wild and beautiful look with that kind of ordered romantic beauty which was achieved by the landscape artists of the eighteenth century who fell under the influence of Jean Jacques Rousseau's romantic ideas regarding Nature. The white house was small but always well painted and prosperous in appearance, and there was no finer barn than Walter's, with its fire-red paint, its big straw shed and its ornate shutters and cupolas painted white, and there were no finer cattle in the whole county than those which stood behind the white-painted wooden fences of the barnyard staring at you, fat and sleek and contented, as you drove past "My Ninety Acres." I mention in particular the fine cattle for Walter Oakes loved all animals, wild or domestic, and could not sleep at night if one of his beasts was sick or uncomfortable. That is one of the reasons why his story is included in this book.

The romantic shagginess appeared, too, in the garden around the small white house with its green shutters that stood beneath two ancient Norway spruces. The patches of lawn were kept neatly mowed, but surrounding them grew a jungle of old-fashioned flowers and shrubs—lilacs, standing honeysuckle, syringa, bleeding heart, iris, peonies, tiger lilies, day lilies, old-fashioned roses like the Seven Sisters and the piebald and the Baltimore Belle. At the back the little vegetable garden was neat enough with its rows of vegetables and its peach and pear and quince trees in a row inside the white picket fence. But beyond the borders of the garden, the shagginess continued. There weren't any bright, new, clean wire fences. The wire along the fence rows was hidden beneath sassafras and elderberry and wild black raspberry and the wood lot on the hill above the creek was not a clean place with the wildflowers and ferns eaten short by cattle. The cattle had been fenced out and the trees, from seedlings to great oaks, grew rankly with a tropical luxuriance.

But, despite the shagginess of the farm's appearance, no fields in the Valley produced such big crops or pastured such fine cattle and pigs. At "My Ninety Acres" the shagginess didn't exist, the neighbors came to understand, because Walter was lazy or a bad farmer—there was no more hard-working man in the whole Valley. They were that way because Walter wanted them like that—Walter and Nellie.

I never saw Nellie Oakes. She died before I was born, but my father told me about her. In his time she had been the prettiest girl in the Valley and she taught school at the Zion School house until, when she was twenty-two, she married Walter Oakes. People wondered why she chose him when she might have married Homer Drake, whose father owned four hundred and fifty acres of the best land in the county, or Jim Neilson, whose family owned the bank and the corn mill in Darlingtown. She could have had her choice of any of the catches of the Valley and she chose Walter Oakes, who had no more than ninety acres of poor hill land he had just bought because he hadn't got money enough for anything better.

In the parlor of the little white house on "My Ninety Acres" there hangs an old enlarged photograph of Walter and Nellie taken at the time of their marriage. It is hand-colored and the bride and bride-groom are standing like statues, each with a clamp obviously fastened at the back of the heads in order to "hold the pose," but even the stiffness and artificial coloring cannot alter or subdue the look of youth and health and courage that is in both of them. Walter, the thin, tough old man who was my neighbor and friend, stands there in the photograph, stalwart and handsome and full of courage, one big, muscular hand on Nellie's shoulder. He was blond with blue eyes and the gentle look which big strong men often have, because there is no need for them to be pugnacious or aggressive.

On a chair, beside and a little in front of him, sits Nellie in a white dress with leg-o'-mutton sleeves and a full, flounced skirt—dark, more beautiful than pretty—with big, dark eyes, holding in her small hands a lace handkerchief and a bunch of lilacs. I think Nellie was beautiful rather than pretty because of the look of intelligence. Even today, you sometimes hear old people say, in the Valley, "Nellie Oakes was a mighty smart girl—the only woman I ever knew who was as smart as she was pretty."

Nellie, so far as I can discover, never told anybody why she chose to marry Walter instead of one of the catches of the Valley, but I know from all the long story that it was because she was in love with him. As it has turned out, she was right, because the big four hundred and fifty acre Drake place which Homer inherited has gone downhill ever since Homer took possession of it, and today, with its worn-out fields and decaying buildings, it wouldn't bring as much as "My Ninety Acres," and Jim Neilson died long ago as a drunkard, having lost both the bank and the corn mill. But "My Ninety Acres" is the richest, prettiest farm in all the county, although Nellie isn't there to enjoy its beauty and prosperity. I say she isn't there because she died a very long time ago. But sometimes when I walked about the fields of "My Ninety Acres" with old Walter, I wasn't at all sure she wasn't there, enjoying its beauty and richness as much as old Walter himself.

I am past fifty, and Nellie died before I was born, when she gave birth to her second son, Robert.

My father was a gentle man. He never went through the Valley without stopping at "My Ninety Acres," and usually I was with him. Sometimes when we stopped at "My Ninety Acres" for a meal or for the night, I stayed and played about the barn with Robert Oakes, who was two years older than I, and his brother John, who was two years older than Robert. Sometimes if it was a Sunday we went fishing or swimming. Sometimes I simply trudged behind my father and Walter Oakes and his two sheep dogs as they walked about "My Ninety Acres," and as I grew a little older, I sometimes wondered that the two men could be together, walking side by side, perfectly happy, without talking at all. I did not know then what I came to know later, that among men who were as close to each other as my father and Walter Oakes, conversation wasn't necessary. They knew without speaking what the other felt when a lazy possum, out in the middle of the day when he shouldn't have been, lumbered across the pasture and out of sight and scent of the dogs (I've seen Walter call the dogs and keep them by his side till the possum had disappeared, safe in some deep hole or hollow log).

And I was always a little surprised at how often Walter would say, "Nellie wanted me to put this field into pasture, but we couldn't afford not to use it for row crops," or "'Nellie was smart about such things," or "It's funny how many good ideas a woman can have about farming. Now, Nellie always said ..." Sometimes in the warm summer heat, I'd return to the house, still trudging along behind the two grown men and the dogs, believing that I would find there the Nellie whom I had never seen, who was dead before I was born, waiting for us with a good supper on the table.

But Nellie was never there. There was only an elderly widow woman called Mrs. Ince, a distant cousin of Walter's who came to keep house and look after him and the boys after Nellie Oakes died. She was a queer old woman, very thin and very active, who was always asking Walter how Nellie had molded the butter or pickled the beets or kept a broody hen on the nest, because she wanted everything to be the way Walter liked it. She could not have been more than fifty, for she was still young enough to create talk in the Valley about her living there alone on "My Ninety Acres" with Walter and the boys, but to a small boy like myself she seemed immensely old. She was, as I remember her, very plain and kind and dull, with the meekness which often characterized indigent widows of her generation who were grateful for a roof over their heads, something to eat and a little spending money. When she came to "My Ninety Acres" some of the old women in the Valley talked of the impropriety of her living there in the same house with Walter. I know now that anyone who had ever known Nellie must have been mad to think that Walter Oakes ever had any improper thoughts about poor, drab Mrs. Ince. She was, at most, a convenience, someone to do the cooking and baking and housekeeping for a vigorous man and two wild, vigorous boys. On Mrs. Ince's side, she had the freedom and security which everyone felt in Walter Oakes's house; she was spared the cruelty and hardship of living with relatives as a widow woman and a poor relation.

People in the Valley couldn't see why Walter Oakes didn't get married again. After Nellie died, they said, "He's still a young man and he's done a wonderful job with 'My Ninety Acres'," or "I don't see how a man like that can get on without a woman at his age. It ain't natural." And a good many widows and spinsters past their first youth certainly set their caps for him. It wasn't only that he was doing well with "My Ninety Acres," he was, as I remember him then, a big, straight, clean, good-looking fellow, with his sun-tanned face, blue eyes and blond hair bleached by the sun. He would, I think, have pleased even a young girl.

But Walter never showed any signs of marrying again. He was always polite, and his eyes sometimes twinkled with humor when he saw what some of the good ladies were up to. He didn't leave "My Ninety Acres" save to go into town to buy or sell something or to go to the Valley church on Sunday with Mrs. Ince and the boys. He'd come home from church and change his clothes and spend the rest of the day walking round the place. Sometimes, to the scandal of the old ladies of the Valley, he'd plow or make hay with the boys on a Sunday afternoon. I remember him saying to my father, "They talk about my working on Sunday or plowing, but when the ground is ready or hay has to be taken in, it has to be taken care of. The good Lord wouldn't like to see his beasts eating poor hay all winter because some old women said it was wrong to work on Sunday. Nellie always said, 'The better the day, the better the deed' and quoted that bit of the Bible about the ox falling into the ditch."

The two boys were nice kids and smart like Nellie. John, the older one, looked like her, with dark eyes and dark hair. Robert, the younger one, who had never seen his mother, looked like Walter. The father wanted both of them to go to college and get a good education. I think Walter always loved John, the older one, best—not because of any resentment of Robert because he had caused his mother's death but because John looked so much like Nellie.

With all my family, I went away from the county when I was seventeen and I was gone for twenty-five years. Sometimes at first my father heard from Walter, rather brief, unsatisfactory and inarticulate letters, written on lined paper torn out of a copybook, but neither Walter nor my father were very good letter writers. They were both the kind of men who could not communicate without the warmth that came of physical presence. Writing letters didn't mean much. When they met again, even after years, the relationship would be exactly the same. They were that kind of men, and that kind of friends.

I know very little of the details of what happened during those years, only a fact or two and what little I have picked up from Walter as an old man in his implications regarding the past. The First World War came and in it John, the older son, whom Walter secretly loved best, was killed at St. Mihiel. He was twenty-one and just finished with agricultural college. Walter had counted on his returning to the farm, marrying and producing grandchildren to carry it on. Robert, when he returned from the war, did not stay on the farm. He was very smart, like Nellie, but he didn't want to be a farmer.

Robert had ambitions. He had had them even as a small boy. Sometimes when the three of us, as kids, sat naked among the wild mint by the swimming hole, we talked about what we were going to do in life, and Robert always said, "I'm going to be a great man and get rich and have an automobile with a man to drive it."

In the twenty-five years I was away from the Valley Robert had achieved exactly what he had planned. By the time I returned to the Valley Robert was president of the Consolidated Metals Corporation and he had made many millions of dollars. I think he must have had both Nellie's "smartness" and Walter's steadfastness.

In the first weeks after I came home I never thought about my father's friend, old Walter Oakes. Indeed, I had very nearly forgotten his existence. And then, one day I heard Wayne, one of the boys on the farm, say something about "My Ninety Acres," and I remembered it all and asked, "Is Walter Oakes still alive?"

"Alive!" said Wayne. "I'll say he's alive. The livest old man in the county. You ought to see the place. Brother, that's the kind of farm I'd like to own. He raises as much on it as most fellows raise on five times that much land."

Wayne, of course, was only twenty. He couldn't know how once people had laughed when Walter Oakes spoke proudly of "My Ninety Acres." Clearly, they didn't laugh any more. Clearly, Walter Oakes was the best farmer in all the county, very likely the best farmer in all the rich Ohio country.

The next Sunday I walked over the hills to "My Ninety Acres." As I came down the long hill above the farm I saw that it hadn't changed much. The house still looked well painted and neat, with its white walls and green shutters, and the barn was a bright new prosperous red. But the shrubs and flowers had grown so high that they almost hid the house. It was a day in June, and as I walked down the long hill the herd of fat, white-faced cattle stood knee-deep in alfalfa watching me. I hadn't taken the dogs because I knew Walter always kept a couple of sheep dogs, and I didn't want a fight.

As I walked down the hill I thought, "This is the most beautiful farm in America—the most beautiful, rich farm in the world—'My Ninety Acres.'"

The corn stood waist-high and vigorous and green, the oats thick and strong, the wheat already turning a golden yellow. In the meadow the bumblebees were working on clover that rose almost as high as a man's thighs. In all that plenty there was something almost extravagant and voluptuous. The rich fields were like one of the opulent women painted by Rubens, like a woman well loved, whose beauty thrives and increases by love-making and by being loved.

I pushed open the little gate and walked into the dooryard, with the neatly mown grass bordered by lilacs and peonies and day lilies. The door stood open but no one answered my knock, and, thinking the old man might be having a Sunday nap, I stepped into the house and called out, "Walter! Walter Oakes!" But no one answered me.

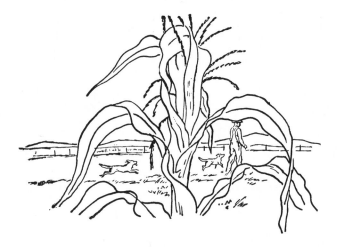

I hadn't been in the house for twenty-five years and I didn't remember very well my way about it, so when I opened the door which I thought led into the long room that had once been used both for eating and living, I found that I was mistaken. I had stepped into the parlor instead.

It had that musty smell of country parlors and the shutters were closed, but there was enough light for me to see the enlarged hand-colored portrait of Walter Oakes and his bride Nellie hanging on the wall above the fireplace. Out of the stiff picture they looked at me, young, vigorous, filled with courage and hope and love. It struck me again how pretty Nellie was.

I stood for a little time looking at it and then turned and closed the door behind me. I went out through the sitting room and the kitchen where everything looked clean and neat as in the dooryard, and I thought, "He must have a woman to look after him."

By now, of course, I remembered enough to know that I should find old Walter somewhere in the fields. Sunday afternoon he always spent walking over the place. As a small boy I had followed him and my father many times.

So I went down toward the creek, and as I turned the corner by the barnyard I saw him down below, moving along a fence row. Two sheep dogs were with him, the great-great-great-grandchildren of the pair I had known as a boy. They were running in and out of the hedgerow yapping joyously. I stood for a moment, watching the scene. The fence row bordered a meadow of deep, thick hay and below, among feathery willows wound the clear spring stream where I had often gone swimming with Walter's boys—John who had been everything Walter had hoped for in a son, the best loved, who was buried somewhere in the Argonne, and Robert who had gone away to become rich and powerful. There was something lonely about the figure of the old man wandering along the fence row filled with sassafras and elderberry. For no reason I could understand, I felt a lump come into my throat.

Then I noticed that there was something erratic in the progress of the old man. He would walk a little way and then stop and, parting the bushes, peer into the tangled fence row. Once, he got down on his knees and for a long time disappeared completely in the thick clover.

Finally, as he started back along the far side of the field, I set off down the slope toward him. It was the barking of the dogs as they came toward me that attracted his attention. He stopped and peered in my direction, shading his eyes with his big hands. He was still tall and strong, although he must have been well over seventy, and only a little stooped. He stood thus until I was quite near him, and then I saw a twinkle come into the bright blue eyes.

"I know," he said, holding out his hand. "You're Charley Bromfield's boy. I heard you'd come back."

I said I'd been trying to get over to see him, and then he asked, "And your father? How's he?"

I told him my father was dead. "I'm sorry," he said, very casually, as if the fact of death were nothing. "I hadn't heard. I don't get around much." I explained that my father had been ill for a long time, and that death had come as a release.

"He was a good man," he said. "A fine man. We sort of dropped out of writing each other a good many years ago." He sighed. "But, after all writing don't mean much." The implication of the speech was clearly enough that friends communicated without writing, no matter how great the distance that separated them. He made the observation exactly as if he expected to see my father again at any time, perhaps tomorrow, and as if he were looking forward to the meeting.

Then suddenly he seemed to realize that I must have seen him for a long time, ducking and dodging in and out of the fence row. A faint tinge of color came into his face, and he said shyly, "I was just snoopin' around my ninety acres. I like to see what goes on here even in the fence rows, and I don't get time during the week."

He looked down at his big hands and noticed, as I did, that some of the black damp loam of the fence row still clung to them. He brushed them awkwardly together. "I was just digging into the fence row to see what was going on there underground. A fellow can learn a lot by watching his own land and what goes on in it and on it. My son John—you remember the one that was killed in the war—he went to agricultural school, but I don't think he learned more there than I've learned just out of studying my own ninety acres. Nellie always said a farm could teach you more than you could teach it, if you just kept your eyes open ... Nellie ... that was my wife."

"Of course," I said, "I remember."

Then he said, "Come with me and I'll show you something."

I followed him along the fence row and presently he knelt and parted the bushes and beckoned to me. I knelt beside him and he pointed. "Look!" he said, and his voice grew suddenly warm. "Look at the little devils."

I looked and could see nothing at all but dried brown leaves with a few delicate fern fronds thrusting through them. Old Walter chuckled and said, "Can't see 'em, can you? Look, over there just by that hole in the stump." I looked, and then slowly I saw what he was pointing at. They sat in a little circle in a tiny hollow, none of them much bigger than the end of one of old Walter's big thumbs—seven tiny quail. They were not much bigger than a good-sized grasshopper and sat very still, not moving a feather, lost among the dry, brown leaves. I might not have seen them at all but for the brightness of their little eyes.

"Smart!" he said, with the same note of tenderness in his voice. "They know! They don't move!"

Then a cry of "Bob White!" came from the thick, fragrant clover behind us, and Walter said, "The old man's somewhere around." The whistle was repeated, again and then again.

Old Walter stood up and said, "They used to laugh at me for letting the bushes grow up in my fence rows, but they don't any more. When the chinch bugs come along all ready to eat up my corn, these little fellows will take care of 'em." He chuckled, "There's nothing a quail likes as much as a chinch bug. Last year Henry Talbot, down the road, lost ten acres of corn all taken by the bugs. Henry's a nut for clear fence rows. He doesn't leave enough cover along 'em for a grasshopper. He thinks that's good farming, the old fool!" and the old man chuckled again.

We were walking now up the slope from the creek toward the house, and he went on talking. "That fence row beside you," he said, "is just full of birds—quail and song sparrows and thrushes—the farmers' best protection. It was Nellie that had that idea about lettin' fence rows grow up. I didn't believe her at first. I was just as dumb as most other farmers. But I always found out that Nellie was pretty right about farmin'. She was hardly ever wrong ... I guess never."

As we reached the house, old Walter said, "Funny how I knew you. I'd have known you anywhere. You're so like your father. I've missed him all these years, especially when anything happened he would have liked . . ." he chuckled, "like these baby quail today.

Come in and we'll have a glass of buttermilk. It's cooler in the sittin' room."

I went with him into the springhouse. It was built of stone with great troughs inside cut out of big blocks of sandstone, and the water ran icy cold out of a tile that came through the wall. Cream, milk and buttermilk, stood in crocks in the icy water, each covered by a lid held in place by an ancient brick with velvety green moss growing on its surface. Coming out of the heat into that damp cool spot was like coming into another world.

He picked up a pitcher with buttermilk in it, and I asked, "Who does your churning for you?"

He grinned. "I do it myself," he said. "Of an evening. I kinda like it."

We went and sat in the living room and he brought glasses and two white napkins. It was buttermilk such as I had not tasted in thirty years—creamy, icy cold, with little flakes of butter in it.

I said, "What became of Mrs. Ince?"

He said, "Oh, she got old and sick and went back to live with her sister. I just didn't get anybody to take her place."

"You mean you're living here all alone?" I asked.

"Yes."

I started to say something and then held my tongue, but old Walter divined what it was I meant to ask and said, "No. It ain't lonely. I've always got the dogs. Jed Hulbert comes down and helps me with jobs I can't do alone, and his wife takes care of my laundry and cleans up once a week. Jed and his wife like the money, and they're nice people." He smiled. "It doesn't seem to me like a farm is a lonely place. There's too much goin' on. Nellie used to say she didn't understand the talk of these women who said they got lonely. Nellie said there was always calves and horses and dogs and lambs and pigs, and that their company was about as good as most of them women who talked that way. And she always had her posy garden. Did you notice it coming in? It's mighty pretty right now. Nellie planted everything in it ... just the way they are today." He was about to say something else, but checked himself and looked at me strangely. A secretive, almost sly look came into his eyes, and he turned away to stare at the glass he held in his hand.

After an awkward pause I said, "Well, Robert did all right by himself. He always said he wanted a big automobile and a driver and a lot of money, and he got it all right."

Then old Walter looked up at me and grinned, "Yes, I guess he got just about what he wanted. He's a good boy, but he's got some funny ideas." The old man chuckled. "He's been trying for years to get me to retire and live in the city where I could take it easy or go down and live in Florida. What'd I do with these big, ugly hands in a place like that? I wouldn't know what to do with myself. And what would become of 'My Ninety Acres?' Or he's always wantin' to buy me a bigger place with a house full of gadgets or to buy me a lot of machinery. What would I want with a bigger place? Ninety acres is enough for any man if he takes care of it right, like he should. And anyway, it wouldn't be the same as 'My Ninety Acres.' And I don't want machinery bought with his money. 'My Ninety Acres' ought to buy its own machinery and it does." A fierce note of pride came into his voice. "All the machinery it needs. Robert wants me to hire a couple to live here and do the work for me, but I wouldn't like that. Yes, Robert's got some crazy ideas and he doesn't understand how I feel. I guess he thinks I'm a little crazy."

It was getting late and I rose, but the old man went on talking. "It's a pity about Robert not having any children. I guess his wife is all right. I don't see much of her. We don't have much in common. But it's a pity Robert couldn't have found a woman he could have loved."

That was the first and last time I ever heard him speak of his daughter-in-law, but out of the meager speech, and the look in his eyes and the sound of his voice, I divined what she must be like. Indeed, I gained a very clear picture of her.

"Robert comes to see me about once a year and stays for a day or two, but he's a pretty busy man with all the big affairs he has to manage."

"Tell him to drive over and see me the next time he comes," I said. "And you come over too."

He opened the screen door for me. "I'm afraid I don't get off 'My Ninety Acres' very often any more. You'll understand if I don't get over soon. The place takes a lot of time when you're working it alone."

I left him and the dogs at the gate and set out over the hill across the pasture with the fat, white-faced cattle, for home.

It wasn't the last time I saw old Walter. There was enough of my father in me to make the friendship between myself and the old man before long very nearly as warm as their friendship had been. And after all, between them, they had taught me many of the things I had come with experience to value most in life. The Sunday afternoon visits to "My Ninety Acres" became very nearly a habit, for I found gradually that old Walter was in himself an education. He knew more of the fundamentals of soil, of crops, of livestock than any man I have ever known. Some of them he had read in books and in farm papers, but he didn't trust the things he read until he tried them out, and many of them he didn't even attempt to try out, since out of his own wisdom he understood at once that they were rubbish. Instinctively and out of experience, he rejected things which ran counter to the laws of Nature.

"Nellie," he would say, "always said that Nature and the land itself was the best answer to all these questions. If it wasn't natural it wasn't right, Nellie would say, and I'd never found that she was wrong. She used to say that there were two kinds of farms—the 'live' farms and the 'dead' ones, and you could tell the difference by looking at them. A 'live' farm was the most beautiful place in the world and a 'dead' farm was the saddest. It depended on the man who worked them— whether he loved the place and saw what was going on or whether he just went on pushing implements through the ground to make money. Nellie was awful smart about a lot of things."

Sunday after Sunday we would make a round of the small empire, while old Walter told me the history of each field and what had happened to it, what he had learned from this field or that one, and why his alfalfa and clover were thicker than those of his neighbors, his corn higher and sturdier, his Herefords bigger and fatter. And after a time I began to understand how old Walter and my father could walk side by side half the afternoon without speaking to each other, communicating by a smile or a nod or without any visible or audible sign. There are times when speech is a poor, inadequate business.

One afternoon I arrived to find old Walter in the garden, standing quite still, staring at something. He did not speak when I came near him, but only raised his hand in a gesture which clearly prohibited any speech or violent movement. Then he pointed at a male cardinal, very handsome in his red mating coat, moving restlessly about the lower branches of a magnolia and chirping anxiously. In a low voice he said, "The poor fellow is looking for his mate. I found her dead yesterday on the ground under that pine over there. He was staying around, trying to bring her back to life and make her fly away with him. I took her and buried her. I hoped he'd forget and fly away and find another mate. But he didn't. He keeps hanging around, trying to find her. It's funny about birds and animals that way."

Then a farmer and his wife came in the gate and interrupted our quiet. We were not always alone on those Sunday walks, because neighbors and even farmers from a great distance came sometimes on Sundays to see his farm and hear him talk about "My Ninety Acres." I knew he took pride in his prestige, but he never showed it. He kept his simple, modest manner when he talked of this field or that one, a kind of fire would come into the blue eyes, like the fire in the eyes of a man talking of a woman he loves passionately. He never came to see me, but he always welcomed me warmly on "My Ninety Acres," and when I missed a Sunday, he was disappointed.

And then, one brilliant day in October, I saw a big, shiny black car coming up the long lane to our house. I knew at once who was in it. I knew by the size and importance of the car, and, as it drew nearer, by the cut of the driver's uniform. It was Robert. He had come on his annual visit and had driven over to see me.

I went down the path to meet him, and as he stepped out of the shiny car, it was hard for me to remember him as the boy I had seen the last time when he was sixteen, slim, muscular, towheaded and athletic. He still looked a little like old Walter, yet in a strange way he appeared older than the old man. He was plump and rather flabby, with pouches beneath the eyes, which looked through the shining lenses of steel-rimmed spectacles. He stooped a little, and there was a certain softness about his chin and throat.

He said, "I'm Bob Oakes. My father told me you had come back to live in the Valley."

"Yes, I know. I'm delighted to see you. Come in."

I found him rather as I had expected him to be, an intelligent fellow, with a good deal of dignity and authority. He was, after all, the child of old Walter and Nellie, and their qualities could not be altogether lost in him. After thirty years the going was a little stiff at first, but after a drink we got together again, mostly by talking about "My Ninety Acres" and the old swimming hole in the creek and maple sugar making time and the other boyhood experiences we had shared.

He laughed once and said, "The old gentleman has certainly made good on his ninety acres."

I asked him to stay for lunch and he accepted the invitation so readily that I suspected he had counted on it from the beginning. I said, "I know it's no good sending for your father. He won't leave the place."

"No, he and Jed were in the field by the creek husking corn when I left." Robert laughed. "He told me if I sat around long enough over here I'd get a drink and be asked to lunch. He said it was worth it to see the house and the place. Privately, I think he wanted to get rid of me for most of the day so he could get on with his work. He doesn't know what to do with me. I get in his way and take up his time."

We had lunch at a table crowded with noisy children with four dogs on the floor beside us. I think, at first, that Robert didn't know quite how to take it, but he warmed up presently and said to me, "You have a mighty good life here. I envy you."

After lunch we sat for a time on the porch overlooking the Valley. The sky was the brilliant blue of an Ohio sky in October and the trees were red and gold and purple, with the green winter wheat springing into life in the fields beyond the bottom pasture where the

Holstein's moved slowly across the bluegrass. He kept watching the Valley, so intently at times that he did not seem to hear what I was saying.

And presently he came round to what was clearly the object of his visit. "I really wanted to talk about my father," he said. "He's quite a problem and stubborn as a mule. I know your father was a great friend of his and that he accepts you nowadays exactly as if you were your father. And I thought you might have some influence with him. You see, I offered him almost everything—I've offered him a fruit ranch in Florida or Southern California, or a bigger farm, or a flat in New York. I've tried everything and he doesn't want any of it. He won't even let me hire him a couple or buy him a new automobile or any machinery that might make life easier for him. This morning he was up at daylight and down husking corn in the bottom field with Jed by seven o'clock."

I grinned, for I could see the whole picture and could understand how the old man's rich, famous, successful son got in his way.

"When I got up," said Robert, "I found some eggs and pancake batter laid out for me and coffee on the stove, with a note to my driver about how to get breakfast for me. In the note he said to come down to the bottom when I'd finished breakfast. What can you do with a fellow like that?"

"What do you want me to do?"

"I want you to persuade him to let me do something for him. He's seventy-five years old, and I'm afraid something will happen to him alone there in the house or barn."

"I'm afraid it's no good," I said. "I couldn't persuade him any more than you could."

"I've tried everything even to saying 'What would it look like if it came out in the papers that my father had died suddenly alone on his farm in Ohio?' That's pretty cheap, but even that didn't move him. All he said was, 'You're rich enough to keep it out of the papers and, anyway, the dogs would let people know if I was sick.'"

We were both silent for a time, and then I said, "Honestly, Bob, I don't think there's anything to be done, and to tell the truth I don't see why we should do anything. He's as happy as it's possible for a man to be. He's tough as nails, and he loves that place like a woman." Then, hesitantly, I said, "Besides, Nellie is always there looking after him."

A startled look came into the son's blue eyes, and after a moment he asked, "Do you feel that way, too?" Nellie, who died when Robert was born, must have been as unknown and strange to Robert as she was to me.

I said, "I think Nellie is everywhere in that ninety acres. He's never lonely. She's in the garden and the fields and his famous fence rows. She's out there husking corn with him now in the bottom forty."

Robert lighted another cigar. "It's the damndest thing," he said. "Sometimes I've felt that he had some resentment because I killed my mother when I was born or that he liked John better because he looked like her, but I know that isn't true. That's not in the old gentleman's character. I think it's more because Nellie is always there and I just get in his way. It's funny," he added, "I always think of her as Nellie—somebody I would have liked knowing because she was so pretty and kind and gay and 'smart' as they say here in the Valley. Sometimes I think the old gentleman gets Nellie and the ninety acres a little mixed up."

We talked some more, and then Robert called his driver, got in the shiny car and drove off. We had agreed that there wasn't anything to be done about old Walter and Nellie. I said I'd keep my eye on him and go over myself or send somebody once every day to see that he was all right. Of course on Thursdays it wasn't necessary because that was the day that Jed's wife came to do the washing and clean up. And so every day for two years I, or somebody from the place, went over. Sometimes we'd have an excuse, but more often we didn't even let him know that he was being watched. One of us would drive past at chore time, or I'd walk over the hills and watch until he appeared in the barnyard or the garden. I knew how much he'd resent it if he suspected that anyone was spying on him or looking after him, and I didn't want to risk breaking our friendship.

I continued to go over every Sunday and each time I went over I learned something about soil, or crops, or animals, for the knowledge and experience of the old man seemed inexhaustible. And then, one Sunday afternoon in early September, when we were walking alone through one of old Walter's cornfields, I made a discovery. It was fine corn, the whole field, the best in the whole county, and as we came near the end of a long row, he stopped before a mighty single stalk of corn which was beautiful in the special way that only corn can be beautiful. It was dark green and vigorous, and from it hung two huge, nearly ripened ears and a third smaller one. Old Walter stopped and regarded it with a glowing look in his blue eyes.

"Look at that," he said. "Ain't it beautiful? That's your hybrid stuff." His hands ran over the stalk, the leaves and the ears. "I wish Nellie could have seen this hybrid corn. She wouldn't have believed it."

As I watched the big, work-worn hand caressing that stalk of corn, I understood suddenly the whole story of Walter and Nellie and the ninety acres. Walter was old now, but he was vigorous, and the rough hand that caressed that corn was the hand of a passionate lover. It was a hand that had caressed the body of a woman who had been loved as few women have ever been loved, so passionately and deeply and tenderly that there would never be another woman who could take her place. I felt again a sudden lump in my throat, for I knew that I had understood suddenly, forty years after the woman was dead, one of the most tragic but beautiful of all love stories. I knew now what Robert's strange remark about Nellie and the ninety acres getting mixed up had meant. Robert himself must once have seen something very like what I had just seen.

It happened at last. I went over one Sunday afternoon a few weeks later, and when I could not find old Walter or the dogs anywhere I returned to the house and went inside. I called his name, but no one answered, and in a little while I heard scratching and whining in the ground floor bedroom, and then a short, sharp bark, and when I opened the door the sheep dog bitch came toward me. The other dog lay on the hooked rug beside the bed, his head between his paws, looking at me mournfully as if he knew that I understood. On the bed lay old Walter. He had died quietly while he was asleep.

I telegraphed to Robert, and he came with his wife for the funeral. The wife was exactly as I expected her to be, and I understood what old Walter had meant when he said it was a pity Robert had never found a woman he could love. As I listened to the service, I knew how much feeling lay behind old Walter's simple observation.

He was buried beside Nellie in the Valley churchyard. The dogs came over to join my dogs, and after awhile they got on together. Robert wouldn't sell "My Ninety Acres," but I undertook to farm it for him, and one of our men went there to live. But it will never be farmed as old Walter farmed it. There isn't anybody who will ever farm that earth again as if it were the only woman he ever loved.

Fragments from a Journal

Wᴴɪʟᴇ ɪ ᴍᴏᴡᴇᴅ this afternoon a whole army of fat, half-grown young rabbits kept coming out of the alfalfa ahead of the mower. There is something very engaging about them. During the morning I uncovered a woodchuck lair and as I came round the second time, I noticed something moving beneath the fresh mown hay. It was the young woodchuck himself returning home. Evidently I had caught him out and he was creeping back under cover of the hay. I stopped mowing until he was safely home again. In a week or two the alfalfa will be grown up again to give him cover. They are odd beasts, full of charm, always fat and always a little lazy. They seem to get all the water they need from the clover and the dew for many of them choose to dig their homes high on the hills away from water. On the other hand the marshes next to our corn land in the Conservancy are filled with woodchuck holes. Often enough, when the lake level rises they are flooded out and have to dig new homes on higher land.

Three times this spring I have had puzzling experiences with wild animals. Early in the year we found a woodchuck in the fork of a sapling a good ten feet above the ground. He lay there resting on his elbows, showing no alarm, not even stirring when I poked him with a stick to make certain he was not caught in the fork of the sapling. He seemed very sleepy. I do not know whether he had just come out of hibernation or had climbed the tree to die in peace. The next day he was gone. I have never before heard of a woodchuck with tree-climbing habits. In June, I encountered another woodchuck in the middle of the road below the Big House. He showed no inclination to run away and when I turned the old Ford slowly toward him, he held his ground and gnashed his teeth at me. At last I drove off leaving him there but when I returned later the same day he was lying dead in the road, the victim of some driver, more careless or blood-thirsty than I.

Yesterday in the Bailey barnyard I came on a young rabbit feeding on the spilled corn from the old crib we tore down. He showed no fear and paid no attention to me, except to move away about ten feet. As I went toward him with caution he kept just out of reach, stopping and turning now and then to regard me without fear but with curiosity. I talked to him for a time and he seemed to like the sound of my voice. I went away and he returned to the scattered corn. Fortunately the dogs were not along.

The only time they do not go with me is when I go out with the power mower. They have learned that mower means long hours or boredom and heat for them while I go round and round a hayfield. And I think they don't like it because they cannot ride on the tractor.

Few things are more pleasant than to sit watching the herd. The big white bull is a docile fellow who pays you no attention. At first the cows and calves will gather round you to study you for a while. If you sit quite still and the dogs are not along, they will go away again to eat lazily. But the young calves stay around, skittering off in mock alarm if you make a sudden movement, only to return in a little while to watch you like children daring each other to come closer and closer. As you lie on your back in the thick bluegrass looking up at the sky you can hear all about you the "whisk-crunch" as they eat their way across the meadow.

The herd seems to lead a very ordered existence, always remaining together and the cows feeding their calves at prescribed hours—morning and evening. During the day they will put all the calves together in a kind of kindergarten well hidden in a copse while the herd goes roaming. If you stumble upon the kindergarten, the calves will lie quite still at first but if you disturb them at all, they will set up a wild bellowing and bawling and are answered at once by the mothers, even if they are a mile away on the opposite side of the big pasture. The calves will high-tail for their mothers who come running anxiously from the opposite direction.

The other herd of Shorthorn cows on the Bailey Place are ruled by Blondy, the patriarchal coal-black Angus bull. He takes his paternal responsibilities more seriously than the white Shorthorn bull, Elmer, and will always stay behind to guard the kindergarten although he is never alone but accompanied by two or three of the cows on watch. I do not know how he selected the honored ladies-in-waiting. I wish I did.

Just at dark Anne appeared, flushed from the long climb up the hill through the woods to tell me she had been found. She had gone up the road toward Hastings and stopped in at the Areharts when the storm broke. She "visited" after the storm and forgot all about dinner. She stayed with me for a while clearing fallen branches out of the path of the mower. The dogs came with her and were glad to see me but disappointed at the sight of the mower. When Anne left they did their best to make me return home too, barking and jumping and carrying on generally. Prince came back twice after Anne started down the hill and finally gave up and went home with her.

Finally, while I mowed, a blue-wet dewy darkness came down and the valleys and woods and farms faded out first into a blue mist and then into blackness, starred with the distant lights of farmhouses and the comets of moving light made by cars on the roads far below, I turned on the tractor lights and kept on mowing and the whole herd found a new curiosity in the lights. The calves frisked round and round me as I mowed and even the cows would stand in front of me staring at the lights until the last moment. When I yelled at them they would frisk off kicking their heels high in the air, their udders bouncing about ludicrously, giving that "rabbit punch" kick which can break your leg if you come into contact with it. Altogether they enjoyed the evening, I think, as much as I did.

About ten-thirty I gave it up and set out for home down the steep, rocky lane that goes through a tunnel of woods bordered by ferns and laced with wild grapevines. All the way down I had an eerie feeling that I was being watched by the eyes of wild things—foxes and raccoons and mice and owls. Once, near Jim Pugh's cabin the lights caught a pair of green, phosphorescent eyes that may have been one of the catamounts that live on the hill opposite the Big House. Or it may only have been a fox or a raccoon. In any case the goose pimples rose all over me and my hair stood on end like the hair of a dog.

Smoky and Baby stayed at the house last night instead of going down to the barracks to sleep with the boys who have come to work on the farm during the summer. Usually they spend the day following Charley who feeds them or following me while I am plowing or working in the fields. With Charley and me both away they were lost and deserted my room for the company of the boys. Prince still slept in my room with Dusky, the cocker. Both Gina and Folly were at Dr. Wadsworth's—Folly to be bred. Gina not to be. While Charley and I were away Prince, Baby and Smoky fought incessantly, once knocking Ma out of her chair on to the lawn.

Boxers are strange dogs. They have no tramp habits and will not go fifty yards from the house unless they have human company. They are affectionate but never groveling. In fact, I sometimes find myself groveling to them, especially to Baby, who is a clown and a ham actor, but still possessed somehow of an immense dignity and indifference. If you do anything foolish or unworthy, they know it and do not hesitate to let you know.

❖   ❖   ❖   ❖   ❖

This afternoon while I was mowing on fallow ground, I flushed a whole family of baby rabbits and their mother. They could not have been more than a couple of weeks old and too young to know how to save themselves. They just hopped about in aimless circles. The dogs—Gina and Folly—were with me and behaved very well. At my command they simply stood still, trembling, and let the rabbits hop away into the thick oats of an adjoining field.

❖   ❖   ❖   ❖   ❖

Among other things the day was marred by two heroic dogfights both staged within five minutes involving four dogs on one side and seven on the other. Prince, Baby, Gina, Folly, Smoky, Susie and Dusky were all with me when I stopped at Harry's house to inspect the improvements he was making. Laddie, his big St. Bernard, came running out, followed by Sandy, the Border collie who has ten new pups, Penny, Harry's boxer, and the big St. Barnard pup.

It was a real brawl with all the ladies joining in a hair-pulling match—six boxers and a spaniel on one side, two St. Bernards and a Border collie and a boxer on the other. We just managed to separate them and lock the Hellers' dogs in the house when one of the children opened a door at the back of the house and all of them came galloping out to renew the battle. The big St. Bernard seemed to have been the chief casualty. Prince got hold of his big floppy ears and wouldn't let go.

❖   ❖   ❖   ❖   ❖

It rained all day—good rain—slow, soaking rain like that of northern France save for an occasional half-hour of flooding downpour, when the heavens seemed to open and hurl down buckets of water. At the end of the day our own brooks were still running clear which is something of which to be proud.

❖   ❖   ❖   ❖   ❖

Tonight while I mowed, the fireflies came up out of the grass almost in swarms as the cutter bar passed through it. Because the year has been so wet there are millions of them. They hung over the field, glittering in the moonlight as the mist came up over the damp ground of the lower pasture. Gina and Folly stayed with me fixing most of their attention on the woodchuck holes I uncovered while mowing.

      ✧   ✧   ✧   ✧   ✧

Yesterday while I worked in the fields I was accompanied by scores of barn swallows which swept over and around me catching the insects driven out of the heavy alfalfa by the mower. Sometimes they brushed my head and I could feel the rush of air from their wings. I know of no bird of which I am fonder. They build dozens of nests each year on the big hand-hewn rafters of the old barns, very close up against the upper floors with scarcely room to enter the nest. They are, partly at least, responsible for the total lack of mosquitoes at Malabar. The fish in the ponds, the frogs and toads, and the good drainage all do their part.

      ✧   ✧   ✧   ✧   ✧

The drawing power of the wild, deserted farm called the Ferguson Place with no dwellings or barns is extraordinary. Everybody loves it—high against the sky overlooking three counties. Tonight the whole farm—men, women, children and dogs—held a picnic there. We built big fires and burned up a lot more of the fallen branches, old fence posts and rubbish that always clutters a run-down abandoned farm. We have been five years at off moments clearing up the Ferguson Place and the job is at last nearly done. I must say Nanny and Anne did most of the work while I ran the mower over about five acres of pasture. The kids enjoyed themselves and Betty Pugh came up from the cabin to join them. It was a cloudy evening with all the farms in the valley far below and among the woods on the opposite side all misty and blue like the trees and houses in a French landscape.

We saved two big old chestnuts killed years ago by the blight for it was evident that the hollows of both, one of them upright and one prostrate, were filled with animal life. At the foot of one lay four blacksnake eggs empty with a small hole where the baby snakes had emerged. Most of us rode up the rough road through the forest on a hay wagon hitched behind a tractor and we picnicked alongside the giant dead chestnuts where every now and then a turn in the breeze brought to us the pungent, musky odor of the raccoons who were inside the old dead trees hiding and listening to the hubbub outside their house. It is a very solitary place and they are rarely disturbed from one year's end to another.

Very late just as we were about to pack up and return, the boys, quite spontaneously, burst out singing "Ghost Riders in the Sky." The older boys sang a kind of accompaniment to the solo performance of young George Cook who has a fine clear voice with that purity characteristic of all boy soprano singing. The effect was beautiful, for it is a good song with a curious sadness about it, and the setting, high on the hills of the Ferguson Place with the clouds scudding wildly across a full moon, was singularly moving. There was something in the sound of the young pure voice, the huge troubled sky and the melancholy of the song which appeared to move each one of us, old or young, deeply and singly, so that for a long time after the song finished there was only silence. It was one of those rare accidental precious moments when the purification of catharsis seemed to take place; even the dogs lay still, staring into the fire.

The picnic was a kind of consolation for the boys to whom I had refused permission to ride the horses up to Vane Close's farm three miles away. Only Sandy claimed to know anything about riding and neither Tex nor Tony are horses to be left in the hands of inexperienced riders. On Friday, Tony even gave Hope, who can handle most horses, a bad time, and Tex is always unpredictable and wicked. She knows the minute someone mounts her how much she can get away with and will go the limit. She is a beautiful mare, very vain and domineering with great intelligence and a prankish sense of humor. Last year a French cavalry officer went out on her to ride with

Hope who was on Tony. After dark Hope came back alone with the news that the Captain couldn't make Tex come home. I drove in the car about a mile up the Hastings Road to find the Captain patiently waiting for Tex to feel like coming home. He had tried everything he knew but none of it was any good. I turned over the car to him and when I mounted her, she went off home gentle as a lamb. The exploit was no credit to me; it was merely that for some reason she had taken a dislike to the Captain, and despite the fact that he was a crack rider in horse shows in New York, Paris and London, he lacked the authority to make her behave.

✿ ✿ ✿ ✿ ✿

To all the family at Malabar, animals somehow are not animals and are not treated as such. We believe that all animals have a dignity, an integrity and an entity of their own and men get back from them in affection, respect, loyalty and the quality of understanding exactly what they give.

All animals and especially dogs are frequently blamed for faults which should properly be placed on the shoulders of their owners and masters. Not a few of the people I know should never have dogs. Worst of all are those people whose possession of dogs is founded upon their own egotism—the people who think it is "smart" to have a dog or have a dog merely to watch the house or one they keep most of the time in the kennel while they travel, or the actress who keeps a dog as an ornament as she might a bracelet or a necklace. If a dog is a dull fellow, it is more than likely that he gets no companionship from his owner or because the owner is himself an even duller fellow. The ill-mannered dog is almost always a neglected dog and not one who is spoiled or loved too much. One can even visit a farm and know from the farm animals pretty much what kind of a farm it is and what kind of farmer the owner or manager may be. All animals, even some cats, the most independent and incorruptible of all animals, take on the qualities of their owners.

For us Tex is not simply a beautiful mare, or a five-gaited Kentucky thoroughbred, but a queen who rules all the other horses, imperious and conscious of her beauty. She leads and dominates them all, even the geldings. It is useless to attempt rounding up the other horses unless Tex is first under control; and, being clever, she is hard to catch in an open field. She knows the tricks of luring her with an apple or an ear of corn and can take them from your hand quickly, too quickly to permit you to seize her halter. She understands when someone who does not know how to ride climbs on her back. She will shy, dramatize every rabbit or blowing leaf and pretend to run away with her rider, like as not to leave him by the side of a lane or in the middle of a field, somehow quietly, without hurting him. With an experienced rider on her back she is a different animal. She will show off her five gaits and even attempt in the middle of a pasture to go into circles and figure eights, as if she were back again in the show ring. In the field she takes care of the blind Percheron mare, Sylvia, never going far from her and whickering to lead her across the creek or up a steep bank. When Sylvia feels herself lost she will neigh frantically until Tex answers.

And there is Tony, Hope's big pony, part quarter horse, part polo pony, who is a clown and shakes hands and does other tricks, one of which is to steal up behind you in the pasture and butt you in the middle of the back with his head. He is neither bad-tempered nor bad-mannered but frolicsome, and it is always well to keep out of the way of his heels if you are on another horse. He once put me out of the running for three days with a side kick delivered on a gallop as he passed Tex and me. Only the steel stirrup saved me a broken leg.

On more than one occasion a woman visitor on the farm, walking with me through the fields has been butted or pinched in a sensitive spot by Tony who has come up unheard behind her, and on more than one occasion I have seen the woman turn quickly and indignantly to upbraid what she believed was someone taking liberties with her.

And Red, who died at last when he was twenty-eight years old, took care of the younger children. Any babe could ride him. He even glanced back occasionally, I think, to see that the small ones were firmly in the saddle. If they fell off he stood quietly by until they climbed aboard once more.

None of the children has ever been afraid of animals; all have always accepted them as companions and equals. In the beginning at Malabar, when they set out on a walk they were always followed by four or five dogs, four goats, a tomcat and a pet lamb.

The goats came into our lives when Kate Tobias, an old friend and childhood schoolmate of mine who kept a grocery store, a filling station and a stable of goats on the Little Washington Road, brought a tiny kid as an Easter gift to the children. Nothing in life is, I think, prettier or more touching than a kid, with its deerlike ears and big, brown eyes. The first kid called for a companion, and we ended up with four. As they grew up as part of the family, they wanted no part of life in the fields. They wanted to live in the house and their favorite resting spot was the porch swing, where all four would lie, gently chewing, to watch what went on in the lane and barnyard. Twice they managed somehow to get into the house and were found on the bed of a ground floor bedroom. Quickly they learned to leap to the hood of a car and thence on the roof, and after that no car ever stopped at the door without all four springing to the roof where they lay peacefully chewing until driven down.

It was impossible to shut them up and we tried vainly to induce them at last to live in the pasture with the sheep, but they would have none of that, and each time I took them to the remote and distant Ferguson Place to introduce them to the sheep they would beat me home from the pasture across half a dozen fences and be there on the porch quietly rocking in the swing to greet me. They would simply walk up the brace of a fence or lie on their sides and squeeze under the fence. One of their favorite pranks was to walk across the top of the hotbeds, breaking glass as they went. In the end they became intolerable. It seemed that at times they actually persecuted us with a special goatish intelligence. The decision to save ourselves from them came at last when one summer day they got inside the car of a visitor and were found placidly chewing up a scattered packet of neatly stamped and addressed envelopes. To save ourselves from further persecution we found homes for them in the suburbs of Cleveland among the Italians who undoubtedly knew better how to cope with goats than we did.

But I am not sorry for the experience of the goats, for it gave me an insight into all the legends concerning goats that have been a part of human history and mythology since the beginning of time. Their intelligence is of a different quality from that of all other animals, almost human and a little devilish. The ancient wisdom in the eyes of a billy goat can shame you. And at courting time they become very nearly human. The sight of a billy goat prancing on his hind legs, tilting his head from one side to another, making sounds that have strange, half-human intimations brings the legends of fauns and satyrs very near and makes them seem very real. It also calls up visions of elderly butter-and-egg men and middle-aged, tipsy seducers in the back seats of cars at the nearest country club. No animal is so amorous or so demonstrative as a he-goat and none more human. Hector, the big Nubian he-goat, was, when courting, the perfect picture of a lecherous, bearded old reprobate. He seemed strangely out of place among the soft, green bills and woods of Ohio, and indeed, almost obscene. He belonged, I think, among the gray rocks of Italy or Greece, prancing and strutting amorously among the olive trees. It is not for nothing that he-goats have long been associated with devils and witches, with Walpurgisnacht and the witches' Sabbath.

And there has been a long line of orphan lambs brought up on bottles as pets by Hope and Ellen. No animal is more touching than a young lamb and no animal more stupid and lacking in charm than a grown sheep, and so, as they grew up, interest lagged and they were returned to the flock, or at least we hoped they were. But they wanted no part of the sheep. They had been brought up among people and dogs and horses and despised the other sheep; when you crossed a pasture they would leave the sheep and join you and the dogs and always they kept returning to the Big House. As Ellen, my then small daughter, once said, "You can't blame them. They don't know they're sheep. We should get a mirror and let them look at themselves."

Certainly one or two of them thought they were dogs. They ran about with the dogs and even chased cars with the dogs, and nothing startled a stranger so much as to see a good-sized lamb frolicking with the boxers and sometimes in the middle of a dogfight. It was only when the breeding season came that the lambs finally gave in to the fact that they were, after all, sheep and we were at last rid of them.

And there were the karakul lambs given Ellen by Grove and Esther Patterson—strange-looking beasts more goat than sheep, who would rather eat weeds and briars than good bluegrass and clover. They came as tiny black lambs, with silky, tightly curled coats and long, drooping, black ears. They grew into a ram and a ewe, still black until they were shorn for the first time. The ram grew great curling horns and, like most of the animals, simply acquired a name which established itself. He had a long, aquiline nose which, with his thick, black coat and his melancholy, dark eyes and skinny legs begged for the name of Haile Selassie. As George observed, "All he needed was a royal umbrella to look exactly like the Lion of Judah."

Haile had a playful disposition and a sense of humor and usually frightened visitors by backing off, rearing on his hind legs and springing toward them. It was rare that he actually butted in earnest, and as a young ram he never did much harm, for he was mostly wool, and, despite his size, weighed only about half as much as an ordinary Dorset ram. He insisted on going for walks along with the dogs, and occasionally had to be lifted over tight wire fences. He became quite accustomed to the hoisting operations, and at sight of a fence would place himself alongside it and wait to be lifted over. More than once he butted visitors gently through the front door of the Big House, on one occasion no less a personage than Vladimir Popoff, animal-breeding expert from the Soviet government.

The visit of the Soviet dignitary was itself accompanied by a certain atmosphere of absurdity. I had been going over the fields with the farm manager. As we approached the Anson Place, I discovered in the near distance an extraordinary figure of middle height. Beginning at the top the figure was dressed in a kind of green hat worn in the Tyrol but made of green plush and obviously too small for it sat on the top of the man's head above a broad ruddy face, with very bright pink cheeks. Indeed, he resembled closely one of those highly colored caricature bottle stoppers carved from wood which one finds everywhere for sale in Switzerland and the Rhineland. Beneath the bottle stopper face was a long green overcoat reaching to the ankles and ornamented with white pearl buttons. The shoes were what the automobile makers describe as "two tone," the upper part white and the lower part tan. They also were fastened with white pearl buttons. He was accompanied by a somewhat bewildered friend of mine, George Ganyard, the county agent.

They came toward me and George said, "Here is a gentleman from Moscow!" Although Ohio has towns called Paris, London, Vienna, Rome and *Moscow*, it was quite clear that the stranger did not come from Moscow, *Ohio*.

"His name," said George, "is Commissar Popoff."

At this one of the farm children, who might be described as considerable of a brat, said in a loud voice, "Gee! You should have heard Mom pop off at Pop last night!"

The crack was lost on the Commissar because he spoke no English but only a little French and German. However, the repetition of his name appeared to give him pleasure for he rewarded the brat with a broad grin. Indeed, he seemed painfully eager to be friendly and to discover someone with whom he could converse. Since George spoke only English, they had been having a rather poor time of it and had been communicating entirely in pantomime, at which neither of them was very good. I tried my French and my German and discovered that by using bits and pieces of both languages, we were able to converse after a fashion. I discovered his mission (that of seeing the crossed Angus-Shorthorn cattle and the general operations at Malabar) and I invited him up to the Big House. It was then that Haile Selassie gave him a resounding welcome. Clearly the Commissar was of peasant origin and he did not mind being practically knocked down by the boxers or being followed by two pet lambs to the threshold of the house. Even when he was butted gently into the front hall by Haile Selassie, he did not lose dignity or poise. In reply to my apologies he said, with a wide peasant grin, "But this is the first time I have really felt at home in America."

It was a remark which had, I knew, a deep and regretful implication for poor Popoff, for I had seen before representatives of the Soviet Republic, even sometimes in fairly high circles in Washington, dressed in clothes from Moscow, ill-fitting, made of cheap materials and resembling the fashions in a play by Chekhov. They were sharply aware that frequently enough they resembled caricatures or figures of fun at a dinner or a ball and always entered the room with a shyness and self-consciousness which instantly isolated them from men and women of other nationalities who were less ludicrously dressed. Tragically there was little they could do about the situation for if they purchased and wore American or English or French clothing they immediately became suspect to the NKVD. Indeed, I think that much of the inferiority complex which tends to make Soviet government officials abroad resentful and surly and ill-mannered arises from the knowledge they have that they are somehow different from other peoples and are perhaps laughed at behind their backs. Much of the same thing is true of their women and accounts for the mad rush to buy wholesale in American shops and department stores when they are recalled to Russia. At home in Moscow good-looking clothing or clothing conventional in the Western sense do not matter so much. At home their sartorial heresy is not so important and undoubtedly gives them a sense of superiority over those who are dressed in what they can buy in the Soviet government stores.

All of this was of course a long time ago when the Russians were friendly with the rest of the world and allowed and even sent some of their citizens abroad to learn what was to be learned in other more sophisticated and civilized areas. Only in 1955 with the visit of the Russians to the corn belt was the iron curtain lifted and even then there were no real farmers in the group, only government bureaucrats.

Alas! Haile developed a nasty habit of *hooking* you with his big horns. Since he usually caught you on the shins, it was a painful habit, and we had to shut him up in the paddock overlooking the courtyard at the Big House. Here he spent his days on a cattle-loading platform watching the traffic of the farm and conversing with passers-by in deep-voiced bleats. When there were no strangers around, I would let him out and play a sort of bull-fighting game with him, letting him charge and catching him by the horns just as he got to me. He would play this game over and over with zest until I was worn out.

He finally came to live with his mate Snowball and a Dorset-Delaine cross ewe who was brought up as a pet. If you entered their pasture, they would follow you and soon Haile would begin his old bull-fighting tricks. You could call him from any distance within hearing range and he would raise his head, bleat and come running. He had a real passion for tobacco and would stand indefinitely with his forefeet on the top rail of the fence begging for the cigarette butts which were saved for him during the war years when cigarettes were difficult to get. In this position his resemblance to the Emperor of Abyssinia was almost unbelievably human and striking.

At last one day he caught Nanny out blackberrying, employed his side-swiping tactics and cut her leg badly. I think it was all meant in fun but one could not be certain and with small children wandering everywhere on the farm he had to be sent away. He went to occupy the poultry runs of a friend in a near-by village where, together with Snowball, he earned his keep by eating up all the coarse weeds which he always seemed to prefer over the best and sweetest of grasses.

He is still alive, a very spoiled, tough and elderly gentleman looking
more than ever like the Lion of Judah.

✵   ✵   ✵   ✵   ✵

Most of the animals at Malabar have in reality named themselves.
That was the case of the wild tom turkey we bought to cross with the
bronze turkey hens in the hope that their crossed offspring would
develop more sense than their inbred, overbred, idiotic mothers who
were hopelessly unable to bring up their young. Certainly the bronze
breed was in the past a very different breed from the bronze turkeys
of today. I remembered well that my grandmother always kept a

big tom turkey or two and a half dozen or more turkey hens who at
nesting time simply took off for the nearest fence row, hatched their
young and lived off the countryside until winter came and food grew
scarce. Nearly every one of them returned with eight to a dozen
nearly full-grown turkeys which, because they had lived wild off the
countryside like quail or pheasant, had a much finer flavor than many
of the leathery turkeys one is forced to eat at banquets nowadays.
Indeed I have seen monstrous turkeys in Texas which were bred to
be all breast and are even known as "double-breasted" turkeys. They
lead a wretched life and are nervous and irritable from never having enough sleep for they are now so overbalanced by the weight of

breast that as soon as they fall asleep they fall off their perches or out of trees. Fundamentally they are impractical freaks like sows which weigh eight hundred pounds or cows which give a hundred pounds or more of milk per day.

The crossbreeding experiment was a failure for the crossed off-spring were just as addle-pated as their mothers and dragged their young great distances through wet grass and did not know how to shelter or dry them off after a storm. But the tom turkey, like the goats and lambs and Haile Selassie, developed such an attachment to the family that he wanted to live in the house and, like them, spent a good part of his time following you about or looking in the windows. He was anything but a *wild* turkey. In summer you could not be rid of him, and his strutting and gossiping and gabbling some-times drowned out all conversation on the veranda or terrace. He was a handsome animal and knew it. For hours he would strut be-side a car, regarding his beauty in the enameled reflection. He was a bird of violent and implacable antipathies, especially for anyone who had ever teased him or kicked at him. He had a hate for Bob, the manager, and would give him no peace when he was at the Big House. He would follow him about, uttering high-pitched, peevish cries, and would attack him with wings and feet and beak at every opportunity. He would chase Bob's car all the way down the lane as far as the road. He had a similar hate for the driver of the Omar bak-er's truck and for two of the boys who work on the farm in summer. And he carried on a perpetual feud with Baby, the clown boxer, who rushed at him and strong-armed him without ever doing him more harm than knocking him over. He acquired the name of Gilbert in honor of a fat acquaintance of the family who never walks but struts pompously thrusting a great stomach well in front of him.

❁ ❁ ❁ ❁ ❁

No chapter would be complete which overlooked Donald. I found him in the barnyard, when he was only a day old, wandering bravely about, a tiny ball of fluff. He seemed to be without father or mother, and to this day I have never discovered where he came from. I took him up to the Big House and gave him to Ellen, who was in bed with a cold. She put him in a shoebox and kept him on the bed with her day and night. When she got up he continued for a time to live in the nursery where he ran across the floor chasing moths brought in for him. Usually the chase ended in a wild and comical skid on the slippery waxed linoleum. He would climb all over you as you lay on the floor and grip you firmly by the ear in his soft bill.

As he grew older, Ellen kept him outside, where he followed her about wherever she went, and although that summer she tended and brought up five hundred ducks, he never showed any desire to leave her and join his own kind.

Then Donald went through the ugly duckling stage between down and feathers and presently grew a coat of feathers which gave some clue to his ancestry. He came out speckled black and white, which led us to believe that his father must have been a half-wild, traveling-man Muscovy duck which flew in one day out of nowhere to join the Pekings on the lower pond.

Donald, even when full-grown, still chose to live at the Big House, ignoring the other ducks and living peacefully with the dogs, the pet lambs, Gilbert, the tom turkey, and the fighting chickens. He never showed any fear of the dogs and would boldly waddle across them as they lay on the grass. It was not until the wild ducks, coming south for the winter, descended on the ponds that he gave any sign of knowing that he was a duck. Tentatively at first, he would join them for a swim which led us to suspect that somewhere in his ancestry there was also a mallard or two. But for a long time he returned every evening to the garage to sleep alongside Dusky and Patsy, the cockers. And then one day he went off to the pond for good and turned out in the classical manner to be a she, but "he" would always come when you went to the pond and called to "him." He would leave the other ducks and follow you along the border of the pond, quacking in a friendly fashion. Then at last, I called for Donald and "he" was no longer there among the other ducks. Unlike the Pekings, "he" could, like "his" father, the Muscovy traveling-man, fly very well and my suspicion is that "he" became enamored of a visiting wild duck and eloped.

✿   ✿   ✿   ✿   ✿

I think I loved as much as any animal I have ever known the big Angus bull—Blondy. He had an extraordinary, sleek, inky-black beauty, with huge muscles and a giant arched neck, great, black, intelligent eyes and a friendly disposition. He lived mostly on the range with a harem of thirty Shorthorn cows, but you could go up to him at any time in the field and scratch his ears without his ever showing either nervousness or anger. Now and then we attempted to shut him up at certain seasons, but always very quietly and thoroughly he used his great shoulders and head to demolish fence or pen or even the side of the barn, and with great dignity and calm he would set out across country over fence after fence to rejoin his harem.

Once we attempted to keep him inside the barn by enclosing his pen with an electric fence. At first the shock awed him into submission and temporary obedience, but Harry, the herdsman, took to shutting off the current at night for reasons of economy. While the current was on, the transformer made a slow ticking noise, and Blondy, after three or four days, came to understand that when the current was turned off the ticking stopped and the wire was harmless. The first morning after making this deduction he was gone again, back to the high pasture with his harem.

And so the stories of the animals at Malabar go on and on. It is a friendly place because of the animals who, to me and indeed to all of us, each has a personality. Fortunately, all the people on the farm and especially the children feel much the same way, and I think the animals know it. They are all good people who understand livestock and could not sleep if any animal were sick or cold or without feed or water. And the children are growing up with a feeling of sympathy and responsibility toward all dumb beasts, a feeling which can bring great richness in life and great understanding of things which others, who do not know that sympathy and responsibility, never understand or fathom. And the odd thing is that the feeling extends to the animals themselves which live together—dogs, barn cats and lambs—in peace. There are times in my own relations with the farm animals when I am tempted to accept the beliefs of the Hindus and the Jains concerning reincarnation and the sacredness of all life. In any case, I know how much poorer life would be without the animals and their trust.

The Bad Year
or Pride Goeth Before a Fall

The rains began, cold and dreary at the beginning of the month of April and day after day they continued through April, through May and into June. Meanwhile, the fields grew wetter and wetter, until at last the hillsides themselves began to weep, the water oozing out of their sides down the slopes onto the lower ground. In the flat country to the west of us the fields became lakes of water, sometimes almost unbroken for miles across the level rich fields.

In our county oats, if one is to have a good crop, should be planted as early as possible, for winter oats, seeded in the autumn, rarely weather the rigors of the northern winter and a farmer cannot afford to gamble on them. Oats planted in March have the best chance of success. Planted after the middle of April the chances of vigor and yield are lessened. Planted after the middle of May the yield is cut in half or if hot, dry weather comes on the results may be utter failure. In 1947 planting in March was out of the question for the fields were still frozen and covered with snow. The usual "false spring" which allowed us to put in early oats did not come at all, and then the rains began, falling day after day, in showers some days, in drenching downpours on others. And always it was cold, so cold that even the wild flowers and the morels (those first delicious woodsy fungi that grow in the deep forests under ash trees or in old and dying orchards) grew confused. A sudden burst of sunlight brought some of them into flower and fruition only to meet disaster on cold frosty moonlit nights. The delicate, tiny Dutchman's breeches all met a frosty death while in full flower and the trilliums turned up stunted, brown-fringed petals toward the gray skies instead of the usual luxuriant blossoms that sometimes covered whole acres of our deep woodlands in drifts of white. The bluegrass, water-soaked and cold, languished instead of growing and kept the restless cattle (who know better than we do when spring should be at hand) prisoners in the barns and soggy barnyards. They mooed and cried out in their restlessness, the sound of their mournful voices drifting far across the woods and hills.

And slowly, throughout all our county, the complaints of the farmers, impatient to get into their fields and worried over the cold, soggy fields, began to rise into a wail.

Charlie Schrack, standing in the doorway of the barn, watching the fields drenched by gray rains, said, "I can't remember anything like it in fifty years." Lots of farmers talk that way when drought or floods by persistent rain begin to spell disaster, but this time it seemed to me that Charlie was right, for it rained when it seemed impossible. Rain seemed to fall in cold, frosty weather out of skies that were comparatively free of clouds. It was as if the heavens were a gigantic showerbath with a small irresponsible child playing with the chain which released the water.

And Nanny said, "I'm beginning to wonder if the Atomic bomb didn't have something to do with all this rain. Maybe the scientists had better stop discovering things before they destroy us altogether. It begins to make you believe in the story of the Tower of Babel. Man can become too pretentious."

And the next morning I read in the papers that government agencies had warned planes to keep below the level of twelve thousand feet since the Atomic cloud from the Bikini tests was passing for the third time around the earth and had just reached us again. That night and for two days, it rained without ceasing.

Walter Pretzer, a prosperous hothouse grower, came down from Cleveland for a dreary, water-soaked weekend. Curiously enough he is both an immensely practical man and a mystic. He said, "The rains are only balancing out. We're getting what we missed during the past four or five years." To which I replied cynically, "Yes, but it isn't raining into your greenhouses."

But he answered me, "Nor is the sun shining." Sun or lack of sun can make all the difference to the grower of hothouse vegetables. The lack of it can delay the crop until fresh vegetables, field grown from some other part of the country, come onto the market and run the prices of hothouse vegetables below the level at which it is even worth harvesting them. Sometimes such a lack can destroy the profits of a crop altogether.

In modern agriculture, too much rain is about the only thing which a farmer cannot somehow control. Against the next most disastrous potential—a sharp disastrous fall in prices—the good farmer can protect himself and manage to survive, but when the rain comes in floods at planting time or refuses to come at all for one dreary week after another, there is not much that he can do. And flooding rains are worse than drought; a farmer can irrigate dry burning soil if he possesses the facilities; he cannot mop up heavy persistent floods.

At Malabar and among the hills of our neighbors we were better off than the flat country people, for the water did not stand in lakes on our hills of glacial gravel loam. The worst we had to face were the seepage spots and "wet weather springs" which appeared here and there, sometimes at the very top of a hill. These we could plow around, leaving them water-logged and fallow, for another and better year. Our soil was loose and open and you could work it wet without too much damage if there was enough organic material mixed with it. And we had the advantage of mechanization—that when there was a break in the weather we could get into the fields and with tractor lights burning, work on shifts all through the night.

And that was what we did during the awful spring of 1947 and so somehow we got ninety acres of oats into the ground, some of it in land which had been rough plowed the autumn before and was all ready for disking, fitting, and drilling. We got in our oats in one of those two-day breaks when, if the sun did not shine, the rain at least did not fall. Then the rains broke again and the cold persisted and in three or four days the oats were through the ground in a pale, misty shimmer of lettuce green across the wet, brown fields. And our hearts and stomachs felt better and our pride rose, because we had in the ground probably more oats than any farmer from the Appalachians to the Great Divide. On our loose, well-drained soil, oats did not mind the cold nor the rain. It was the kind of weather from which it benefited in the early stages. We were having March weather at least a month after March had passed.

There is in every good farmer a curious, overwhelming, almost malicious pride common to the human race but especially well-developed in the cultivator. It is born of satisfaction in being "smarter" than his neighbor, in having his acres look greener, in getting in his crops earlier, in having fields where the hay or the pasture is heavier. And conversely there is in every good farmer a kind of perverse satisfaction in the discovery that his neighbor's fields look poorly. The sight of a poor crop in someone else's field somehow warms the heart of the farmer whose own fields are lush and green.

Often when I have been driving across Ohio with David, he will grin, as we pass a miserable pasture or field of yellowish weedy hay and say, "I suppose that makes you feel awfully good!" And I'm afraid that sometimes it does. The pride of a good farmer is often his worst sin, but it is also what makes a good farmer and what helped to feed this nation and the rest of the world in the difficult years when lack of machinery and labor made farming a back-breaking, long-houred job. It is that same pride which makes the good farmer resist subsidies and government payments and all the paraphernalia of a "kept" agriculture. In his heart a good farmer wants to show that he cannot be "licked," and that without help from anyone he can grow abundant crops despite every handicap.

That is why a good farmer grows short-tempered and desperate when the weather turns against him. With each day of drought or flooding rain, he becomes more frustrated and savage, because the weather alone he cannot lick altogether either by machines or muscle or long hours in the field.

And so farmers everywhere that spring of 1947 grew ill-tempered and angry. They did not wail. It is only the poor farmer who wails and looks for scapegoats or excuses for his own failures of energy or intelligence. But that, of course, may be true of the whole human race. It just stands out clearly in the case of the farmer who long ago discovered what many others rarely discover—that in life there are no "breaks" except as one makes them for himself.

Still it did not stop raining. Time for planting oats receded into the distant unchangeable past and time for corn plowing came along, and still it rained and stayed cold. It was the year when Al Jolson's old song, "April Showers" had a great revival and every jukebox and every radio program was blaring it forth. It was a song that sounded very sour to the farmer that spring. The violets, which grew on banks like weeds in our country, were small, shriveled and frost-bitten. There were no warm showers. There were only flooding downpours, day after day as May slipped past toward June, and Ellen, my youngest, said, "They ought to change that song to April showers that bring the flowers that bloom in July."

Slowly countless farmers abandoned all hope of planting oats. They talked of other crops and of putting all their land into corn. Corn planting time came along and still it rained. Here and there in our hill country one could see farmers dripping wet on their tractors, turning over sod ground for corn planting. Sod ground, especially in soil like that of our county, can be plowed fairly safely when it is still too wet because the roots and vegetation help to keep the ground open, aerated and keep it from packing. We too plowed sod in the rain and turned under the acres of rank sweet clover on the loose, alluvial soil of the farm we rent from the Muskingum Conservancy. We dared not even put a tractor wheel on the small acreage of water-logged clay.

But even after the ground was plowed it was too wet to fit for planting. Day after day went by, each rain bringing us nearer to the last date at which corn could be planted and have any chance of maturing before the average frost date of October fourth. Then the rain stopped for a couple of days and again we worked night and day until all but ten acres of corn were in the ground. By our own standards at Malabar, we were three weeks late but with luck that corn, changed at the last moment to a quick ripening, short season hybrid, would mature if the frost held off.

We were thankful that we had all our corn in save for the ten acres of clay which we could not touch because it was as wet and sticky as glue. So we planned to put that into buckwheat, let it serve the bees and then plow it into the soil for the benefits it would give us the following year. "At any rate," said Kenneth, "it will look pretty, and it's better than leaving the ground bare or to grow up in weeds."

And again, smugly and pridefully, we settled back, aware that we had probably more corn in the ground than any of the farmers to the west of us all the way into the corn country where the fields were still more like the carp ponds of Austria and Czechoslovakia than the fertile fields of the Midwestern bread-basket country. But still it rained and remained cold, and we began to worry over whether the seed would rot in the ground. Then for three days the rain suddenly stopped and capriciously the weather changed from cold to oppressively hot with a hot baking sun and a new peril developed—that even with all the organic material we had pumped into the soil for years and the fresh crop of sweet clover turned under, the soil was so wet that the hot sun might bake the surface and prevent the tender, germinating corn from piercing the surface. So on the third day I climbed aboard the tractor, attached the rotary hoe and drove it full speed back and forth across the surface of the cornfield because the faster you drive it, the more efficiently it works, breaking up the surface and throwing the tiny weed seedlings and bits of crumbling earth high into the air.

Driving at full tractor speed, I felt good. The sun was shining. The alluvial gravel loam was dry enough for the rotary hoe to work efficiently. The Conservancy farm lay alongside the big artificial lake formed by one of the dams of the Muskingum Flood Prevention Project. The lake beneath the clear skies and hot sun was a brilliant blue. The distant wooded hills were tropically green and lush from all the rain. The birds, mute during the weeks of downpour, chorused from every tree, bush and hedgerow and from the marshy land along the lake came the sound of splashing caused by the thrashing about of the big carp engaged in an orgy of reproduction. And in my heart was that gnawing old farmer's pride that we had outwitted even the weather. It was one of those fine days which is recompense for weeks of bad weather.

At sundown I drove happily home and ran the rotary hoe briskly over the plantations of beans, peas and sweet corn. And then at supper time as the shadows began to fall across the valley and the lush forest there came a sinister note of warning. Out of the symphony of birds singing and the music of the frogs in the ponds below the house, there emerged a note which fell on the ears and assaulted my senses as violently as a shrill fife playing loudly and discordantly in the midst of a great orchestra. It was the cry of the tree frogs calling for rain. It came from all sides, the same monotonous, trilled note which in time of drought can be the most lovely instrument in the whole symphony of Nature.

I said, "Listen to those damned tree frogs! Haven't they had enough? I'd like to go out and strangle every one of them!" And from across the big table I heard a loud chuckle from my daughter Anne.

When I asked, "What's so funny?" she said, "Just the picture of you going around the farm strangling every tree frog with your bare hands."

Tree frogs do not, as legend has it, "call for rain." On the contrary they call when the atmospheric conditions foretell rain. They are not suppliants; they are prophets. I looked out of the window and against the brilliant sunset, big, dark, unmistakably wet clouds were piling up at the end of the Valley. I couldn't believe it could rain again. There couldn't be any more water in the skies.

That evening everybody on the farm was feeling good and on such evenings the men and the kids on the place are all likely to gravitate to the lower farm. It is a kind of public forum in the center of the thousand acres and when the rain is falling people gather in the machine shop where Kenneth is kept busy during the bad weather repairing machinery or ingeniously making machines which we can't buy because they are in short supply or don't exist. On fine evenings we seem to gather there spontaneously just to talk or enjoy the evening or sometimes to go fishing in the pond that lies below the shop.

We were feeling pretty good because our oats stood high and strong and green in the fields, and because our corn was in the ground, the grains swelling and popping, in the dark ground, warmed for the first time by a hot sun. While we talked, pridefully, the dark clouds at the head of the Valley piled up higher and higher and the tree frogs sang more and more shrilly. When I pointed out the clouds, Bob said, "Well, we haven't got anything to worry about. Think of those poor guys in the flat country with their fields still under water. Even if it stopped raining it would take two weeks for the ground to dry out enough to get a plow into them."

Yes, we all felt pretty good.

We all went home at last, still feeling good. Two things were certain—that we were ahead of most farmers and that no matter how hard it rained we had lost and were losing none of our precious soil. It stayed where it was meant to stay, held in place by that thick pasture and hay sod or the protecting sodded strip which prevented it ever getting away from us.

Tired from the all-day jolting ride on the rotary hoe, I fell into that deep sleep that comes only after physical labor in the open air, the kind of sleep which you can feel yourself enjoying with an almost voluptuous pleasure. Even the dogs were tired from the long day in the field and forgot their snack in their eagerness to go to bed. They fell asleep in their chairs even before I found myself lying with eyes closed and the book I was reading fallen aside. I awakened long enough to turn out the lights and fell into that warm, pleasant oblivious sleep which must be like the reward of death to very old people who have led long, full and happy lives.

I slept "like a log" until about two in the morning when a prodigious clap of thunder which rocked the whole house awakened me. The thunder was bad enough but there was another sound even worse. It was the sound of rain on the roof, a sound which in the dry hot days of August comes like a celestial benediction. Now it sounded like a curse from Hell for not only was it the sound of unwanted rain but of ropes and buckets and torrents of it, the sound of Niagaras of unwanted water streaming from gutters and spouts which could not carry it off fast enough. And above and through the sound of the rain on the roof came another sound of water even more menacing—that of the spring brook which ran through the garden below the house.

It was a sound I had not heard in seven years, since first we controlled run-off water on the hills and pastures above. Now, after all these years, the clear little creek was roaring again. It meant not only that it was raining hard and that the water-soaked land could drink up not one more rain drop, but that this was flood and perhaps disaster. I rose and went to the door and Prince who sleeps always on the foot of the bed, jumped up and went with me. There I heard another sound, even more ominous—the roar of Switzer's Creek a quarter of a mile away which had been clear and well-behaved, never going out of its banks since farmers upstream had begun taking proper care of their fields. Now it was roaring again. It could only mean flood.

With a feeling of helplessness I went back to bed, to lie there sleepless and worrying over the fact that all the work I had done with the rotary hoe was useless since these torrents of water would pack the earth harder than ever, worrying over the cattle, the calves, the horses in the bottom fields. I knew from the roar of Switzer's Creek that this time it was not merely rain but a cloudburst of the proportions that sweep away bridges and houses and drown livestock in the fields. I slept a little more, fitfully, and each time I wakened I heard the unwanted hateful rains streaming down and the increasing roar of the streams.

At daylight I went to the door and looked out over the Valley. Part of the lower pasture was flooded but the livestock was safe on high ground, drenched and grazing peacefully in the downpour. Through the middle of the flooded field ran the swift, muddy current carrying with it whole fences, trees, rubbish, bits of hog pens and even a brand new milk can bobbing along on its way from some spring house upstream to the reservoir lake below.

It rained thus until nine o'clock in the morning when suddenly the awful downpour ceased and everyone on the farm—men, women and children—streamed out of the houses toward the bridge over Switzer's Creek. There was the kind of excitement among us which comes perhaps as a recompense to people in the face of destruction and disaster, a kind of exhilaration which brings all people, whatever their temperaments or differences of character, together on a common level.

The first concern of the men was the new floodgate that Bob and Kenneth and Jesse had constructed only a day or two before to separate the two bottom pastures. It hung from a heavy piece of steel pipe between the two concrete buttresses of the township bridge, made thus so that when the water rose it would swing out and float. To build it had taken a great deal of time and hard work.

The gate was still there, swinging out almost flat on the surface of the rushing water. Now and then a log or a whole tree swept swiftly beneath it without lodging or tearing it loose. It was a good piece of engineering. Everybody was proud of it.

Then with all the dogs, the men crowded into the jeep to inspect the rest of the farm. The wheat fields, so green and lush even the day before, were beaten down in spots as if a giant had flung great pails of water against the wheat. In the wild swamp and woodland we call the Jungle, the water poured through the trees high above the banks. Here and there a log or a tree had become lodged, collected a bundle of flotsam and jetsam and the diverted waters had cut out a whole new channel. We stood there on a high bank, silent, watching the flood, awed yet somehow exhilarated by the terrible, unpredictable, incalculable power of rushing water.

And last of all we set out for the Conservancy farm on the edge of Pleasant Hill Lake built years ago to check just such floods as this. We went with forebodings for we knew that the dam would be kept closed to hold back the water and protect the helpless people in the towns downstream along the Muskingum River all the way to the Ohio and perhaps even down the Mississippi to the Gulf of Mexico. As we neared the Conservancy farm the forebodings grew for the rising waters of the lake had already covered the lower road. There had never been such a flood before in all our experience so we could not know what that high water meant to the fields of which we had been so proud because our oats were all above ground and flourishing and our corn planted even in the midst of the weeks-old rain.

Cautiously I felt my way with the jeep through the high water. We just made it and as we came out the other side on the high ground we found out what the water on the road meant. It meant that our pride, the oats field on the Conservancy farm lay under four to six feet of muddy water. In the shallow water near the banks we could see the rippling wakes left by the big carp as they moved in to take advantage of the plowed muddy oats field which they found ideal for spawning. For a long time we stood there watching the water-traced movements of the big invisible carp.

Then Kenneth said, "I guess we might as well make something out of this mess. I think if you all make a drive we might corner some of these big carp." So the men and the boys down to George Cook, who was nine, took off their pants and waded out in their shorts into the cold water making a chain to trap the carp in shallow water. Even the five boxers joined in. As if they understood the game they moved forward in a line with the men and boys trying to drive the carp into the shallows. Only Bobby, who was four and might have found the water over his head, stood on the bank and shouted advice as one big carp after another turned swiftly and darted between us, sometimes even between one's legs.

It wasn't any good. Every carp escaped but somehow the game raised our spirits. We all decided that probably the water would be released quickly from the dam and the oats field would be left free of it again before the crop and the beautiful stand of sweet clover sowed in it would suffer any damage.

At last we made our way home to disperse to the monotony of regular tasks which could and did bring a kind of numb solace and resignation in such occasions.

That afternoon the air cooled and the bright sun came out and two days later the gravelly cornfield was dry enough to repeat the whole process with the rotary hoe, all the long hours of rough tractor riding at top speed, to break up the crust all over again and let the young seedlings through. While I worked back and forth across a big sixty-acre field, the air turned muggy and hot once more and the wind shifted a little to the south which is always a bad sign when there is too much rain. I kept listening above the rumble of the tractor for the sound of train whistles. In our country when one hears the whistles of the Pennsylvania locomotives it means dry weather; when one hears the B&O, it means rain. In midsummer one prays for the B&O. For once I wanted to hear a Pennsylvania whistle. Presently as I was finishing the job with the rotary hoe, I heard a whistle. It came from a B&O freight train pulling up the long grade to Butler and never have I heard it more clearly!

At about the same time great black clouds began to appear again at the head of the Valley and the accursed tree frogs began to sing. I knew that once again I had gone over that cornfield only to have all my work undone.

At twilight I rode the tractor the two miles back to the house. The setting sun disappeared beneath clouds, and as I rode the drive up to the Big House, great solitary drops of rain began to fall. Before I got into the house the drops began to come down by the trillions, in torrents. I thought, trying to deceive myself, "Very likely it's only a big thunderstorm and will quickly be over." The water in the reser-

voir had already gone down about two feet in two days leaving part
of our oats field bare in time to save it. If we had another heavy rain
it would mean, with the lake level above flood stage, that instead of
the young oats plants being released before they were drowned, the
whole field would be flooded again and perhaps the cornfield that
lay above it.

I was wrong. The rain was no thunderstorm. It was the same kind
of flooding rain that had come down two nights earlier. Indeed it was
worse, if possible. Eight o'clock came and nine and ten and still it
poured. The little brook in the garden began to roar once more and
then from the Valley came the louder roar of Switzer's Creek.

I took a couple of good drinks and went to bed to read, thinking
I could take my mind off what could only be disaster. But it wasn't
any good. I tried reading novels, agricultural editorials, magazines,
but through all the print and ideas, good and bad, came the devilish
sound of torrents of water pouring off the roofs and the rising roar of
the little brook. And at last when my eyes grew tired and I began to
feel drowsy, I heard the ring of the telephone. I knew it was someone
on the farm ringing because the sound is different when the ring
is made by cranking the phone handle instead of pushing a button
in the central office. I thought, "This is it. Something bad has happened on the farm!"

Bob's voice answered me. He was calling from his house below
not far from the creek. He said, "I think we've got a job. The horses
in the bottom are scared. They're running up and down crying out.
One of them tried to get across the creek and is marooned on the
island. We've got to look after them and the cattle."

I asked, "Is it worse down by the bridge?" And his voice came
back, "Brother, you ain't seen nothing."

I dressed, gloomily, worrying about the animals and especially the
horses. Cows and steers are generally phlegmatic. They either take
things calmly or go completely wild, but horses and especially highly
bred horses, get frightened, like people, and for me the horses, like
dogs, are people. I took only one of the dogs with me. I chose Prince
because Prince owned me—I didn't own Prince—and he was the

steadiest of them all save old Gina who had always been wise and calm. But Gina was too old and plump for wild adventure. Too many dogs might only make confusion. And besides they were likely to follow me into the water if I had to go there and be carried away in the flood. Prince was a good swimmer and he would obey me and not get panicky. So Prince, delighted and excited, jumped to the seat of the jeep.

Bob met me at the bridge, water streaming from his hat and jacket. He had an electric torch and with that and the lights of the jeep I saw quickly enough that I hadn't seen anything until now. The water was so high that it was seeping through the wooden floor of the bridge and sliding past beneath with a terrifying speed. A whole log struck the edge of the bridge and made it shudder and then slipped under the water out of sight in a second. In the earlier flood there had been backwaters and whirlpools beneath the bridge where rubbish gathered but now there was nothing but rushing water going past so fast that I felt a sudden dizziness and instinctively stepped back from the edge.

He told me about the panic of the horses. "I heard them all the way up at the house."

I said, "Get in. We'll take the jeep out in the field and use the lights." He didn't think we could make it with the jeep but I knew better than he did what it could do.

He said, "I'll get my car, leave it on the road and put all the lights on the field and join you."

While he got his car I opened the pasture gate and drove through. Even the high ground was running with water and wherever there was a depression the water stood in deep pools. I put the jeep into four-wheel drive in low gear and she did what she was supposed to do. She plowed through mud and water until the lights penetrated a little distance into the mist and driving rain, enough for me to see that only a rim of bluegrass remained above the flood. The lights picked up two things, both white, the white spots of the Holstein cows who had gone to the high ground and were either grazing or ly-ing down and the white blaze on the forehead of Tex, my own mare, as she came toward me splashing through two feet of water.

Tex is a beautiful Kentucky mare, chestnut with a white blaze, and the proudest and the most spirited of horses. She rules the oth-ers and it is impossible to catch any of the others in the field until you have first captured Tex. But in the flooded field she wasn't behaving that way and now ran straight toward the lights of the jeep followed by another horse. As I got down she came up close and whickered. There were no antics now. She was afraid and wanted to be taken care of. Then the lights of Bob's car were turned into the field and I saw that the other horse was Tony, my daughter Hope's horse, young and strong, who is by nature a clown. But tonight he wasn't clown-ing. He too whickered when I spoke to him.

I recognized Tony with a sinking heart because I knew then that the missing horse marooned on the island in the flood was Old Red. Either of the others were strong and spirited and could have taken care of themselves even in the terrible current that was running, but Old Red was old and tired. He was a little deaf and nearly blind. He was the one you felt sorry for.

Old Red had brought up the little children until they had learned to ride well enough to handle the younger, more spirited horses. If they fell off he would stand still until they picked themselves up and climbed back on. He never got flustered or showed off and reared like Tex and never clowned as Tony did. He was twenty-one years old when we bought him, because he was calm and docile. He was just a horse, never a high-spirited queen like the thoroughbred Tex nor a wild, impish polo pony like Tony. Sometime in his youth when perhaps he had been a carriage horse on some farm, he had been abused for on his shoulder he bore the scars of old galls from a collar. He wasn't a clever horse or a spirited horse or a beautiful one. He was always just a kind, patient, old slob. And now, at thirty years of age with his joints stiffened and his teeth mostly gone, he was marooned on an island in the midst of a roaring flood such as the county had not seen in half a century. I wished it had been one of the others.

As I took hold of Tex's halter, for the first time without her giving an indignant toss of the head, Bob came up out of the darkness and rain and mist with the light. He was carrying a long rope.

"I thought," he said, "we might need this to get over to the island to get the horse off."

I told him the missing horse was Old Red and that I'd better take the other two to the barn before they turned completely panicky and uncatchable.

Tex led easily enough. She wanted the dry safety of the barn and Tony followed as always at her heels. Prince, despite the fact that, like most boxers, he hated getting wet, trudged along beside us, his ears down and his stub of a tail pressed low in an effort to get it between his legs. Bob went off through the water to check on the cattle on the high ground. On the way back the roar of the flood seemed to grow steadily louder. After the two horses were safely in the barn, I discovered on my return to the field that the water was still rising.

Far off through the rain I could see the faint glare of Bob's torch as he checked the cattle and in the light from the two cars I could see the stream of logs, trees and driftwood moving swiftly down on the surface of the current, but I couldn't see the island or Old Red.

I waded into the water and was joined presently by Bob but as the water rose deeper and deeper above our ankles and knees, it was clear that we were never going to make the island.

Then out of the mist, the willows of the island emerged but there was no island. There was only swift flowing water covered with leaves, bits of sod and branches. And then out of the mist, catching the light from the cars, appeared a ghostly Old Red. He was walking up and down, whickering loud enough to be heard above the sound of the water.

I called out to him and he stopped, looked toward me and then started in my direction but as soon as he reached deeper water he turned back to the island and the shallow water.

There wasn't any way to get to him. The water had risen so high that on the whole of the farm there wasn't a rope long enough to permit us to reach the island, and even with a rope tied about your waist, there wouldn't be much hope of getting through the torrent. Knowing horses, I knew that even if you made it, there was small chance of getting a horse in a panic to follow you.

I shouted to him again and again and each time the old horse started toward me and each time when he got into deep water he turned back to the island.

Meanwhile both Bob and I were drenched. The water ran inside our jackets and down our bodies. Prince, miserable in the dampness, crouched beside me. At last I gave up.

"There's nothing to do," I said, "but hope that he'll stay there and that the water won't get much higher."

And so we turned away with a sickening feeling through the rain and water, leaving the old horse where he was. The other horses were in the barn and the cattle all safe on high ground. There wasn't anything to do but go home. We had hot coffee at Bob's house and as I said good night to Bob, he said, "Maybe I opened my big mouth too soon—saying we hadn't anything to worry about." I laughed but I knew what he meant—that probably sunrise would find most of our corn and oats deep under the waters of the big lake.

By the time I got back to the bridge the planks were under water and before I drove across it I got down to make sure that the planks were still there and the bridge safe. You could not make sure but I got back into the jeep and took a chance. I speeded up the jeep and made a dash for it. The water flew high on both sides so that together with the pouring rain and the rushing water it seemed for a moment that all of us, Prince, myself and the jeep, were caught in a raging torrent of water. The planks were still there and we made it.

At home Prince and I dried ourselves off and joined my wife for hot soup and a snack with all the dogs, who treated the wet and miserable Prince with such resentment for having been the chosen one on the expedition that a fight developed between him and his brother, Baby. Then I went to bed after taking two sleeping pills so that I would not waken in the still early hours of the morning and hear the terrible rain and think of Old Red marooned alone on the island in the rising flood.

It was nearly eight when I wakened and the rain had stopped. The old orchard on the hill above my room was streaked with early morning sunlight and the red sandstone rock looked brighter and the trees lusher and more green than I had ever seen them. But in the back of my mind there was a sore spot which could not be healed until I went to the windows at the other side of the house which overlooked the bottom pasture. I had to know what had happened to Old Red.

It must have stopped raining sometime during the night for the water had gone down and the surface of the island, littered with branches and trees and old boards, was now above the flood. But among the willows there was no sign of Old Red. I felt suddenly sick and in a last hope I thought, "Perhaps he is all right after all. Perhaps he's just around the corner below the slope." And I went back to the far end of the house and looked out, and there behind the slope, peacefully munching bluegrass with the few teeth he had left was Old Red, behaving as if nothing had happened.

After breakfast Kenneth and I climbed into the jeep with the dogs and set out for the Conservancy farm. The jeep was the only car which had a chance of making it. We already knew the worst for from Mount Jeez we could see the lake—an enormously enlarged lake covering twice its usual area with clumps of trees here and there barely visible above the water. This time we couldn't get through the lower road at all. Not only was the road under ten feet of water but

Charley Tom's pasture was under ten feet of water also. The bridge structure was out of sight.

So, turning round, we took the only other course of reaching the Conservancy farm; we took to a rutted abandoned old lane and the open, soggy fields and somehow we made it. As we came over the crest of a slope we saw the full extent of the disaster. All the oat fields and half the corn land was covered by water and here and there in low spots in the field there were great ponds of water as big as small lakes.

This was, in reality, a disaster. We sat for a time in silence looking at the wreckage. It wasn't only the money loss but the loss of the long hours of work and care we had all put into these fields.

Then Kenneth said, "There's a new milk can bobbing on the edge of the current. We might as well salvage something."

So together we set to work to get that solitary milk can out of the swirling torrent. It was not easy but by the use of long tree branches and poles we maneuvered the floating milk can to a point where, wading in up to his hips, Kenneth salvaged it. He fastened it to the back of the jeep and we climbed in and set out for home. There wouldn't be any recompense in cash for the damage done by the waters of the lake; we rented the whole farm from the Conservancy District with the gambler's chance that some day there might be just such a flood and disaster. And anyway money is poor recompense to a good farmer; he wants his crops and the satisfaction that goes with raising them.

For three weeks most of the Conservancy farm remained under from five to twenty feet of impounded water, kept there to prevent its menace from being added to the already disastrous floods on the Mississippi. When the water went down at last not one living thing remained but only the desolation of logs and fence posts and driftwood scattered across the barren fields. Even the trees were killed along with the blackberries and elderberries that filled the hedgerows. We had not only lost our crops, but we had to clear the fields of their desolation. What little corn or oats remained on dry ground was growing but looked pale and yellowish in the water-soaked ground.

And elsewhere on the upper farm more rich wheat was beaten to the earth to mildew and smother the precious seedings. The blue-grass behaved in the water-soaked earth exactly as it did in time of drought. It grew tough and went to seed early and it was possible to clip it only on the high ground. Everywhere else in the fields, the power mower bogged down and had to be pulled out.

Good farmers are by nature optimistic; otherwise the uncontrollable vagaries of Nature—the floods, the droughts, the plagues of locusts—would long ago have discouraged them and the world would have been left starving. We were no different from other farmers—we hoped that the great flood had marked the end of the persistent intolerable rains.

We were wrong. June passed into July and still the rain continued, not simply showers or simple rains but cloudbursts coming sometimes twice a day. Even the fish ponds, fed from tight sod-covered land and springs, overflowed their barriers and big trout and bass escaped into the Clear Fork and the lake below. Came time to fill the silos with grass silage and we began cutting and hauling but quickly found that every tractor had to carry a log chain so that we could pull each other out of the mud, a minor disaster which happened ten or fifteen times a day. Twice the big John Deere dug itself into the mud up to its belly and a string of four lighter tractors, chained together, could not drag it out. In the end with four-by-fours chained to its giant wheels it succeeded in lifting itself out of the mud.

Somehow the silos got filled with the lush, heavy alfalfa, brome grass and ladino, but even the grass was so filled with moisture that it had to be wilted a long time before it could be safely put away. Weeds grew in the corn and more wheat was beaten down in the fields of which we had been so proud. The oats which remained grew more and more lushly and all but the tough, stiff-stemmed new Clinton variety were beaten to the ground while weeds began to grow up through them.

Then the weather turned warm but the rains continued and at night when the air cooled the whole Valley was blanketed in heavy white mists which appeared at sundown, rising in smokelike writhing veils above the trees. For days the Valley seemed more like Sumatra or Java than midsummer Ohio country. Rust appeared for the first time in our experience on the ripening wheat and mildew on the leaves and fruit of the fruit trees. Some of the grapevines began to die back from the tops, a sign that their water-logged roots could no longer stand the lack of oxygen and the wetness of the earth. Three times the vegetable garden was replanted and three times drowned out, sometimes standing for days under three or four inches of water.

Then came a brief respite which in itself was very nearly a disaster. There was no rain but in its place there was a brilliant, burning sun accompanied by hot winds which burned the moisture out of the topsoil but not out of the subsoil where the water still soaked the roots of all vegetation. It baked a crust over open ground and burned the overlush leaves of the crops. At night the moisture still rose from the soaked ground in heavy blankets of fog. It was as if now it was the earth rather than the sky which was raining.

Somehow we managed to combine the wheat, although we lost from five to fifteen bushels per acre of wheat literally beaten into the earth by the torrents of water. Except for thirty acres of good oats on the highest ground, the crop was ruined. In the heads there were no grains at all but only chaff. And from over the rest of the Middle West there arose a cry that drought was ruining the corn crop just at the crucial moment of tasselling and pollenization. Because there had been so much rain the corn had set shallow roots on the surface of the soil and now suddenly that surface had been burned, baked and hardened.

But in our Valley even the short, vicious heat was only a delusion. As it came time to make hay and clip and bale straw, the rains began again, not simply rains but the old cloudbursts. Ragweed grew higher and higher in the standing straw and the hay, partly dry and then soaked, rotted in the fields. Weeds everywhere grew like the fierce tropical growth that overwhelms settlements and plantations in a few weeks in the Tropics when the battle against them is relaxed for a season. The whole farm, usually so neatly and proudly kept, acquired a disheveled, unkempt, half-tropical appearance.

And so it went, on and on, through the end of July and then August and well into September. There was no hay-making season at all, even for the second cutting, and when there was a day or two of sunshine the hay, dried during the day, became drenched again each night from the moisture rising out of the water-soaked ground and from the heavy, damp fogs which settled at sundown in the Valley. At last we took in hay which was still damp. Some of it molded, some of it heated and turned brown and a little came through as the good green hay which we always made in a summer that was even vaguely reasonable.

Only the pastures and the new seedlings gave us any pleasure or satisfaction, for they were lush and green, but even this was small compensation for all the lost labor and seed and fertilizer and the depression which arose from the sight of wet hay and weed-choked cornfields. The buckwheat planted later on wet ground produced a bumper crop but few farmers take pride in lowly buckwheat and the season was so wet that the bees could not even work the blossoms.

And then presently in the beginning of September the rains stopped and miraculously two weeks of hot weather day and night set in, and suddenly the corn, after dawdling along all of the summer, began to show signs of ripening and making a crop. The soil began to dry out for wheat plowing and that miraculous resiliency which preserves farmers against utter and paralyzing despair began to assert itself.

Gradually the season began to recede into the past. It was becoming the "old season." It was time now to plow and fit for wheat, to clip the bluegrass pastures and the weeds for the last time in the evil year of nineteen forty-seven. With the turning of the first furrow the pride which was humbled began to rise again. The fields were full of moisture and the plowing was easy. The earth turned over behind the plow, dark and crumbling, and you smelled already the wheat harvest of the coming season which you knew would be the greatest harvest we had ever known. The lime trucks began moving across the remaining worn-out high pastures, raising visions of deep, thick clover. In the desolated oat fields of the Conservancy farm and on the poor strips of the Bailey Place the sweet clover stood deep and rank. The new season had begun.

One more disaster in the "Bad Year" still lay ahead—a hard frost with a clear, full moon which burned the alfalfa and the grapes before they were ripe and covered all the landscape of Pleasant Valley with glittering white rime. For a moment our pride rose again, even in a bad year, for our corn was ripe and hard, while to the west of us in *real* corn country thousands of acres of corn had been frosted while still green and soft. And then came the warm, clear weather of October, brilliant with the deep green of the new springing rye and wheat and the burning colors of the forest. From brilliant blue skies the sun shone all day long while the work for the new season went on its way and all hearts sang.

What was past was past but 1947 would go down among the legends of our Valley as the "Bad Year," the worst year that any of us, even old Mr. Tucker who was over ninety-one and had lived all his life in the Valley, could remember. We would be proud again of our fields and we would feel a certain wicked satisfaction when other fields looked worse than our own but after the bad year it would always be a pride that was not quite so confident.

The Cycle of a Farm Pond

Of the three ponds at Malabar, the low, shallow one at the Fleming Place is the most productive of big fish. This is so because it is the oldest and the richest in vegetation. It was made out of an old ox-bow left when Switzer's Run was foolishly straightened by the County Commissioners before we came here. We raised the banks about two feet by a day's work with hand shovels and thus raised the water level by the same depth. It is fed by a big spring in the bottom which has increased its flow by at least one hundred percent since we began keeping the rainfall where it fell on our land, and by the flow of an abandoned gas well which has turned into a first-rate artesian well flowing hundreds of gallons a minute of ice-cold water. Drainage from the neighboring barnyard during heavy rain occasionally reaches the pond and fertilizes the heavy vegetation in it. It is a comparatively shallow pond with a gravel bottom long since stopped tight by layers of decaying water vegetation.

The natural balance and cycle of this pond is very nearly perfect. The population is made up of bass, bluegills, sunfish and innumerable hybrid variations of the sunfish family which occur in fish ponds. There is also a single large carp caught by the children in Switzer's Run as a small fish and dumped into the pond along with a miscellaneous assortment of minnows, shiners, suckers, etc. All but the carp have long since disappeared, devoured by the big bass. On the richness of the table set for him by Nature beneath the surface of the water, the carp has grown to nearly three feet in length and must weigh in the neighborhood of thirty pounds. He is occasionally accompanied by a gigantic goldfish which seems to have for him a romantic attachment—a situation not unusual since carp and goldfish belong to the same family and in Lake Erie where huge goldfish, descended from a few which escaped from a pond in Cleveland years ago during flood times, are not uncommon and frequently breed with the big carp to create new crossbred strains puzzling of identification to the amateur and sometimes to the commercial fishermen who find them in their nets.

The goldfish also came into the Fleming pond through no design but through the zeal of the children who, several years ago, dumped into the pond a dozen fingerling-size goldfish bought at Woolworth's. On the rich diet of the pond they have grown to eighteen inches and more in length and to a weight of two or three pounds. They are very fat and lumbering and awkward beside the swift-moving streamlined bass and bluegills and have the appearance of red-gold galleons wallowing through the deep green-blue water moss and weeds. Some have the appearance of large luminous streamlined carp and others have long flowing tails and fins which trail behind them in the clear blue water like the veils of brides. Some have their red-gold scales variegated with silver. It is easy to see why the Japanese and Chinese long ago regarded goldfish as works of art, of high artistic value in their shallow ornamented pools, and made a science and an art of breeding them into fantastic almost artificial shapes and colors. A glimpse of these big, brilliantly colorful fish seen moving through the gently undulating weeds in the blue, clear water from the high bank of the Fleming pond gives the beholder the sudden delight that comes from the contemplation of an old Chinese painting or from the luminous beauty of Redon's flower pictures.

Neither the goldfish nor the great carp belong in a properly managed Ohio fish pond but all efforts to remove them have failed. The goldfish, fat and contented, will sometimes nose about a worm-baited hook but never take the worm. The great carp has refused all baits persistently and has even managed to escape the marksmanship of the boys who regularly attempt to shoot him with a twenty-two calibre rifle.

However, beyond consuming some of the food supply of the pond, neither goldfish nor carp do any serious harm. I am not at all sure that they are not an asset in the cycle of the pond and to the food supply of the big, small-mouthed bass. They have never succeeded in producing a single surviving descendant and there is consequently no way of knowing whether the romance of the great carp and his love-lorn accompanying goldfish has ever been fruitful. Each year the goldfish gather, after the fashion of carp, in a herd in the shallowest water and there thrash about in the ecstasy of reproduction for several days at a time. But apparently the big bass immediately devour the roe or any young goldfish which by chance have hatched out. Thus they continue—the great carp and his fleet of goldfish cousins—to lead, if not a sterile existence, a fruitless one, taking their place in the cycle of pond life and producing a perpetual supply of caviar for the bass.

I have seen literally acres of great carp spawning in the shallow waters of the big Pleasant Hill Lake at the end of the farm in late May or June. In the late spring they gather from the deep holes of the Clear Fork and the deeper waters of the lake itself by some common and terrific urge and then move into the shallow waters where they indulge in a wild orgy of reproduction continuing for several days. At such times it is possible to walk in water up to one's knees among hundreds of thrashing, wallowing carp, which in their ecstasy pay little attention to one's presence—so little indeed that it is possible to knock them over with blows of a club. In Lake Erie at spawning time, the big carp put on a similar performance in the shallow waters along the beaches and boys amuse themselves by shooting at them with rifles.

The fresh-water shad which exist in great numbers in the waters of the lake and the Clear Fork have another way of spawning. They will gather in schools on the surface of fairly deep water and swarm and flash, jumping in and out of the water in the brilliant sunlight of June. They are prodigiously fecund and reproduce themselves by the hundred thousands and their offspring are devoured in great quantities by the big bass which fit into the cycle of life in the streams, ponds, and lakes of most of the Mississippi basin. So intent do the shad become during the season of breeding that you can swim among them while they continue their gyrations and silvery leaps above the surface of the clear, blue water.

There are no shad in our ponds but their place is taken in the pond cycle by the bluegills and sunfish which also reproduce themselves in prodigious numbers. Tom Langlois of the Ohio Fish Laboratories, one of the great authorities on mid-American fresh-water

fish, tells me that not only are there many distinct and identifiable members of the sunfish family, but that they have an indiscriminate way of crossbreeding an infinite number of variations. Many of these are sterile, like the mule, and each year go through the fiercely compulsive process of breeding and laying eggs without producing anything. It appears also that the urge to breed overtakes them earlier in the season than it does the accepted and recognized members of the sunfish family. Very often they will pre-empt the available nesting grounds on shallow gravel beds in their fruitless and sterile efforts and fiercely fight off the fertile members of their tribe when these attempt a little later to find nesting places, a fact that can upset the regular cycle of pond life and food supply within the pond.

The mating habits of many fish and of most of the sunfish family in particular are fascinating to observe. In our ponds, they begin to nest about the end of May and all along the edges of the ponds in shallow waters, you will find them in great numbers beginning to clear away the mud or the decayed vegetation that cover the clean gravel which they like for nesting purposes.

The bass, the bluegills and the other members of the sunfish family all follow a similar urge and procedure. Each one will select, not without considerable fighting, a chosen site and then begin to clear off the silt or decayed vegetation that has settled over the gravel during the year. Each one will take a place above his selected site and without moving either backward or forward will set up a fluttering motion with his fins which in turn creates a current in the water that washes the gravel clean. This procedure sometimes requires a day or two of work. When the gravel has been washed clean and a slight depression of from one to two inches deep has been created (similar in appearance beneath the water to the nest of the killdeer plover which lays its eggs and hatches its young on a nest of gravel on the adjoining dry ground), the female will deposit her eggs in the nest and the male will swim over them and fertilize them. From then on the duty of guarding the nest becomes that of the male and until the young are hatched he will remain over the nest, moving his fins very gently, unless another fish of any species comes within an eighteen-inch radius of the center of the nest. Then he will attack furiously until the molesting fish is driven off. The bluegills and some varieties of sunfish build their nests in clusters side by side, each with a male fish fiercely guarding his own nest and darting angrily at his nearest neighbors if they attempt to cross the invisible line which guards his nursery from that of his neighbors.

I am not certain that the male fish is aware of the exact moment when the tiny fish he has fathered hatch, nor of how long the period of gestation is but overnight the whole pond will become infested with millions of tiny fish no bigger than a pin which move about in schools of thousands and promptly seek refuge in very shallow water or among the algae which by the time they have hatched covers large areas of the pond. There would seem to be some purpose in the presence of the algae as a protection for the tiny fish not only because its fabric makes it impossible for the big bass to swallow the young fish in a single sweeping gulp but because the larger fish find the algae itself distasteful and unpalatable. I have observed that even the smallest filament of algae attached by accident to a baited hook or fly will prevent the bigger fish from swallowing or striking at the bait.

I doubt that the male fish is aware of the moment when the young fry hatch out and flee the nest for the safety of the very shallow waters or of the webbed, clinging algae. I suspect that very often, driven by an urge which covers a comparatively fixed period well overlapping the period of gestation, the male fish often remains on guard long after the roe have hatched and fled the nest.

In certain parts of the pond which the fish have chosen as nesting and spawning beds, the whole character of the pond bottom has changed over a period of years. On bottoms which once were clay and muddy, the clay-mud element has been entirely washed away by the motions of countless small fins season after season until they have become clean, gravel shelves, bars and beaches. If, as sometimes happens during the spawning season, which usually coincides with a season of rains and thundershowers, floodwaters cover the nests with a thin layer of silt, the male fish will immediately and frantically go to work washing away the deposit of silt to make the nests clean once more.

During the spawning season, the male becomes fierce and even the little male bluegill will stand by his particular nest and give battle to a stick or a finger thrust into the water near him. I have had my finger "bitten" by big male bass when I thrust my hand into the water above his nest. At other times when the fish are not nesting my mere presence on the bank or a shadow cast over the water will suffice to send them in a darting brilliant course into deeper water.

All of these elements play their part in the "balance" of a good fish pond. The algae and vegetation shelter and produce vast quantities of minute animal life upon which the fiercely fecund and reproductive small-mouthed, purse-lipped bluegills and sunfish largely feed along with the flies and insects which fall on the surface of the ponds during the long, hot, insect-breeding months on a fertile Middle Western farm. In turn the small-mouthed sunfish produce millions of small fish which provide food for the big, predatory bass and trout and some of the larger-mouthed and predatory green sunfish.

Weather and flood conditions occasionally alter the nesting habits not only of fish but of marsh-nesting birds. During the disastrously wet spring and summer of 1947 the red-winged blackbirds provided a remarkable example of the effect of weather upon nesting habits. These lovely birds which normally nest among the sedge grass and bulrushes of marshes, creek banks and ponds, abandoned their usual habits and took to nesting on the high ground in the alfalfa fields. When I began mowing alfalfa in mid-June I started up considerable numbers of fledglings just old enough to fly and found several old abandoned nests set into clumps of alfalfa exactly as the birds normally set their nests in a clump of sedge or marsh grass. The fact raises again the old question of whether birds by some instinct are aware in advance of weather or the exact time of changing seasons. The migration time of many birds varies a great deal. In this case I do not know whether the birds anticipated the floods which later inundated their usual low-ground nesting places or whether they took to the higher ground because the whole of the spring had produced continuously flooding rains and abnormally high water. In the same season of disturbed and turbulent water in the ponds, the sunfish and bass did not breed and nest until five or six weeks later than usual. Whether they attempted to do so earlier at the normal time and found their efforts thwarted or whether their later nesting and breeding period produced the usual results I do not know. In that same summer, the red-winged blackbirds developed or at least exhibited habits that in my observation were new and strange. They appeared in great numbers, indeed in flocks, following the mower and gorging themselves on the leafhoppers which infested the alfalfa. Except at migrating time the red-winged blackbirds had generally flown about in pairs or occasionally appeared in groups of five or six all of the same sex. It scarcely seems possible that the birds through nesting on high ground suddenly and for the first time discovered the leafhoppers as a rich source of food supply. The occurrence, however, was one more proof of the benefit to the farmer of supplying adequate cover in fence rows or isolated patches of undergrowth and marshland for the bird population.

In the same season the killdeer plovers, which also nest on low ground along creeks, made no apparent change in their nesting habits. They are among the most careless of nest-builders, taking no trouble at all beyond hollowing out a shallow nest on a bare spot of gravel or sand in a low pasture by a creek. Presumably the eggs and the young killdeer which were not yet old enough to leave the nest were destroyed by the floods. Like quail, however, the young of the killdeer are extremely precocious and leave the nest very early, running about on the sandbanks and on the short bluegrass pasture even before they are able to fly. The young of the red-winged blackbird, on the other hand, must be fully feathered and well grown before they are able to leave the nest. They live almost entirely in the air or by clinging to high bulrushes and weeds, rarely making excursions on the ground as walking birds.

The green sunfish is the broad general name in our part of the country for a group of fish with varying characteristics. Although they rarely attain a length of more than eight inches, there is no fish which fights more gamely. Indeed, if their size is taken into consideration, I know of no fresh- or salt-water fish which puts up so valiant a fight. They are, so far as I have been able to discover, the only group of the minor sunfish which feed upon the young of other fish. I have observed them greedily pursuing young bass which is a little like the fox turning upon the hounds. Naturally they are equipped with much bigger mouths than the other minor sunfish and some of them actually resemble closely small bass in appearance. When they get out of balance in a pond or lake they may become a menace even to the predatory bass population. The green sunfish is altogether a very aggressive little fish and a gallant fighter which will provide good sport on a light fly rod.

All will take a worm from a hook and, of course, artificial flies, but at times it is difficult to take the bluegills or some of the varieties of sunfish because of the extreme smallness of their mouths. The bass, even the small-mouth which is the variety which inhabits our ponds, has an immense mouth and gullet, sometimes making up very nearly half his length. The great mouth and gullet permits him to swallow a good-sized sunfish at a single gulp. In the case of the Fleming pond, the bass provide an absolute check or block upon the increase of carp or goldfish by devouring their roe or their young very soon after they are hatched.

This process and control and the operation of a natural cycle and balance of life is observable not only in ponds but in the free, open, fresh-water streams. In almost any clear running stream with abundant vegetation throughout most of the Mississippi basin, the balance and life-cycle will include some carp and catfish as well as bass, crappies and other members of the sunfish, game fish family. If the stream becomes polluted either by sewage or siltation or is swept clean of vegetation by periodic floods, the balance is upset and the game fish will gradually disappear and the mud-loving fish will presently dominate in overwhelming numbers until gradually and finally only coarse mud-loving fish—carp, catfish, et al.—alone exist.

This has been the history of many once fine fishing streams and lakes in the Mississippi basin where either sewage pollution from cities or steadily increasing siltation coming from ignorantly and poorly managed farm lands gradually produce conditions which exterminate all the game fish and leave only the coarse fish and finally exterminate all stream life save turtles and frogs.

This is what happened to countless streams in the South which were once famous for good sport fishing. Increasing erosion has turned many of them at certain times of the year into what is little more than a mass of viscous, thin, slow-flowing mud in which all fish life becomes impossible.

For the sportsmen this gives the problem of soil and water conservation and reckless deforestation an important place in the scheme of things. In the past, stream after stream, pond after pond, and bay after bay in the bigger lakes which were once famous fishing grounds for sportsmen have been reduced, by incessant floods and siltation coming from bare, poorly farmed fields, to the category of coarse, mud-fish territory or of no fish at all. In Lake Erie even the commercial fishing business, representing millions of dollars a year, is being threatened by the pollution of the big industrial cities and the siltation of spawning beds in its shallower waters. On the other hand, in a few streams in limited areas where good soil, water and forestry practices have come into existence, clean water and vegetation have come back into the streams, ponds, and lakes, and periodic floods have been largely eliminated with the result that in streams which only a few years ago had been reduced to the level of coarse-fish carp and catfish waters, the proper balance and cycle is being restored and the waters are becoming known again as fine places for game fishing.

In our own farm ponds every effort has been made to prevent siltation. The practice of proper forestry and soil conservation and a program of grass farming has reduced siltation virtually to zero, and after and even during the heaviest rainfall the excess water reaching at least two of the ponds is as clear as the rainwater itself. In one pond the water becomes discolored from the run-off of a neighboring gravel lane which cannot be controlled, but the siltation amounts to little more than discoloration and is mostly very fine sand which settles quickly leaving the water clear and blue after a short time. Under these conditions the balance of aquatic life quickly establishes itself and the ponds rapidly become filled with too many fish, so that fishing becomes not only a pleasure but a duty, for unfished ponds existing under proper conditions need no stocking; on the contrary it is necessary to fish them constantly in order to keep down the population. Otherwise the population exceeds the food supply and the pond becomes filled with innumerable fish which are too small either for good sport or for food.

The pond on the Fleming Place has long since reached the point of ideal balance and cycle. If fished steadily it goes on producing quantities of big game fish providing both unlimited sport and "fish for supper" for every family on the farm as often as they want it. Because the pond is a fertile one filled with vegetation, it produces a constant supply of food for small fish and the small-mouthed sunfish which in turn provide food for the bass and the bigger fish. The cycle of production for sport and food is constant and prodigious despite the fact that the pond is little over an acre in size. Constant fishing is in itself a part of the cycle of abundance since the pond is land-locked and would quickly become overpopulated and the fish small and bony if a considerable poundage of fish were not removed from it annually.

The Fleming pond is an old pond. Those on the Anson and the Bailey Places are newer. The one on the Anson Place was constructed fourteen years ago and the one on the Bailey Place nine years ago. In the Anson pond the perfect balance and cycle has not yet established itself. It is a deep pond with a comparatively small amount of shallow water. In the beginning no stocking was done, save the fish caught in other ponds or in neighboring streams and dumped into it. Two years ago about five hundred fingerling rainbow trout were put in. The fish from local ponds and streams were largely bluegills and varieties of sunfish with a few suckers and minnows. Among them were a score and more of big small-mouth bass weighing from one to two pounds upward. These were taken out of the older Fleming pond which at the end of each summer is cleaned systematically by worm and hook fishing to eliminate the biggest fish which turn cannibal and devour not only the "food fish" within the pond cycle but also the young and half-grown bass.

Of all the fish put into the pond on the Anson Place, the minnows and suckers very quickly were eliminated, either by being eaten or by going out of the outlet into the flowing streams which were much more their natural habitat than the still ponds. A heavy winter following the transplantation of the big bass kept the pond frozen over solidly and the lack of oxygen and sunlight was apparently too much for the bass for when the ice thawed in the spring nearly all of them were floating dead on its surface. They never had a chance to nest or breed.

Fish ponds and even lakes of considerable size throughout Ohio suffered similar losses of the bass and some other fish during the same severe winter. Open streams did not suffer similar losses because the movement of the water kept them open wherever there were ripples. Ponds, of course, are not the natural or ideal habitat for the small-mouthed bass which prefers streams, varied by deep pools and swift-flowing water over steep gradients. The fish for which the pond is a natural habitat suffered much less from the shortage of oxygen and sunlight.

As it turned out, this worked into the plan of control on the Anson pond. Its waters ran to a depth of twenty feet and it was spring-fed both at the inlet and from springs in the bottom and even in the hottest days of August the deeper water remained cold, at a temperature of about fifty degrees. This depth and temperature made it a possibility as a trout pond. Trout could never have survived in the old shallow Fleming pond which was too warm and which already contained a flourishing population of bass. We found long ago that trout and bass cannot exist indefinitely in the same waters; the bass inevitably exterminate the trout, perhaps because they have much bigger mouths and can outswallow the trout both in number and size of fish. Therefore, the elimination of the big bass by a severe winter left the deep, cold, six-year-old Anson pond ready for stocking by trout, especially since the food supply of the smaller fecund sunfish of all varieties was already well established.

Rainbow or brown trout were chosen as the most likely to flourish in the Anson pond and eventually we put in the five hundred fingerlings not more than three or four inches in length. During the first summer there was no evidence of them whatever. They were never seen at all, either alive or floating dead upon the surface, and I came to the disappointing conclusion that they had all left the pond through the open outlet. When spring came the following year there was still no evidence of the rainbows. None of them were seen either dead or alive or in the shallow waters where the sunfish could be watched nesting.

During the first six years of the pond's existence, following the "amateur" stocking of native fish from neighboring ponds and streams, the fish population increased immensely until by spring it became evident that there were far too many fish and that we should have to go to "work" fishing them out. There were thousands of them, mostly too small for table use. When we went to work, we made a remarkable discovery. Among the scores of fish which we took out as rapidly as the hook struck the water, more than ninety-nine per-cent were of two varieties—either long-eared or green sunfish with some odd unidentifiable hybrids. There being no big predatory fish in the pond, we came to the conclusion that these two varieties had survived and dominated because the green sunfish had the biggest mouths. They could swallow the other varieties of smaller, purse-mouthed sunfish like the bluegill, the punkin-seed and even the long-eared sunfish. They had simply eaten the other fish out of ex-istence, and themselves had no control placed upon them since the small-mouthed fish could not swallow them once they were above a certain size, even if they had been inclined to include other fish as legitimate articles of diet which, as a rule, the small-mouthed fish do not do.

In any case, we were made sharply aware of the vast population of green sunfish, which I suspect in our case, may have been a crossbred variety in that particular pond, for their mouths and gullets appear to be much larger than the ordinary green sunfish described and pic-tured in all books dealing with the fish of the Mississippi basin.

These voracious green sunfish, although they never attain much size even under favorable conditions—and I have seen only a few that approached a pound in weight—make excellent sport with a fly rod. They take the fly with a rush and ounce for ounce put up a fiercer and longer fight than any trout or bass. That summer we did not look for sport in the Anson pond so much as to reduce the population of fish, so we used cane poles and worms to fish. Even with this steady tackle, I have seen the little fellows take a worm on the rush and bend the bamboo pole halfway to double.

"Cleaning" a pond to reduce the fish population is a pleasurable procedure. Armed with cane pole and worms and with a big milk can at one's side we take fish after fish off the hook at half-minute intervals and throw them into the milk-can for transference to a new pond or to the neighboring streams, but there is not much real excitement in it. At times eight or ten of us will spend an evening simply "cleaning" a pond.

I began the "cleaning" process when the Anson pond was six years old to cut down the population of green sunfish and I got my excitement, even with a bamboo pole and worm-baited hook, when, after I had half-filled the milk can with fish, the bait was taken by a fish which behaved differently from the ones I had been catching. I brought him to the surface and the sight of his silvery speckled body gave me one of the thrills of a long fishing career. He was no sunfish. He was a rainbow trout, ten inches in length, one of the five hundred I had put in a year earlier and bemoaned as lost. He was not only still in the pond but he had grown in the span of a year from three inches to ten. I raised him reverently from the water. I had hooked him through the cartilage around the mouth and he was unhurt. Reverently I threw him back into the pond to go on growing into a two or three pound big fellow who later on will make wonderful sport and wonderful eating.

And about every tenth fish we took out in the process of "cleaning" was a handsome, silvery, speckled fellow, one of the rainbow fingerlings we had put in a year earlier. Most of them were uninjured and were put back to grow some more.

It is clear what happened. The trout fingerlings stayed in the clear, cold, deep water and never appeared in the warm shallow water where the sunfish nested, frolicked and ate. They are still staying most of the time in the deep, cold water but now the fingerlings are big enough to go foraging into the shallow haunts of the sunfish, clearly in search of food which meant that they were after the young sunfish. The latter are now having competition from predatory fish with as big or bigger mouths than their own and it is probable that a balance and cycle like that between bass and sunfish in the older Fleming pond will establish itself between trout and sunfish in the Anson pond. In the evenings we see the trout foraging on the surface for insects.

The vegetation and life growing in the algae of the pond are clearly already sufficient to support a considerable population of food sunfish, enough to give the rainbow trout as fat a diet as the bass already have in the older Fleming pond. Whether the trout whose breeding habits are different from those of the bass-sunfish family will manage to reproduce themselves as rapidly as the bass have done in the Fleming pond or even at all, remains to be seen. I am hopeful. If they do, the productivity and balance of the newer pond will be established and we shall, in order to maintain it at the maximum level of food and sport, have to fish it regularly, a hardship any fisherman is willing to suffer when it means that he is getting fish from a pound to four or five pounds, all fighters whether they are big bluegills and sunfish or bass or rainbow trout.

The life cycle of fish is a subject of some dispute among scientists and, to be sure, varies greatly with the species. Legend has it that there are carp in the moats and ponds of Fontainebleau and Chantilly which were there at the time of François Premier and guides point to the rings set in the snouts of the huge, mangy old carp with the statement that they were thus ringed two hundred years ago. All this may be true for certainly the carp are immensely old and very large. Recently a female sturgeon weighing 175 pounds was taken in Lake Erie and the press attributed to it an age of over a hundred years. This particular fish was a female and yielded many pounds of caviar at the time of the catch. It is a sad fact that the sturgeon population of the Great Lakes like that of many other fish, has been steadily decreasing as siltation, sewage and industrial pollution has increased.

Growth and size of fish and perhaps their age are determined largely by food supply. A green sunfish in the controlled Fleming pond will reach what is apparent maximum size much more rapidly than in the Anson pond where the population of its own kind, feeding upon its own diet, is much too great at present. In the Fleming pond where its food is abundant, a bass will reach a weight of three or four pounds in approximately the same number of years. The largest bass taken from the pond weighed a little over five pounds. I do not know its exact age. But because the Fleming pond is comparatively small and shallow it is possible to observe and check with a considerable degree of accuracy the age and growth of the fish. There always appears to be at least four sizes: (1) The newly hatched pin-sized fry. Those which survive apparently reach a length of three to four inches in one season. (2) The two-year-olds which at the end of the second season have grown from the four-inch length to a length of eight or more inches. (3) The three-year-old crop which runs a foot to eighteen inches. (4) Those fish of all sizes above eighteen inches which are the biggest ones and whose cannibalistic habits with regard to the five- to eight-inch bass lead us to clear them out of the pond at the end of each summer.

The newest of theories among fish experts is that if a pond or stream provides the proper conditions, and is not subject to violent periodic flooding, siltation or pollution and the food supply is adequate, there is no need for stocking and that, on the contrary, there is a need to fish the stream or pond constantly in order to control the population and secure bigger fish and better sport.

The Ohio State Conservation Commission, of which the author is a member, has opened several lakes and some streams where the food and control conditions are right and pollution is virtually non-existent, to unrestricted fishing without season, size or bag limit, and the results tend to show over a short period of time that such wholesale fishing improves both the size and quality of the fish without diminishing the amount of the catch. Other states are making similar experiments and if the final results are in line with the early indication of the experiment it is likely that stocking fish in polluted or heavily silted streams where they cannot live or reproduce will be abandoned, together with bag and season restrictions, and the emphasis and expenditure of taxpayers' money will be diverted from expensive fish hatcheries and stocking programs to the cleaning up of streams and lakes and the establishment of conditions which permit and encourage almost unlimited fish populations which actually *demand* unrestricted fishing to keep their populations in control.

Among the great and beautiful artificial lakes created in the Tennessee Valley Authority area all restrictions as to season, bag and size limit have been removed. The result has been to create a veritable fisherman's paradise. The creation of proper conditions, clean water, vegetation, etc., has proven that legal rules on take, season, etc., are unnecessary and that actually the more fish taken the better the fishing becomes. This is both a reasonable and scientific procedure since a single female bass will produce as many as a hundred thousand and upward of eggs which when fertilized become small fry. Sunfish, crappies and coarse fish reproduce themselves at an even more prodigious rate. Not long ago I happened along the shore of Pleasant Hill Lake at the end of the farm when a Conservation Commission employee was dumping five thousand fingerling small-mouth bass into the lake. As he poured the bass into the lake he remarked cynically, "Each one of these fish cost a lot of money to produce and all this stocking is a lot of hooey. Maybe it makes some ignorant sportsmen feel they're getting something, but a couple of pairs of good bass could do the same job without any expense at all." The man was not a scientist. He was an unskilled laborer but he had learned a great deal of wisdom through observation. I am told that in Colorado where hatchery-raised trout are introduced into streams, the cost of each trout is about $4.75. This, of course, is paid out of the sportsman license fees which could be expended far more profitably in providing clean streams and proper habitat where the fish could reproduce themselves successfully by the million. The new belief that money expended upon clean streams and habitat is better spent than on hatcheries and stocking is growing among state fish and game commissions and sportsmen generally. The same theory is spreading to the realm of hatchery bred and stocked quail, pheasant, partridge, to raccoon "farms" and all fields of game conservation and propagation.

This is a revolutionary idea, but it is also a wise development in reason, science and common sense. If the streams and lakes of the country were cleaned of pollution and siltation and floods checked by proper agricultural and forestry methods, there would be fine fishing in unlimited quantity for the whole of the population which enjoys fishing. Certainly our own experience with both ponds and streams has proven that this is true and that fishing becomes not only a sport but at times a duty and occasionally a real job.

One of the most fascinating spectacles in the world is the fashion in which Nature herself will take over a naked, newly constructed pond and set to work to make it into an old fertile pond in which natural controls are set up throughout the whole cycle of its life.

We have had an opportunity during the past years to observe the process in the case of the new ponds constructed and particularly the one on the Bailey Place. The site chosen for this pond was the corner of a field which even in midsummer was too wet for use as cultivated ground. Nearby was a very fine, big spring and several smaller ones as a source of water. In two days' work with a big bull-dozer and scoop a pond was constructed of about three acres in size varying from under a foot to fourteen feet in depth. The shallow area is large and makes an ideal feeding and breeding ground for fish once aquatic life is fully established. The barrier was made by excavating the soil from the bottom of the pond and piling it up as a dam which also serves as a roadway to and from adjoining fields.

Nearly seven weeks were required to fill the pond to its full depth for some of the water evaporated and much of it seeped through the bare, newly created bottom.

Watching the pond carefully, I observed a number of things. The first life to appear was the native killdeer, accompanied now and then by a dozen or more of their cousins, the rare golden plover. They waded about, crying and fluttering apparently in delight over the shallow rising water. They did not appear to feed but simply to wade about screaming and flapping their wings. Then a few frogs appeared from the damp spots in the neighboring fields and numbers of water skaters and water beetles. In the water warmed by the sun a few thin strands of algae, possibly carried in on the feet of the killdeer and plovers, appeared and began to grow in long strands, like the green hair of mermaids, and presently as the frogs increased in number the smaller herons appeared, and at last the pair of great blue herons which had been with us winter and summer for six years and ranged the ponds and the shallows of the big lake at the end of the farm, acknowledged the existence of the new pond by visits to do a little frog hunting. What new life they brought to the pond clinging to their feet or in their excreta I do not know, but they too undoubtedly made their contribution to the growing, expanding life of the pond.

On the naked sides and on the newly constructed dam we put a layer of barnyard manure and sowed rye to bind the soil with its deep, wide-spreading fibrous roots and stop all erosion. In the manure there must have been millions of undigested seeds of ladino clover and other plants for there quickly grew up a carpet of vegetation which included ryegrass and bluegrass, white, sweet, red alsike and ladino clovers, and within a few weeks all danger of erosion or siltation from the naked soil surrounding the pond was eliminated. Even after a heavy rain the water remained clear. The apparent high rate of germination in the manure-sown clover seeds could doubtless be traced back a season or two to the activities of thirty hives of bees which we keep on the farm to provide honey and pollenize the legumes. During all that first summer the level of the pond continued to rise and fall, varying according to the seepage in the pond bottom as it settled itself. By autumn there was a thick growth of algae over a considerable part of the surface. The winter came, the vegetation froze hard, the frogs and beetles disappeared, the killdeer and plover went south and the great blue herons abandoned visiting the pond for the richer, shallower, unfrozen waters of the big lake. Then the pond froze over and went dormant.

With the coming of spring, the ice melted and presently the crying of frogs and spring peepers was heard from along the shallow edges. The vegetation came back with a rush. Then in the shallows occurred the mating orgies of the hundreds of toads which appeared out of nowhere, and presently great strands of frog and toad spawn appeared in the shallow waters. In the same shallow waters the coarse hardy dock plants, submerged the summer before where they grew, thrust their tough heads up through the water and presently began to turn yellow and drown to slow death to be supplanted by the new growth of seedlings and water grasses brought in as seeds clinging to the feet of water birds. And the seepage problem seemed to have solved itself. The pond had settled, the weight of the water closing up the open places in the bottom. And the algae had done its part for with the coming of winter it had sunk to the bottom and laid a network of fine webbing over the whole of the pond bottom. The clay which had been squashy the season before so that when you waded into the pond you sank very nearly to your knees, became firm and hard under the weight of tons of water and remained only a little sticky on the top surface. What had once been a naked excavation walled in by a naked earthen dam had become within a year a watertight reservoir, its banks covered with protective vegetation, its shallow waters alive with vegetable and animal life.

The beetles and water skaters and water flies reappeared in vastly greater numbers and presently the shallow water was filled by millions of animated exclamation points that were tadpoles. And along the banks one came upon various kinds of water snakes which had discovered the new pond and taken up residence there to feed upon the young frogs and fish which their instinct told them would soon provide a rich source of food. But most curious of all, there appeared presently in a pond completely shut off from outside waters, among the myriad tadpoles, a few pin-sized fish. Where they came from I do not know unless the eggs became attached somehow to the feet of the plovers and herons as they waded over the nests of fish in the other ponds or in Switzer's Creek. They were, at the time, still too small to be identified as to species save through the use of a magnifying glass or microscope. The eggs may have remained wet, the germ still living during the flight of the birds from one pond to another or from the creek or the shallows of the big lake at Pleasant Hill dam. Those who live near to water know that in the business of carrying on life, Nature can be incredibly tough and resistant and overwhelming. As the summer progressed all of these small fry turned into varieties of sunfish indicating that their origin probably lay in neighboring ponds.

In the case of the frogs and tadpoles which appeared early during the second year of life in the pond, we were indeed overwhelmed. The tadpoles appeared by the thousands in the shallow waters and presently were turned into myriads of small frogs, mostly of the handsome green and black-spotted leopard varieties, none of them too big to sit comfortably on a silver half-dollar. As we walked along the banks they went into a panic and leaped into the water like flights of grasshoppers in a grasshopper year. One could understand easily the Old Testament plague of frogs brought upon Egypt in Moses' time. One could understand too why Nature produced tiny frogs in such vast quantities for their behavior during panic was idiotic and made them an easy victim of any predator, snake, fish, or raccoon. As one approached, they went into a panic-stricken hysterical flight, some jumping into the water, some away from the water. The truth was that the new pond, still partly undeveloped by Nature and with no natural balance established, contained not yet enough enemies and predators to cope with the prodigious fecundity of the frogs which produced in the scheme of things thousands of frogs in order that a few score might survive. There were in the waters of the pond no bass or trout or pike which would have made short work of the hysterical young frogs which leaped into the open water, and not yet enough snakes, raccoons and herons to devour the more foolish of their numbers on land or in the very shallow waters.

It is easy to see how the frogs of the world, unhampered by natural checks and predators, could soon increase to such numbers that they would overrun everything, fill the whole of the land, and leave no room for the rest of us.

The muskrats were certain to be the next settlers at the new pond. Always in the second year they make their appearance, coming up the narrow silver thread of overflow water in the moonlight from the marshes in the Jungle, a wild piece of wet land in the middle of the farm, and from the marshes about the big lake where they exist by the thousand. One rarely sees them save sometimes in the moonlight when the nose of a muskrat moves across the ponds leaving a long V-shaped wake behind it in the still, silvery waters. One rarely sees them but the evidence of their presence is all around the edges of the pond, in the holes they dig for dens in the banks, in the nibbled foliage of certain plants and in the runways they make along the edges of the streams that feed the ponds. Usually they migrate during the second winter of the life of a pond and once they are established they like the easy living and remain there. When their numbers exceed the food supply, the younger ones go back to the marshes about the big lakes which are a muskrat's paradise.

The ones which remain are an endless source of trouble. They devour the succulent roots of the water lilies and the bull rushes and the tender underwater shoots of the arrowleaf which we try to establish in a new pond, and they attack even the tubers of the irises in the flower garden only fifty feet from the house. Two years ago during a hard winter when the ponds were frozen over for three months they burrowed beneath a tree wisteria and ate off all its roots so that in the spring, it simply fell over, rootless and dead. They burrowed into the dams and threatened to destroy them until we discovered that twenty-four-inch chicken wire laid along the dam at the surface of the water, where they like to dig, prevented further burrowing. They are tough and shrewd and sly and prolific and no amount of trapping by the boys on the farm, who pick up a good many extra dollars that way during the winter, either intimidates or discourages them. Now and then one of the dogs catches a foolish young muskrat offside and ends his career, but the dogs do not serve as a sufficient check upon the fecundity of the water rodents. There are no more wolves in our country but there is an abundance of foxes which at night bark from the wooded ridge back and forth in the moonlight. Save for the dogs they are the only check upon the woodchucks and the muskrat and they get only the young and foolish ones. A big muskrat is too shrewd for a fox and a big, old woodchuck can outfight him. Without the dogs, the woodchuck would, like the frogs, eventually take us over.

It must be said, however, that one of the last things we should desire at Malabar is the total extermination of woodchucks. The holes they dig and their generous hospitality in sharing them with other animals make them a great asset in building game and wild-life populations. Their holes serve at all times, but particularly during the winter months, as shelter and refuge for rabbit, quail, possum, skunks, partridges and other animals and birds. Female raccoon, when natural tree dens are scarce or nonexistent will house their litters in woodchuck holes. So valuable does the Ohio Conservation Commission consider the place of the woodchuck and the hole he digs in the whole cyclical balance of wildlife that in 1947 it established a closed season from March, when the woodchuck wakens to emerge from his hole, to August, by which time the young are able to take care of themselves. The ruling does not prevent a farmer from reducing the woodchuck population which gets out of control but it does put an end to the idiotic and unsportsmanlike habits of some city dwellers who go into the countryside merely to use the woodchuck for target practice. Among emigrant Southerners, both white and colored, woodchuck is considered a delicacy.

Rarely have I seen a muskrat by daylight and then only when ly-ing very still among the sedge grass and weeds, I have been so well hidden that he was unaware of my presence. His habit is to travel in the shallow water of a creek close to the bank and even though the water is clear he is difficult to notice or to see. The concealment arises less from his fantastically protective coloring than from the undulations of his wet shining body which are like the movements of the flowing water itself. He moves, half-swimming, half-walking with a flowing motion and only a sharp eye can detect his presence where there is any current at all.

Perhaps the most beautiful newcomers to the pond during the second summer were the dragonflies. They appeared in prodigious numbers, looking like gaudily painted miniature planes. At least three varieties were noticeable. One variety, the largest, was about three to four inches long, with purple-black body and with bars of black on the widespread transparent wings. Another smaller dragonfly came in various shades of green with deep emerald green wings. The third, smallest and most beautiful was a fragile dragonfly all of one color, an iridescent turquoise blue with body which appeared to be almost transparent as it hovered over the surface of the water. All three varieties spend the whole of their brief lives in frantically eating and breeding. They dart and hover over the shallow water, the floating algae and the water weeds, devouring hosts of tiny gnats, mosquitoes and other insects which deposit their eggs in the water where they hatch into larvae to feed the sunfish as well. The prodigious number of dragonflies over the new pond probably arose from the fact that the fish population has not yet become established to devour the larvae and act as a check upon the almost unlimited increase of insects.

The great numbers of hatching insects brought not only hordes of the delicate dragonflies, but wild, soaring flights of deep, iridescent blue and red swifts and barn swallows which each year build their neat mud nests on the beams of the big Bailey barn beside the pond. In the evenings they circle, hover and dive-bomb the newly hatched insects, dipping their tiny, swift wings into the water, sending up tiny jets of spray in the evening light.

Of course, within the depths of the new pond there came quickly into existence trillions of amoebae, rotifers and tiny plants and animals invisible to the naked eye which flourish in the warm shallow waters of ponds and in the form of fresh-water plankton which makes up a large part of the food supply of the fish from the smallest pin-sized fry up through the larger sunfish. These animals and plants, seen under a microscope, reveal complicated and brilliantly beautiful patterns of life. Although invisible they comprise a vital part of the natural life cycle of a pond. Doubtless they are carried there upon the feet of birds and muskrats or the damp skin of frogs and on the bellies of slithering water snakes from adjoining ponds and streams. Many already existed in the wet ground of the pond site. The Natural History Museum in New York City contains a truly wonderful exhibit of these organisms executed brilliantly in colored glass many thousands of times larger than life.

Nature has a million subtle ways of quickly converting a raw, new pond into an old pond, fertile and teeming with life, but in all our ponds we have helped her as much as possible to speed the rate of conversion. One thing which a good farmer quickly learns is that in fighting Nature he will always be defeated but that in working with her, he can make remarkable and immensely profitable progress. Beside the barnyard manure and the seeding of the banks we have thrust young willow butts here and there along the banks and every three or four feet along the crest of the dam. Within two or three years the fast-growing willows, the particularly beautiful and hardy, semi-weeping variety known as *Babylonica*, will grow twelve to fifteen feet and along the dam their roots create a solid mat which binds the earth together and makes it resistant to the waters of the most devastating cloudbursts. Along the edge they provide the shade which the big bass love and a resting place for insects which drop into the water and feed the hungry fish waiting below.

The Conservation Commissions of many states send out free to all farmers of the state bundles of shrubs and trees for planting around farm ponds. These hasten the efforts of Nature to convert a new pond into an old one and provide food and shelter for small game. The bundles include native flowering wild crabapple, standing honeysuckle, fruit-bearing viburnums, hazelnuts, pines and many other shrubs and trees. These are now planted in the areas about the ponds and help to build up that balance and cycle in the pond and the area about it which is a part of any successful fish pond. The new ponds are treated with fertilizer along the edges in the shallow water to encourage the growing of vegetation which plays so large a part in the cycle of pond fertility and life. A little fertilizer—particularly phosphate—will increase the number and size of the fish enormously. At Georgia State Agricultural College experiments with the fertilizing of fish ponds achieved an increase in fish production of up to five hundred pounds to the acre.

During the first summer of the Bailey pond's existence we transplanted to its borders a few roots of arrowleaf and some of the water plants already growing in the older ponds. It was a simple enough process, simply that of thrusting the roots into the soil in the shallow water. These took hold immediately and increased prodigiously during the summer, as much as many hundreds of times, joining the water and marsh vegetation already seeded there through visits of muskrats and water birds in providing shelter for all sorts of minute animal life as well as for the small fry which appeared mysteriously and those hatched out after the stocking of the new pond in the early spring with mature bass, bluegills and sunfish from the older ponds.

By the end of the second summer the first evidence of balance had become apparent. The plague of small frogs and toads had leveled off to a normal population, the number of dragonflies diminished and the whole cycle of birth, life, death and rebirth had begun to operate.

At the end of the third year the new pond on the Bailey Place already took on the aspect of the older ponds. The shallow water had been invaded by thick growths of arrowhead, bulrush, water lilies and a great variety of water grasses and subaqueous vegetation. Within the refuge they provide against the attacks of the bigger fish, the watersnakes and birds, there appeared in due course of time literally thousands of young bluegills, sunfish and young bass up to three or four inches in length. The fingerlings of the pound-size bluegills and the big bass which will make the sport of tomorrow.

The annual "cleaning" of the older ponds with bamboo poles, worms, and a couple of big milk cans, transferring fish wholesale from the fertile older ponds into the newer ones, is a serious task that becomes a sport in which all the farm takes part. The boys, the older men and even some of the women join in, and in the crowded ponds every cast means a strike, and one never knows what one will get—a bluegill, a bass or any one of the varieties of sunfish and sometimes in the Anson pond, a nice-sized trout. Only the trout are thrown back because we want to establish in the Anson pond that cycle of trout and sunfish based upon the bass and sunfish cycle which has proven itself so productive in the old Fleming pond.

Fish after fish, the catch is tossed into the milk cans, kept aerated by changing the water and pouring in fresh bucketfuls constantly from the pond. There is a wide range of beauty in the catch from the lovely deep sea-green of the bass and the silvery-spotted beauty of the trout, through the whole range of sunfish up to the iridescent, fantastic beauty of the long-eared type with his brilliant yellow belly, his stripes and changeable colors and the jet-black spot behind his gills.

One night we sat among the willows along the old Fleming pond, fishing, nine of us, as the sun went down and a virgin crescent moon appeared as the sky changed from scarlet and gold to pale mauve to deep blue. The women sat in the grass shelling the glut of peas from the garden for canning and the quick freeze and the small children yelled with excitement each time they managed to hook and bring in a fish. We fished until it was too dark to see the bobber, and then set out with a flashlight to transfer the fish to the new ponds. There was at least thirty pounds of fish ranging in size from a few baby sunfish to a fine big bass of about four pounds which somehow had eluded us in "cleaning" the pond of big fellows the preceding autumn. And everyone had fresh fish for breakfast the next morning.

The farm pond is becoming rapidly not only a pleasure but a necessity. State Conservation Commissions are encouraging them. Ohio aids the individual farm without cost in their construction. Missouri plans to construct two-hundred thousand farm ponds during the next few years. They tend to catch and hold the precious rainfall on thousands of farms, to supply water for the livestock, swimming holes, and fish for the table. On our farm whenever a family wants fish for supper one has only to take a pole and a line and in a half-hour or more get all the fish he wants.

But there are other advantages to farm ponds which are not wholly utilitarian. Our ponds are each one a spot of beauty, a small

universe teeming with life. The big herons visit them and the lovely red-winged blackbirds build their nests in the rushes along the
borders. They are the delight of the big fierce Toulouse geese and
the tame mallards. They are the source of much music in the night
from the peeping of new young frogs to the booming bass of the big
Louisiana bullfrogs which we put in as tadpoles years ago and which
now measure as much as eighteen to twenty inches when stretched
out. In April their borders turn green and gold with the lush foliage
and flowers of the marsh marigold, and later they are bordered with
the blue of Siberian iris and the purple and gold of the native wild
flags. At night the muskrats move across the surface in the moonlight and the raccoons and foxes and possum come down out of the
thick woods to drink and catch unwary frogs, leaving the imprint of
their small paws in the wet mud along the banks. And there are the
scavenging mud turtles and a few big destructive snapping turtles
which the mallards avoid by shrewdly never taking their young onto
the ponds until they are well grown. And there are countless birds,
the swifts and barn swallows which skim low over the ponds in the
blue evenings, to catch the insects hatching from their depths, and
the flocks of goldfinches which finally mate off and build their nests
from the down of the purple thistles growing in the damp ground.
And in spring and autumn there are the visits of the wild ducks which
join our mallards and feast off the richness of the farm ponds and the
neighboring fields for three or four weeks at a time. For a lonely
farm a pond provides life and fascination.

Each year, spring and autumn, we have been accustomed to visits
of wild ducks. Usually these were mallards and so-called shallow-
water ducks, but with the establishment of the Bailey pond we began to receive visits from flocks of bluebills and other deep-water
ducks. We discovered presently that they were attracted by the tender shoots of the fast spreading arrowleaf, spending hours diving and
burrowing for the young growth. Wherever they burrowed their bills
left tiny holes in the mud bottom of the pond. Dessie and Al often sit
on the veranda of the big, old Bailey house in the evening watching
the life on the pond until darkness comes down, the swallows take to

the barn and the muskrats and raccoons come out to haunt the reeds and the shallow water.

In a way, a farm pond is a symbol of life itself. It is a bright spot on any farm, a whole universe in which the laws of Nature operate under the close and intimate gaze of the interested. One can find in farm ponds and along their borders almost everything. They change with the season, awakening from the frozen, silent sleep of winter, going into the beginning of spring and the fierce breeding life of early summer. They provide skating in winter and swimming in summer and good fishing for three seasons of the year, as well as an unlimited supply of water near all farm buildings in case of a fire. Around each pond, enclosed by a thick hedge of multiflora rose, which itself is the best all-game cover and source of food, there have been established small game reserves planted to sheltering pines and a great variety of food plants and shrubs. These have, in the wilder ponds, become impenetrable refuges for pheasant, quail, raccoon, rabbits—indeed every kind of wild life. Here they may hide in summer from killers, in the brilliant autumn from the hunter, and in midwinter they are sheltered from the blizzards and the cold northwest winds. For the children the ponds are a source of inexhaustible delight. And like the fish ponds of the abbeys and castles of medieval Europe and the Dark Ages, when all the world fell apart in anarchy and disorder, they provide not only food for the table but peace for the soul and an understanding of man's relationship to the universe.

All of the foregoing observations and experience are the results of the initial years of pond building, and as each pond at Malabar has aged, matured and taken on what might be described as a balanced and permanent state, other changes have occurred, and it is possible that more changes may occur in future years. These ponds and their changes are an endless source of interest and fascination, for the ponds never remain the same. Even the climate of a single summer will have its effects; a drought will produce one set of conditions and results, a wet summer quite a different one. Invasion by domestic ducks and geese, but especially ducks in large quantities, can revolutionize the conditions and ruin a pond as a place for good fishing. A sufficient number of ducks, especially in a shallow pond, can reduce its status to that of a mudhole. The harm done in a large deep pond, even by considerable numbers of ducks, is negligible save on the land area surrounding the water.

These ponds have of course continued to attract great numbers of birds of almost every kind, but particularly water and shore birds which for me always exert a fascination, since their migrations, their manners, their habits are frequently very special and more discernible at close range than those of the field birds or the hedge and meadow birds, and especially birds which, like the tanager, frequent the very depths of our dense Ohio forests. In a busy life occupied with many interests, the element of time alone exerts limitations and makes necessary a rigid process of choice, not only in work, but in pleasure. One can observe the water birds which frequent the small ponds as one can observe the antics and gossip of my favorite domestic animals the pigs, in passing, without making of the pleasurable occasion an organized expedition. They are always there close at hand, almost a part of the domestic rather than the wild side of farm life. At Malabar they go unmolested and are even fed; an effort is made to provide them with the conditions which suit them and which they find attractive and agreeable, so that the colonies become a little larger each year. For a very long time now the wild ducks, the mudhens and occasional wild geese and other migrating birds have come to understand that on the Malabar ponds they are fed and protected. They stay with us sometimes for two or three weeks, both on going north and returning to the south. They even frequent in great numbers the pond at the Big House with the farm traffic circling the pond in many places on the very edge of the pond itself. The only sign of alarm and fear in their behavior is that they move slowly and with dignity to the other side of the pond. There is great pleasure in being able to look out of the window or sit on the terrace and watch them from less than a hundred feet away. By now the original migrants must be bringing with them friends and children and grandchildren.

There are also of course the red-winged blackbirds which frequent the reeds on the edge of the pond and build their nests in the marsh grass and the tall bulrushes. And there are the night herons which are nearly always there standing placidly on a rock waiting for a minnow to come along, and the magnificent big blue herons which stay with us the year round, frequenting the unfrozen waters in their fishing. And the killdeers and even the rare golden plovers, which are never very far from water and even build their careless nests between the rows of vegetables bordering the pond, screeching and trailing wings which are not broken at all to lead you away from their hiding places among the beets, the carrots and the lettuce.

On the pond high up on the Ferguson Place, a pair of wood ducks have returned for three successive years. Far down below them in the Valley run the streams with deep pools and riffles which they love. But high up on this solitary pond where no one ever comes but the quiet cattle, they live in a world of their own. The male is perhaps the most brilliant-colored of all birds.

Long ago we abandoned the idea of attempting to keep bass and trout in the same ponds. The big bass have enormous mouths, and unless the trout are stocked at a length of ten inches or more, there is little chance they will escape being swallowed eventually by the bass. As the bass have grown even to the size of the monster of them all, nearly eight pounds, even a big trout has a good chance of finding himself suddenly, like Jonah, in the stomach of a giant fish.

In and about the ponds we have a chance to observe day and night and from day to day the workings of the universe as it was far back in the ages when the earth was first cooling off and life began to appear. One learns that a foolish frog who allows himself to be caught off base can be the victim of the nearest big bass or water snake, but one learns too that, but for the water snake or the bass, even man would eventually be dispossessed from the earth by frogs and not one frog but millions of them would die a slow death of bitter starvation.

One learns things which go deep into the very fundamentals of man's own existence—that perhaps one day of necessity there will be no more sentimentalists who would keep on the bare margin of a wretched existence millions of babies and children and people who suffer throughout their lives from the most painful and wretched of all diseases—hunger and the miseries of near idiocy and deformity and degeneration which go with it. One becomes quite certain that if man continues increasingly to meddle with the natural order of things he will only bring upon himself new and more terrible disasters. For man has the intelligence, if he chooses to employ it, to work *with* the laws of Nature and to prevent the coming into the world of millions of unwanted individuals whose only prospect, through a short and troubled lifetime (which is not in reality life at all), is disease and misery and wretchedness of the most abysmal sort.

Indeed I can think of few experiences more satisfying, profound and illuminating than to be involved for a long time and in an intimate way with the life of a farm pond.

Goodbye to a Friend

I HAD BEEN FISHING for three days among the islands of Lake Erie, escaping just ahead of a great equinoctial storm which shut the islands off from the mainland for three days. Friends drove me from Catawba down to the farm with the rising wind and the towering black clouds just behind us all the way. We won the race, driving up the long lane, between trees whipped by the wind, scattering showers of early falling leaves across the road. The Big House had never looked pleasanter nor the farm more green than in the sulphur-yellow light from the approaching storm. But in my heart there was always that uneasy misgiving which always troubles me when I return after an absence. At Malabar there are many people and animals of all ages and sizes and kinds which have a deep hold on my affections. And always there is a fear in my heart that, while I am away, something bad might have happened to one of them. It is the penalty for having affections and attachments. Life would be much simpler, I suppose, and the emotions less distressed if a man lived alone in a cave without either affections or attachments of any kind; but life would also be less warm and less rich and infinitely and painfully sterile. Like all else, about which Emerson was so right in his clean, transcendental thinking, these things are a matter of compensation.

Always when I have been away I am almost sure to be greeted, as the car comes up the lane, by a troop of dogs. There were always Prince and Baby, Gina and Folly, the four boxers, Dusky, the cocker and Jo, the Border collie. Once there had been the great liver-colored cocker, and Midge the boxer pup, but they have been gone now for an even longer time, although the family talks of them as if they were still alive. It is always the dogs who give the signal of my approach and my wife, recognizing it, comes down the path from the house.

On that wild September evening, the arrival of the car was heralded by the rush of dogs, but almost at once I saw that two things were wrong. Prince was not with the dogs, leading them as he always did, and the door did not open and my wife did not appear. Instead it was Tom, the man of all work, who came out of the kitchen across the lawn.

The old uneasiness rose again and then, as we unloaded the bags and fishing tackle, Tom was suddenly beside me and without even greeting me, he said, "Mr. B., Prince is dead!"

"Dead!" I asked, "What happened?"

"He was coughing badly and we sent him up to Doc's. He died during the night."

I know now why my wife hadn't appeared. She couldn't face telling me because she knew about Prince and me. So Tom had been delegated and it was hard for him, so hard he didn't even accompany the news with the prelude of a greeting. I knew it was hard on him too because when my wife and I were away, Prince attached himself to Tom, following him everywhere all day long. Each morning when I wakened, Prince would get down from my bed, have his part of my breakfast and then go off to Tom in the kitchen to have his back brushed. Tom always used a whiskbroom. Animals and especially dogs are very conventional. The back-brushing was a regular ritual.

My friends expressed sorrow at the news and I was grateful but they couldn't know how I felt. I asked them in for a drink before they drove off to Columbus. My wife joined us and acted as if nothing at all had happened. We talked and my friends left, eager to continue their race against the oncoming storm.

When they had gone, my wife looked at me without speaking and I said, "I think I'll go and have a look at the farm before dark." She said, "I think that would be a good idea."

It was always Prince who went everywhere with me in the jeep. He loved it, partly, I think, because it was open and he could catch every scent on the breeze as we drove and partly because in the jeep we went to the wildest parts of the farm where there were always squirrels and rabbits and woodchucks to chase. Now as I climbed in, Prince's brother Baby jumped quickly into the seat beside me.

I wasn't going to look over the farm. I was going to one place where all of us on the farm go instinctively when we are worried or depressed or something unhappy occurs to us. I was going to the pastures of the Ferguson Place which lie high above the valley just beneath the sky. It is a lovely place which has no buildings, a farm which is all forest and bluegrass, but it is not lonely. Without being told my wife knew where I was going.

Prince had slept on the foot of my bed since he was a fat puppy. Never once in the eight years of his life was he absent from his accustomed place. He spent twenty-four hours a day with me. If I moved across a room to another chair, he moved with me and lay down at my feet. People came to say that I did not own Prince: he owned me.

And now as I drove up the long, wild lane through the woods, his brother Baby was beside me and something curious happened. Halfway up the lane he leaped into my lap and began to lick my ear, exactly as Prince had done so many times when we set off alone together in the jeep—as if the pleasure was always too great to be borne. It was exactly as if Baby *knew.* Baby had always seemed a strange, self-contained dog, little given to demonstrations of affection of any kind. The sudden outburst was so violent that I laughed and said, "That's enough, Baby! Let me alone! I have to drive!" And he quieted down for a moment only to break out a little later with another wild and affectionate assault. Boxers are big dogs and when they demonstrate their hearty affections, the demonstrations can only be described as an assault.

We reached the high farm just as the clouds of a storm were blackening out the last rays of the setting sun. There on the green pasture the Holstein heifers and Pee-Wee, the bull, were grazing quietly, scarcely looking up as the jeep drove among them, and then, when I had turned off the motor and climbed out, followed by Baby, to lie on the grass, the cattle came up one or two at a time to stand there, very close, watching the two of us. Baby did what Prince had always done. He sat close to me, his back against my chest, to protect me from the peril of the docile heifers.

I don't know how long I lay there but the smell of the bluegrass and the friendliness of the heifers made the hurt seem a little less. This was a place where Prince had come with me countless times to sit in the evening looking down over the valley. It was all just the same. Despite the oncoming storm, the evening seemed quiet but for the wild beauty of the great black clouds touched at moments by the crimson and gold light of the setting sun. The thick woods shut out the rising wind and the only sound was the soft swishing, crunching sound made by the heifers and the bull as they ate their way along the bluegrass and white clover. Then there was a wild clap of thunder and another and another. I heard myself half-thinking, half-saying, "It's all right, kid! I'm coming back! Don't worry!" And I thought, "That's silly!" But somehow it made a difference.

It was what I always said to him when I went away on a trip. He always knew all the signs. He knew what a suitcase meant. He grew worried and miserable even if I put on store clothes to go into town for a few hours. So I'd always say, "It's all right, kid! I'm coming back! Don't worry!" And always when I came back I'd say after I'd recovered from the first affectionate assault of welcome, "You see, kid! It's all right! I told you I'd come back and I did." He came to understand it all and although the sight of store clothes or a suitcase never failed to depress him, understanding the situation and knowing I was not leaving forever made it all easier for him. On the occasions when I went away he never rushed to the door with me but stayed behind in my room till the car drove off.

Then as I lay there on the grass, Baby turned suddenly and again began licking my ear violently and quickly, and out of the threatening sky, the wild storm of the equinox broke. The heifers and Pee-Wee took to a sheltering thicket and Baby and I climbed back into the jeep to drive home down the wild, rough lane through a wild wind and a driving rain with flashes of lightning which illumined the very depths of the thick wood.

I know that much of what I am writing sounds sentimental and much of it is. And so I am a sentimentalist and so what? It is inevitable that anyone who likes and understands animals should be a sentimentalist. I think too that such people sometimes find in animals and especially dogs consolations and sympathy in time of hurt which no human, however close, can ever bring them. And there is much truth in the sentimentality about animals, much which brings a special warmth and satisfaction in living and a clue to much that is a part of understanding and of God. Some people will perhaps not understand at all what I am writing about and others will know, instinctively and rightly.

All that night and for days afterward Prince was always with me in a way for, as when great friends die, one thinks of them almost constantly—they are indeed even present in one's dreams. And so I thought a great deal about Prince, remembering all the small things about him and a hundred small incidents, good and bad. For he was a very human dog, neither wholly good or bad. He was willful and demanding in his love for me and very jealous. He fought with Baby and was even known to snip at Gina and Folly when they became too affectionate and intimate. Always in his mind, I was his special property.

He was a big and handsome dog, the child of Rex, a noble father, and Regina, a mother with an immense store of feminine wisdom, calm, and poise, affectionate and pleasant as a good wife and mother should be. She brooked no nonsense from her children and grandchildren nor from her in-laws. When she was quite an old lady she could quiet them all simply by making faces at them and she could make really ferocious and terrifying faces.

Prince was different from any of the fifty or more dogs I have had in a lifetime. He was different because he was a boxer and boxers' owners will know what I mean by that—but he was a King, even among boxers. Above all he was a good companion. To drive with him over the farm or to take him with me across the fields and woods was like having the company of a great friend who was intelligent and amusing. When I walked three or four miles, he would joyously run ten or fifteen, but in all his excursions he kept returning to me again and again to tell me what a beautiful morning it was or how he had treed a squirrel. And sometimes he would return with a woodchuck, proudly, to show me, and would insist on carrying it all the way home. He was obedient too for when he uncovered a nest of young rabbits or, as happened once or twice, came on a baby raccoon offside in the daylight, I needed only to say, "No, Prince!" and he would stand quite still, quivering with excitement, without touching the young animals.

And like all boxers he was clever with his paws, using them with dexterity, almost like hands. Once his cleverness at opening doors nearly caused disaster which might have ended in the death of himself and his wise old mother.

I had left them inside the car on a slope above the deep pond below the Big House, planning to return quickly, but once inside the house a long-distance telephone call distracted me, and temporarily I forgot Prince and Gina, still waiting in the car. When at last I was free to return, I stepped out of the house just in time to see the big car with the two dogs inside slipping down the steep slope toward the deep waters of the pond. It was the dogs I thought of and not the car. Running down the slope I arrived at the pond just in time to see the car slipping slowly beneath the surface. Fully dressed, I went into the water, dived, opened the car door and dragged them both out under water. They swam ashore, shook themselves and seemed unconcerned over what had happened. Indeed, I think Prince took it as a lark.

It did not take me long to divine what had happened. The car was heavy and the emergency brake never held it properly, so, on leaving them, I had put the car in second gear and turned the wheels against a nearby bank. Prince, left alone for so long, had grown impatient and tried to open the door to get out and find me. In doing so he had put one paw on the gearshift, pulling it out of second gear and turning the wheels at the same time away from the bank. The rest was easy—the car simply rolled into the pond.

He had the dignity and the nobility of his father, Rex, but with more sensitivity and intelligence, and this difference made him a sufferer, for he worried as I have never known any dog to worry. He worried about my going away and as soon as I returned, he would begin worrying lest I leave again. After the first roughhouse welcome on my return, he would be overcome again and again during the day by the realization that I had really come back after all, and at such moments he would leap from the floor into my lap and place both paws on my shoulders and lick my ear. Sometimes he would jump from the floor onto my big desk scattering ink and papers in his excitement. I couldn't punish him. How could you punish such a whole-hearted demonstration of affection?

His brother, Baby, the show-off, would talk and talk, very audibly to any circle of friends, but Prince rarely raised his voice. He would open his mouth and his lips would quiver but no sound would come forth, and then he would sigh as if he knew that no matter how hard he tried, he could never make with his dog's mouth the articulate sounds of speech that I was able to do, that he could never really talk to me, no matter how much we understood each other. At such times I would say, "It's all right, kid. I understand everything you say." And immediately he would be happy again.

It was a saying in the family that you couldn't talk confidentially in front of Prince because he understood everything you said, and indeed he appeared to understand perfectly all conversations or the plans made in his presence. He knew perfectly well how to wangle his way onto a sofa despite all rules to the contrary. He did it by degrees and insinuations, almost imperceptibly, until presently he was curled up on the fresh chintz as if that was where he belonged. Like all boxers he hated drafts or cold floors.

Five or six dogs sleep in my bedroom. It is on the level of the garden with two doors which Prince opened easily, sometimes for himself and sometimes for the others. When the "coon-huntin'" season opened, life at night in my bedroom was not placid, and sleep was interrupted, for after midnight when the neighboring boys started running their hounds, the sound of baying drifted down from the ridge across the ravine and the dogs in my bedroom knew there were strangers on what they considered their territory. With a whoop and a halloo they were off, led by Prince who opened the door. Then for an hour or two, all hell broke loose as the boxers, with Dusky, the cocker spaniel trailing them, set out after the coon hounds, driving them out of the valley. Once the hounds were clear of the boxers' land, the boxers all returned with Prince leading to open the door for them to enter, to go back to their beds on chairs and sofas.

If any other dog even approached the bed at night, he was in trouble at once. But for the period of my after lunch nap, he had made some sort of an arrangement with Folly. I do not know when or how it was made but it was one of perfect understanding. He never prevented her from joining me at nap time and never made any attempt to push her aside or to take his accustomed place. But at night it was different, the rug at the foot of my bed belonged to him.

That animals communicate and come to understandings, I have no doubt, for I have seen these things in operation too many times. I recall an afternoon when a group of visitors stopped at the lower garden with a strange boxer in their car. It is always a risky thing to bring a strange dog in a car to Malabar for it is difficult to prevent the boxers from removing half the paint from the car; so on this occasion I held Prince by the collar and told my friends to leave the car down on the road where it would be concealed, with the strange dog inside. Together we walked up the long hill and when we arrived at the house, where three or four empty cars were parked, the other boxers rushed out to greet us. Then after a moment's exchange of communication they all began leaping at the windows of the empty parked cars, one after another, to discover which one contained a dog. Clearly and unmistakably Prince had spread the word.

When they found all the cars empty, they returned with disappointment to sit by us on the lawn, still convinced that there was a strange dog somewhere about. Then suddenly I noticed the hair begin to rise slowly on old Gina's back. She sniffed the wind and suddenly, followed by the others, all save Prince, she set off at top speed down the hill toward the hidden parked car. The odd thing was that Prince did not follow. I think it was because I had warned him to leave the strange dog in peace. He had told them there was a strange dog in a car on the farm but he did not tell them where.

In the mornings when I have breakfast in my office, each of the boxers was given milk from a saucer. They had their own order of being served, apparently by arrangement among themselves. First Prince, as if this were his divine right as the leader and best friend of the boss, then old Gina, perhaps out of respect for her age, then Folly, the pretty, frivolous one, and finally Baby, if he had not already gone out on the farm. The order never varied, nor was there any quarreling nor any attempt to return for a second helping.

Prince was a sociable dog and a great welcomer. Like all the boxers, he loved picnics and parties and after the first uproar of barking had died away, he would welcome and say a few words to every member of the arriving party. Boxers are ferocious in appearance but they have the hearts of big babies. Sometimes the welcome to a small child would create more consternation than pleasure. Like all boxers he was wonderful with children, and on the farm and among the visitors, there are many children of all sizes. Instinctively a boxer will take care of children. I have seen little fellows on the farm pinch and ride and bedevil the boxers and even take bones from them without coming to any harm. When the assaults become unendurable the boxers will simply walk away out of reach without any loss of dignity. I have heard of bad-tempered boxers but I have never seen one. If they are bad-tempered it is because they have been kept tied or shut—things which no boxer can endure.

On one occasion a small nephew of two years came to stay on the farm. He was one of those happy children with no fear of dogs and he moved in on the boxers at once. He liked them all but he adopted Prince and Prince adopted him. The bond became so great that he even insisted upon having his afternoon nap with Prince. He would play with Prince for long periods of time, climbing on him and rolling over him. The friendship reached a climax and a test one summer afternoon while he was rolling on the lawn with the big dog. To the surprise of his mother and the rest of us, the boy was observed biting Prince's lip while the dog lay perfectly quietly with an expression not only of patience but of satisfaction.

Prince had many friends from all over the world and whenever or wherever I met them, they always asked, "How is Prince?" It was as if we belonged to each other and I know that when I was at home no one ever saw us separated, day or night. They asked about him as if he were one of the family. He liked people and remembered them when they returned, giving them a hospitable and friendly welcome.

During the three days I spent among the islands of the lake I should have enjoyed myself. I was among a dozen of my very best friends. We drank some and fished and played poker. We had an attractive and comfortable cottage and wonderful food. Yet, all the time I spent there I suffered from an unaccountable sense of depression and slept badly, an exceptional thing in my experience. I tried to believe that it was the weather with the approaching equinoctial storms, but never quite persuaded myself. By the third day the depression had taken the form of foreboding, of what I did not know. Like Dr. Carrell who was certainly no sentimentalist but a great and pure scientist, I believe that there are in the realms of intuition, of telepathy, of psychic communication things as remote from our understanding or knowledge as the knowledge of the physiology of man is remote from the most primitive savage. I know that in those three days, when for every reason I should have experienced a happy, carefree enjoyment in the open air and on the water, there was some force which dimmed the whole of the holiday and gradually assumed the proportions of menace and foreboding. I am certain now that somehow I knew that Prince was sick.

After returning with Baby through the storm from the high farm, I went to bed early and took a sleeping pill so that I wouldn't wake up and lie awake thinking about Prince. The place on the foot of the bed where he had always slept on an old green rug was empty for the first time since he had come there as a puppy.

Presently I fell asleep but twice during the night I was wakened despite the sleeping pill, once by the feeling of something stirring and pressing against my leg. The feeling was so real and so intense that I thought one of the other dogs had taken Prince's place. But when I sat up and reached down, there was nothing there.

After a long time I fell asleep again only to be wakened this time by the sound of scratching on the screen door. It was exactly the sound made by Prince when, in wet weather, the door stuck and he was forced to crook his paw against the grille covering the lower part of the door and give it an extra tug. I listened for a moment and then concluded one of the other dogs had gone out, and, without Prince to open the door for him, could not return. I put on the light and went to the door. The storm was over and the moon was shining high over the ravine. Outside the door there was nothing.

The two experiences were not imagined nor were they the result of drowsiness for each time I lay awake for a long time afterward. I do not know the explanation—save perhaps that no creature, in some ways not even a human one, had ever been so close to me as Prince.

For weeks before he died he had seemed melancholy and looked a little thin but I thought only that it was the hot weather. Then two days before he died he began to cough violently and my wife sent him up to Doc Wadsworth's and thirty-six hours later he was dead of a hemorrhage which could not be stopped. He died of cancer of the lung and could only have lived a few weeks longer, perhaps in pain. If I could not have been with him myself I was glad that he was with Doc Wadsworth and his wife and sister-in-law for they feel as I do about animals and particularly about boxers. When Doc comes to the farm, they all rush out and leap all over him. On two occasions they have knocked him flat with their joyous and affectionate welcome. I'm glad Doc was with him and gave him something to quiet the coughing and keep him asleep. But I wish I had been there to hold his head on my knee and say, "You see, kid! It's all right! I told you I'd come back!"

He's gone to join old Rex and the charming frivolous little boxer, Midge, who was like a ballet dancer, and little Patsy, the cocker who used to act as "sitter" for Old Gina whenever she had puppies, and Dash, the Don Juan of all Scotties. I have a feeling that I'll see them all some day and that as they rush down the path to welcome me with Prince in the lead, I'll be able to say to him, "You see, kid. I told you I'd come back and I did!"

The story perhaps would not be complete without relating the change in Baby, our show-off, in the days after Prince's death. Despite the unfortunate circumstances of Baby's birth and upbringing he was always a stout and hearty dog and early took to farm life. Of all the dogs, he has always been the real farmer, spending most of his day in the fields riding on the machinery or following the plow. He is perfectly happy to follow the plow or mower round and round the field for hours, unlike his brother Prince who hated tractors and would leave me when I gave myself over to plowing. Unlike most boxers, who dislike bad weather and hate rain, he has never minded either, and in winter sat in the snow looking down the road while the other dogs scratched at the door to be let in.

I have recounted earlier Baby's talents as a clown and a ham actor. His love for showing off frequently brought him into trouble with the other dogs, male and female, who detested the showing off and when he began high-diving would pounce on him to beat him up. He would certainly have been a great dog performer in vaudeville or a circus if he had ever had the opportunity. During the whole lifetime of Prince, I had thought of Baby as a peculiarly impersonal dog, egotistical and less affectionate than the others. It was only after Prince died that I discovered how badly I had misjudged him.

I discovered that he only appeared indifferent and egotistical because Prince, in his devotion to me and his jealousy, would not permit him to be otherwise. It was the ancient, classic case of the domination of the older brother. I know that whenever Baby tried to be friendly with me, a light of fury would come into Prince's eyes and a ferocious fight, sometimes damaging to tables, glassware and lamps, would ensue. I did not, however, realize that Baby was really a frustrated dog and that all his tricks and showing off were in a way merely a device to get attention and praise. He behaved exactly as a child behaves under the same circumstances, especially a child who seeks to attract notice away from a more favored brother or sister.

I do not know how much he understood immediately concerning the death of Prince, but he came presently to realize that Prince was no longer there to attack him when he entered the room where I was or if he tried to sit nearer to me in the jeep. For weeks after the death of Prince he never entered the house or my room save walking on tiptoe, his back arched and bristling, as if expecting attack. Gradually the old apprehension and complex began to disappear and his behavior became more normal. Then it was that I came to understand his troubles. I discovered that the big dog was perhaps the most affectionate of all the boxers. He really didn't want to be a show-off. He only wanted attention and all the privileges Prince had had. He developed Prince's trick of jumping eagerly into my lap or on my desk. His whole character seemed to change. Instead of seeming to alternate between moodiness and showing off, his temperament became even and happy. He still carried on his long conversations, conducted with a remarkable variety of rumbles, growls, barks, and whines; they were no longer complaints but outbursts of happiness. And gradually he became as inseparable from me as Prince had been.

One thing, however, did not change. He could not be induced by any kind of command or blandishment to take Prince's place on the rug at the foot of my bed. He would hold long conversations obviously in an effort to explain the situation to me but nothing would induce him to take the place of his brother. He clung always to the smallest chair which as a puppy he had chosen as his bed although he had long grown into a seventy-pound dog whose head and stub tail overhung both arms of the chair.

But he has become a happy dog with less and less inclination to do his tricks. He has moved into the place left by Prince which long ago had been occupied by their father, old Rex. He was Boss! The thing that is most endearing about dogs, and especially about boxers, is that each one has his own personality and that they are so profoundly like engaging children.

A Hymn to Hawgs

WHOEVER has really looked into the eye of a shrewd old sow should feel humility. It is a bright clear eye, more like the eye of a human than the eye of any other animal. It looks at you quite directly, even with what might be described as a piercing gaze. The look sizes you up, appraises you and leaves you presently with the impression that the old sow has indeed a very low opinion of you; an opinion tempered by scorn and contempt and perhaps even a little animosity. Clearly she does not think that you amount to very much and that, given a difficult situation, she could cope with it far better than you could do. It is as if she said, "You think you can shut me up and confine me. Well, that's what you think! Ha! Ha! and again Ha! Ha!" And any farmer knows what she is thinking—that if she really wants to get out she'll find a way. Sometimes, I have a feeling that she is thinking, "You think you know how to manage me and bring up my litters with all your disinfectants, your heat lamps, your violet rays, your antibiotics, your supplements, your inoculations, your vaccinations. Just let me alone and give me my freedom and I won't have any troubles nor will the pigs I feed."

Yet she can be friendly too and even understanding, as any farmer knows when a seven-hundred-pound sow comes running to have her back scratched. You don't have to scratch her back a dozen or a score of times. Once is enough and she gets the idea and after that she'll always be on hand when you enter the field. She may be using you and undoubtedly knows that she is, and there *may* be some affection involved, but I doubt that she ever really loses her scorn for you. In some ways, about many basic and fundamental things she knows, both by instinct and intelligence, quite a lot of things you don't know.

Animals at Malabar are likely to be well treated and most of them sooner or later come within the category of pets and sometimes very troublesome pets. Alton knows all his cows, what each one likes and doesn't like, in what order they prefer to enter the milk parlor, which cows have best friends, which ones are bullies and which ones are timid and retiring. He knows the bad temper of Inez who just never could be milked without being tied down and the comic ways of Lauren who on more than one occasion was found shaking a barn cat in her mouth when the impudent cat attempted to walk across her parcel of feed. And he knows old Mary whom he rides home from pasture to the milking parlor as if she were a horse. There are no ill-treated animals at Malabar for the first consideration of employment in connection with any livestock is that the man must be able to imagine himself a cow, a pig or a chicken and so to know what would make that particular animal or bird happy and comfortable. And so you get to know animals pretty well and the more you know them the greater respect you have both for them and for God and Nature. The people who think all cows are exactly alike are merely stupid or ignorant; cows can sometimes be as individual as the people of any group and not infrequently more interesting.

But pets can be tiresome too, like the hand-raised lambs at Malabar who, growing up with the boxer dogs, came to believe they were dogs and not sheep at all. The most troublesome of all farm pets at Malabar were the goats which persecuted all of us and all visitors until they had to be sent away to Italian families who know better how to cope with them. If there is any animal more difficult to confine or to shut out than a pig, it is a goat. Both are certainly gifted with great powers of logic, reflection, judgment, deduction and mockery, qualities which man has usually and often mistakenly reserved for himself.

Out of an excessively busy life, pigs have cost me more time than fishing or golf or any of the usual activities in which men are accustomed to find relaxation, amusement and exasperation. When I am really busy, I dare not visit the pig lots, for inevitably I find myself standing there for indefinite amounts of time, watching the little pigs horsing about with their own games, listening to the conversation and gossip of the old sows, watching the pigs line up to feed, even on occasion watching a new litter arrive in this world to get up immediately on their feet, shake themselves and run around to their outside source of supply in the new world which they have entered only a moment before. If I had ever doubted a pig's capacity to think things out, I lost it forever when I discovered one pig's trick of escaping through what was by every reasonable evidence a thoroughly pig-tight fence.

He was one of some two hundred half-grown pigs enclosed for feeding in a ten-acre lot. Every day, week after week, this particular pig got outside the fence and no one was ever able to discover how he accomplished this feat, until late one afternoon as I stood in the far end of the field I saw what I found difficult to believe. At the opposite end of the field I saw a pig actually *climbing* the fence.

The fence was a typical hog fence with graduated openings from those too small for even the smallest pig to negotiate at the very bottom to openings at the top that were reasonably large. But the designer of the fence had reckoned without this special pig who possessed advanced powers of reasoning. He had discovered that the higher the openings were from the ground the larger they were and he managed to climb high enough to reach an opening big enough for him to slip through. With the greatest dexterity he worked his way upward until he reached an opening of sufficient size and then slipped down on the opposite side of the fence.

I watched the whole operation, even to his scuttling across the road into a neighboring cornfield where he was just able to reach up and drag down the ears of corn. I must add that so great was my weakness for pigs and my admiration for this particular pig, that I never betrayed the fact that I had learned his secret. The end of the story was that eventually he ate himself out of his freedom, for each day he grew fatter, heavier and larger in girth, until the day came when he was unable to find an opening large enough to permit his escape or to reach the top of the fence without falling backward again into the prison of his hog lot.

And there was the mentally handicapped pig who never did learn to use the self-feeder and who, as a consequence, developed a psychopathic and extremely bad and aggressive disposition. For the benefit of the city-bred who may be reading, a self-feeder is constructed with a kind of trap door which the average pig, or indeed every other pig I have ever known save this one, learns very quickly to raise by putting his snout beneath it and forcing it upward. Once he has his snout inside the feeder, the trap door rests on his snout or rather his forehead until he has eaten his fill. Then, as he backs away, the trap door falls down again by gravity and the feeder is closed. Just why this trap door is necessary or why it is supposed to be useful I do not know, unless some bright fellow believed that it saved feed, although any farmer knows that any good healthy pig allows no feed to be wasted whether it is in the feeder or outside on the ground. The self-feeder, however unnecessary, has been forced into the consciousness of the average farmer, like many another dubious and expensive agricultural equipment product, by high-pressure advertising and the general pressure in colleges, industrial plants and other places where new gadgets are constantly being thought up for farmers to buy. At this stage in the Malabar program, I was still naïve enough and inexperienced enough to believe that one could not raise hogs without a self-feeder, an idea which I long ago abandoned, for we at Malabar have never belonged to the school which invests in gadgets simply to make a hog lot or a building look "prettier."

In any case, we had in one lot of hogs this special backward pig who never learned to raise the trap door with his snout. He always

took the lid between his teeth and raised it and always as he let loose
of it the trap door fell shut again before he could get his snout under
it to hold it open. I have watched him try again and again countless times to perform the operation so rapidly that he could outwit
the falling trap door. He never won and so in order to get his fill he
turned, like many a delinquent and mental deficient, into a bully.
He would approach the self-feeder, take up a stand and allow some
innocent good-natured intelligent fellow pig to open the trap door
with his snout. Then with a combination of a slashing and shoul-
dering side movement, the backward pig would shove the innocent
aside and thrust his snout into the opening to feed his fill. The odd
thing was that he never learned, either by reasoning and logic as did
our fence-climbing friend or simply by observing how the other pigs
did it. He just never learned. But I think we need not be too criti-
cal or scornful of him; I have known a great many fellow men who
suffered from the same handicap. He was the dumbest pig I have
ever known and in fact the only "dumb" pig with whom I have ever
been acquainted. He was also a bully, like many a human bully with
a strong sense of inferiority—like Mussolini or Molotov.

Much discussion and argument has been spent regarding the
ability or inability of animals to communicate with each other, but
nowadays I believe there are few people or even experts who any
longer doubt that animals have means of communication which are
quite beyond our understanding. Turn a bull into the far side of a
field away from a herd of cows and heifers with a hill or woodlot in
between. All he need do—and he always does it—is to give one loud
bellow and all the cows and heifers, tails high in the air, leaping and
cavorting coquettishly regardless of age, will come running. What
man has ever had the eloquence or the blarney to command so easily
such a harem? Beside the bull Don Juan was merely a piker.

Or what about the cantankerous cow who manages to ride down a
fence or find an opening and who with a single bellow of peculiar volume
and timbre will bring all the rest of the herd to join her in breaking out?

Again and again I have seen one of my dogs soundlessly communicate to the others that there is a strange dog on the place or in

a visiting car which must be put in place or given the bum's rush. I have seen one of them tell the others that Lester the Cat was behind the greenhouse and in a vulnerable situation. A certain kind of bark surely communicates at least a certain variety or kind of information. But among all animals there is none which has such a variety of sounds designed obviously for the purposes of communication and even gossip as the pig.

Waste your time as I do, leaning on the fence, and you will see among the pigs everything from a directors' meeting to a ladies' discussion of the attractions of the visiting boar. There are the sounds which a sow makes when she feels it is time to feed her young, and there are the frightful squeals of discontent from her pigs when she will not give in to their demands and lie on her side to let them feed. And there is what is distinctly the most ferocious name-calling that can occur during the equivalent of a hair-pulling match between two old sows. Pick up a small pig and he will let out the most hair-raising shrieks for help that will bring running not only his own mother but all the sows in the neighborhood. He is the most blatant of small frauds, for the minute you put him down again on the ground the shrieks stop instantly and are replaced by the pleasant "oink! oink!" noises of a contented small pig. Come unexpectedly upon an old sow and her litter in a swamp or a thicket and, especially if there are dogs along, she will give the signal of alarm, gathering all the litter around

her where they form a circle with all their small noses pointed outward like a Macedonian phalanx both for attack and defense, making
at the same time the most threatening and bloodcurdling sounds.

These sounds made among pigs are not merely signals or crude
symbols of speech. Observe a gathering of sows when they are not
eating or feeding their pigs but are merely having a good gossip.
The hog wallow is clearly a favorite spot for woman's talk—the kind
of talk you might hear on "Ladies' Night" in a Turkish bath. There
is a whole variety of sounds including not only pitch but intonation
and the actual formation of given sounds. I once assisted at such a
conversation among a group of sows who came to give advice at the
birth of a new litter by one of their number.

The sow who was brought to bed was either taken unexpectedly
in labor or was a plain fool, which is the more likely situation. She
chose or (like a woman giving birth in a taxi) failed to start for the
shelter of the barn in time and consequently had her litter in the
middle of the hog lot on a day of great heat and blazing sunshine,
something no sensible sow would dream of doing. In any case, the
family came rapidly, all ten of them, popping up on their wobbly
feet and going around at once to feed at the waiting cafeteria. The
spectacle attracted several other sows who stood about very clearly
making comments of a disapproving nature. When the last of the
pigs had entered this world, or, as the fashionable birth announce-
ments in the French newspapers put it, "were given the light of day,"
the sow stood up and apparently either became aware of her foolishness in having her pigs in the midst of a hot field or heeded the
reproaches and advice of the surrounding sows. She attempted to induce the pigs to follow her toward the shade of the nearby barn with
no success, for the pigs were still so new to this world that, beyond
the instinct of eating, they were without adjustment and clearly did
not yet understand pig language. She made an astonishing variety of
sounds, in which her friends joined—sounds that were now cajol-
ing, now scolding, now clearly meant as commands. But the tiny
shaky pink pigs merely wobbled about, aimlessly. Then abandoning
temporarily all hope of getting them into the barn, she relaxed for

a time and held what was clearly a discussion of her labor pains and prenatal condition with her friends. There was the most astonishing variety of sounds and intonations in which the other sows, their heads close together, all joined. This continued for some time with what was growing animation, for all the world like a group of women during a bridge game which has been interrupted by the more absorbing topic of whose labor pains were longest and hardest. Then after a time she returned to her futile efforts to herd the tiny pigs into the shade.

Nothing came of her efforts and I went to get Bob and Carl to help rescue the pigs. They were of the Yorkshire breed, naturally white in color and at this stage a delicate pearl color subject dangerously to heat and to sunburn. By the time I returned, the other sows had apparently exhausted the subject of labor pains and wandered away, possibly with the conviction that their friend was a damned fool and there was nothing to be done about it.

To rescue the pigs and get them into the shade of the barn, we used age-old tactics well known to the experienced hog farmer. Bob fetched a bushel basket and put it over the head of the sow so that she would not attack. The bushel basket blinds her and her only impulse is to back away constantly from it to free herself, and as a sow can back only slowly, a fairly agile man can keep her under control for a limited length of time. While Bob controlled the sow, Carl scooped up the little pink pigs into two pails and headed as fast as possible for the barn, but like all small pigs they set up, even at their tender age which was not more than an hour, the most ungodly racket, bringing a whole troop of sympathetic mothers to the rescue. At the same time, the mother, excited by their devilish and unwarranted shrieks of distress, leapt forward to the fray instead of backing up as she was supposed to do, demolished the bushel basket, and set out in hot pursuit of Carl. Carl is a big and long-legged fellow but never has he made such speed as during that hundred-yard dash for the barn pursued by a whole troop of Yorkshire Niobes and Boadiceas, each one a sympathizing mother. The sounds they made were terrifying but Carl won his race. He managed to make the inside of the barn and drop both pails and clear the barrier of a feeding creep with scarcely an inch between the seat of his Levis and the gnashing teeth of the outraged sows. Both Bob and myself had long ago cleared the fence, barbed wire and all.

At the same moment the wretched little devils spilled helter-skelter out of their baskets, stopped their shrieks and immediately began "oink-oinking!" in the most contented possible fashion while what was clearly conversation of indignation and outrage broke out among the sympathetic sows.

Such an example as this taxicab foolishness is rare indeed among sows, but this one was only young and perhaps a little giddy and like many a young woman merely stayed out a little too long.

Few animals and indeed few people are quite as shrewd or gifted with such a remarkable natural instinct as a sow—instinct with regard to what to eat and how much, how to forage off the countryside, how to find shelter for herself and her young. Give a sow her freedom and she can take her litter right across country feeding off the land. No animal has a diet so varied and so closely resembling that of man. The pig is both herbivorous and carnivorous. Our own pigs make most of their growth off alfalfa, brome grass and ladino clover. No animal, including man, can find a greater delight in good sweet corn, tomatoes, cantaloupe, cucumbers and watermelon, as many a farmer has long since discovered to his sorrow when the hogs raid the farm gardens. Like man, pigs thoroughly enjoy meat, eggs, cheese, milk and will even on occasion go off on hunting expeditions and bring home chickens, ducks and occasionally unwary wild animals.

But man and in particular the mean or ignorant farmer does not always give the hog or sow a chance to take care of their own comfort and needs. A hog is by nature the cleanest of animals and will never foul his own nest unless forced to do so by the laziness or ignorance of his owner. A sow, who is either properly fed or given her complete freedom, has never been known to eat her young. It is only the desperate sow shut into a dark and filthy sty without sufficient protein feeds and with a lack of minerals which she cannot obtain by searching and rooting for them in the open field or swamp.

When we first took over the farms which now make up Malabar, we purchased the livestock as well. On one of the farms there was a sow shut up on concrete about to farrow. So bad was her forced diet owing to the ignorance of the farmer, that she was desperately tearing up the concrete with her teeth in order to obtain calcium and perhaps other minerals vital to the development of the pigs inside her.

Our own hogs are innocent of rings and their rooting activities are not worth notice; indeed the little rooting they do is good for the alfalfa, brome grass and actually stimulates their growth and increases the yield of good high protein forage.

The hog has followed man everywhere on his wildest pioneering ventures. Few frontiersmen ever set out into the wilderness without a sow and a boar pig and wherever he arrived, he had only to turn them loose to forage off the countryside until he could raise crops. Only an animal as big and as ferocious as a mountain lion or a bear was a match for the sow or boar, and even such formidable animals could never be sure of defeating the wits and the tusks of a boar or a ferocious old sow. Wherever man has gone, the pig has gone along to provide him with food, with litters which grew rapidly at very little cost or labor even under adverse conditions.

And no animal has ever provided anywhere near the variety of delicacies that can be obtained from the carcass of the hog. There is fresh pork and hams and bacon and sausage. There are pig's knuckles, and liver and headcheese and tenderloin and pork chops. Indeed less of the hog is wasted than of any other animal. If I were forced to make a choice of a single meat (despite the offense such an opinion may give my beef cattle friends), it would always be pork. A good steak is fine and so is a good roast beef, but for my taste, both can become monotonous. Mutton is a meat that could best be described as "so-so." Lamb is a delicacy but one can grow sick of an unvaried diet of lamb, as many a sheepman knows.

By now it must be evident that this is one farmer who would not consider a farm a farm which did not include hogs in its program. They are the most utilitarian of animals and have justly been referred to as "mortgage raisers," even when uneconomically and badly raised and fed.

Much as I love pigs, much as they entertain me, there is one warning I would issue against them. Never take a pig as a pet. The dangers are far greater than the menace of a good bite from an old sow or being gashed by the long tusks of a boar. There are two principal difficulties and dangers. In the first place no animal comes more rapidly to think that he is "people," and, worst of all, a pig grows. The cute and funny little pig who follows you everywhere "oinking" affectionately will, before you realize it, be a tremendous animal weighing six or seven hundred pounds who thinks not only that he is "people"—indeed he is absolutely sure of it and you cannot dissuade him—but also thinks he is still a very small and charming pig. No animal is more easily housebroken but never let him get his foot in the door. If, by any chance, a small chubby pig does succeed in victimizing you, harden your heart, send him or her away for breeding purposes, preferably to some utterly unknown destination. Otherwise when, out of desperation, you put an end to his existence, you will suffer for the rest of your life from remorse as a cannibal and a murderer. Look at pigs over the fence but never bring a pig into your life. You will not have a chance, for a pig is even worse than a goat when he learns that he can push you around.

From all of this the reader has perhaps gathered the belief that the writer has a higher opinion of some hogs than he has of some people; in this the reader would be quite right.